Bureaucracy and Society

Bureaucracy and Society

IAS at Work

Edited by

Rakesh Hooja

RAWAT PUBLICATIONS

Jaipur • New Delhi • Bangalore • Guwahati • Kolkata

ISBN 978-81-316-0300-0

Reprinted, 2023

Published by
Prem Rawat for **Rawat Publications**
Satyam Apts., Sector 3, Jawahar Nagar, Jaipur 302 004 (India)
Phone: 0141 265 1748 / 265 7006
E-mail: info@rawatbooks.com
Website: www.rawatbooks.com

New Delhi Office
4858/24, Ansari Road, Daryaganj, New Delhi 110 002
Phone: 011-23263290

Also at *Bangalore, Guwahati* and *Kolkata*

Typeset by Rawat Computers, Jaipur
Printed and bound in India

Contents

II
Remembering District Tenures

III
Afterword: What is Desirable in the Civil Service

RAKESH HOOJA

Introduction: Reminiscences of the Civil Servants at Work

It is not just the structures and systems of governance but also the men who man the structures and operate the systems, who together make up a country's administration and determine the ensuing impact upon its successes as well as failures.

From the point of view of its multifunctionality, size, status and impact the Indian Administrative Service (IAS) is perhaps unique in the world. A successor to the Indian Civil Service (ICS) of the days of the British Raj, it has inherited part of the elan of the ICS; and its expanding role and responsibilities have resulted in its importance and prestige in the country. From the impacts of partition onwards it has borne the brunt of numerous challenges faced by India and Indians. The perceived omnipotence and omnipresence of the IAS in all matters related to government has made the members of the IAS a subject of sustained criticism, some of which has been unfounded. Commentators scholars, politicians and observers from various walks of life have highlighted the positive as well as negative sides of the performance of the IAS.

There is a need to understand the role of the IAS in terms of the changing environment in which it has had to function, as also the fact that the administrative acumen and character of individual civil servants can and has significantly influenced the pattern, orientation and productivity of the administrative system. Such understanding can come through scholars, researchers and others who analyze government and administrative systems. It can also come by listening to or reading about people who have worked in the administrative system and helped shape the administrative reality, and who reflect upon the experiences that they have undergone.

In this volume we have brought together the recollections or reminiscences of *The IAS at Work* by 14 persons who served in IAS careers (one of the contributors still being in service) with two contributions by one of the authors. While those who are in the IAS, or who are otherwise familiar with the details of Indian Administration, may not require any assistance in appreciating and understanding the background, the ground realities, the nuances and the implications of what is being set forth in the various essays in this anthology, others may require some guidance. Accordingly, this editor, who himself has spent almost 35 years in the IAS and has a couple of years to go before retirement, has provided some idea about the setting in which the IAS works and which forms the backdrop for the reminiscences in this anthology, so as to facilitate readers in achieving a better appreciation of the recollections being provided in this book. This has been done through the sectional introductions provided by this editor for each of the three sections: on reminiscences about their entire service careers, on recollections of their district postings as Collectors, and on what are the qualities and 'spirit of the service' desired from the civil service. The vast variety of assignments on which IAS officers may end up working, the common elements of the career path that most IAS officers follow, the numerous activities and roles that district Collectors perform, some views about what is expected from the IAS as a service, have all been mentioned in the sectional introductions. These sectional introductions have been kept brief as it is intended to let the narratives written by the contributors of this volume to stand out and speak for themselves.

Many of the incidents and episodes highlighted in the narratives may be seen as case studies of how the protagonists and others concerned responded leading to successful handling of the situations in some cases and failures in others. They also indicate how Indian administration has been effected in actual practice during the last 60 odd years.

This biographical approach to the understanding of the IAS at work, and thus of Indian Public Administration, has been influenced by a number of factors. One is the knowledge of some similar attempts made earlier.

In 1965 K.L. Punjabi brought out an edited book, *The Civil Servant in India* whereby he had invited some of his colleagues in the ICS to narrate their experiences. The aim was "to explain how delicate and intricate is the work of an administrator and the discipline and training necessary for the performance of his duties which need hard toil, a spirit of devotion and a fair measure of ingenuity and enterprise" and also to "bring in bold relief the traditions and practices of the service". This book containing narratives by 20 civil servants had been a great source of interest for the IAS officers of my father's generation who followed in the footsteps of these ICS luminaries, and the book was still well known in bureaucratic circles when my generation joined the IAS in the 1970s. A similar well-known compilation, *Memoirs of Old Mandarins of India* edited by Raj K. Nigam came out in 1985. It contained write-ups on their service memories by 21 ICS officers and brief comments by six more such officers. One article from K.L. Punjabi's book was reproduced with due permission in this volume. The contributors had felt that their narratives would serve as "a shot in the arm", to many an IAS officer to emulate them and serve the country in the best traditions of the civil service, and as reference material for present and future generations of administrators and students and scholars of contemporary Indian history and public administration. Both these books were edited by former government servants, one of whom had served in the ICS, and they had specially solicited reminiscences from various ICS officers for their books.

I am aware of only three collections of IAS reminiscences, though it is possible that others exist.

One, *Governance and the IAS: In Search of Resilience* edited by R.K. Dar came out in 1999. It primarily concentrates on reminiscences by officers of the 1958 batch of the IAS (of which Dar himself was one) which was the twelfth and last batch to be trained at Metcalfe House, Delhi before the IAS training shifted to the National Academy of Administration at Mussoorie. But it is more than the recollections of 14 officers who wrote about their early years in service, their working at the middle level in government, as well as their senior level postings. Twenty officers of the IAS 1958 batch (including the 14 whose service recollections are set forth in the first part of this book) gathered at the National Academy of Administration in Mussoorie for five days in 1997 along with 18 experts from other government services and other walks of life, including academia, to discuss (some in closed sessions of the Twelfth Metcalfians, and some in interactions with the experts) their memories and insights regarding certain administration related themes. The report of these dialogues forms the second part of this book, some commentaries by the experts form a third part, and then there is a section on the IAS in Uttar Pradesh. Though reasonably well known, this book cannot be deemed to be one where former IAS officers 'tell' about their experiences—it also goes into much analysis based on the 5-day workshop, the views of the experts, etc.

Another book is *The Collectors Recollect* (1987) edited by Mohan Mukherji (a former IAS officer who had earlier risen to the level of Chief

Secretary) and Ramesh K. Arora (an academic), which concentrates on first-hand accounts by 15 members of the Indian Administrative Service of their experiences as District Collectors, some of which, via their being used as training reprints brought out by HCM Rajasthan State Institute of Public Administration (HCM RIPA) Jaipur, have found their way into Section II of this book. Ramesh K. Arora who has since joined as Visiting Professor at HCM RIPA is to be thanked for the use of these essays.

Mohan Mukherji and Ramesh K. Arora had planned another book on the reminiscences of the IAS to further the understanding of the role played by the "men at the top" in State Government in operating and transforming administrative structures. Following the demise of Mukherji, the volume came out as, *In the Corridors of Power* (1997) edited by Ramesh K. Arora and contained reminiscences of 13 administrators, both direct recruits and promotees to the IAS.

For both the above books the editors pursued and persuaded IAS officers to provide contributions.

All the above mentioned books and their contributors have been inspired (and some books specifically refer to it) by Philip Woodruff's, *The Men Who Ruled India* (2 volumes) 1954, which, as one of the contributors to Section II of this book mentions, "still finds a revered place on the bookshelves of senior district officer's personal libraries ... official dinners and farewell parties were often punctuated with an anecdote culled from these pages by careerists, who always hoped that at some point of their service tenure, they would go through similar travails and that some modern Woodruff would write about their efforts in overcoming the built-in resistance in the system which has always been an important part of a district officers functioning". However it is felt that the younger recruits to the IAS may not be as familiar with this book which continues to remain in print in India.

Of course, *The Men Who Ruled India* does not contain reminiscences of the ICS and its predecessor HEICS (Honourable East India Company Service) as especially written for Woodruff's book as was the case of all the other publications referred to above, since the persons concerned were long gone when Philip Woodruff wrote the book. Instead letters, journal entries etc., of and about the protagonists have been studied and biographical accounts of prominent 'civilians' or administrators of the British Raj along with extensive quotations in their own words as well as paraphrasing have been provided by Woodruff who himself served in the ICS in the years preceding independence (real name Philip Mason). His work has followed a chronological approach with the first volume tracing the story till the events of 1857 and chronicling the work of 'the founders', and the second bringing up the tale till India's independence and describing the endeavours of 'the guardians'.

Recently, in 2005, David Gilmour has brought out, *The Ruling Caste: Imperial Lives in the Victoria Raj* which some reviewers feel will replace, *The Men Who Ruled India* as the definitive book about the British administrative (or ruling) class in India, whereby through exhaustive research in official archives and family papers, Gilmour has provided a panorama of what it was like to administer the British Raj. Gilmour has focussed on individuals who manned the civil service so as to understand the HEICS/ICS institutions through their members. It becomes clear that many concerns regarding issues like recruitment, training, allotment of provincial or state cadres, cadre management, promotions, secretariat assignments versus field postings, retirement and pensions, hobbies and other intellectual or leisure related non-official activities, their ambitions, and the role and views of spouses and families, which concerned British Indian Civil Servants during the approximately 70-year period of the Victorian age (which was punctuated by the change from Company rule to that of the Crown in 1858), are very similar to those which concern today's IAS officers.

Both the books highlight the high standards set by many of these civilians, but do not omit the warts of some members of the civil service and even refer to some social scandals regarding some officers. Both books provide inspiring reading, more so, *The Men Who Ruled India*. Both are a joy to read.

I have also come across favourable references to Roland Hunt and John Harrison, *The District Officer in India 1930–1947* (1980) which could perhaps serve as a useful point of comparison with the essays in Section II of this book, but have not yet been privileged to read that work.

Mention may also be made of Sanjoy Bagchi's, *The Changing Face of Bureaucracy: Fifty Years of the IAS* (2007). Bagchi had joined the IAS in the early 1950s but left after 25 years to spend a couple of decades abroad. On returning to India he "decided to make an honest and objective study" of the IAS with a view to coming up with recommendations to reverse what he perceived as the decline in the IAS, which in his view had commenced after the 1960s. He has consulted many reminiscences and recollections, both published and unpublished, by IAS and ICS officers and also much of what has been written analyzing the IAS and its actions. So, strictly speaking, it is not a biographical book, nor has it concentrated upon of narratives by officers remembering their years in service.

Having gone through the above mentioned efforts makes one feel that compiling the memoirs of some officers of the IAS will not only provide an interesting and useful read today, but would also provide relevant material for posterity to analyze. It may even inspire the younger officers and those who are still to come, just as some of the books mentioned above have inspired earlier generations of administrators.

One factor why it was felt appropriate to put together the present compilation was the fact that at HCM RIPA I have, over the last 3–4 years, been soliciting IAS officers to write about their experiences which may prove useful and relevant for younger serving officers or trainees since they not only describe actual situations and challenges that were faced but also contain lessons for the future. In fact, all but one of the contributions in Section I and the sole essay in section III of this book were originally brought out as training booklets by HCM RIPA. Similarly, five of the contributions in Section II were earlier published as training reprints by HCM RIPA. Some other contributions were published in the HCM RIPA journal, *Prashasnika*. All of these were very well received not only by young officers and trainees, but also by scholars and researchers, senior and retired officers and the intelligent lay person. This encouraged this editor to put them together in book form in the shape of the current anthology.

A number of IAS officers have now started producing autobiographical books and finding publishers for the same. However, it is felt that combining the experiences of a number of IAS officers in one volume would provide a much better (and varied) overview of IAS officers at work, than the views of a single officer as may be available in a book length autobiography which contains a single world-view and a single approach to administration and may become too personalized and invidividualized.

Accordingly, this book has been put together in the hope that the knowledge, understanding and appreciation of the realities of IAS working that it provides would prove equally useful to the critic who wants to reform the civil service, the scholar researcher who wants to study and analyze Indian administration and government including the constraints and the opportunities available, the teacher or trainer who can use many of the incidents and issues as case studies or teaching material, the media commentator, the officer looking for learning as well as inspiration from the experiences of the others, the people wanting to understand how Indian administration particularly at the State and district levels has been undergoing change, the general reader desirous of an interesting read, and the youngster wondering whether or not to attempt joining the IAS.

And so, on to the words of the contributors…

I

IAS Careers Remembered

SECTIONAL INTRODUCTION

Career Progression in the IAS

Rakesh Hooja

The IAS has been referred to as a generalist service par excellence. Its members shift from one department to another, one sector to another, from generalized administration to more specialized working, from field and implementation—related assignments to secretariat and policy-making postings. The variety of experiences that members of the IAS undergo during their career may be unmatched in any other career service in the world.

A fresh IAS probationer or 'officer-trainee' reporting to Charleville, the National Academy of Administration at Mussoorie, after having successfully negotiated the grueling Union Public Service Commission recruitment process can never imagine what sort of postings would be in his/her fate over the next 30 to 35 years. Nevertheless, there is a rough pattern which most of the IAS officers follow in this career.

The first two years comprise induction training. The Mussoorie training starts with a foundation course in common with other Central Services. Thereafter, the professional course for the IAS at the Mussoorie Academy is in two phases which sandwich the State and district training conducted in the officers' state of allotment. The Bharat Darshan during the first phase of the professional course at the Academy when the trainees visit various regions of the country may be the only time in their lives that some officers visit certain parts of the country. In fact, the day in Mussoorie when the officer-trainee learns as to whether he/she would be getting one's home state or would be going to the cadre of another state, has always been a defining moment determining the region in which much of the working life of the officer is to be spent. Though they do not know it then, and are raring to report for their regular first postings, the trainees are destined never again to cross paths with some of their batch mates allotted to other State Cadres, or may only meet up with them in some meeting or training course, 20 or 30 years later.

A short stint as Sub Divisional Officer/Sub-Divisional Magistrate is common for virtually all IAS officers. In the last decade or so some young IAS officers have been moving on from the Sub Divisional posting to that of Executive Officer of a municipal council at a district headquarters. In the early 1960s when Panchayati Raj was new and receiving much importance a posting as a Block Development Officer could also occur.

Thereafter, comes one's first promotion from the junior scale. In some states this has meant an assignment as Additional Collector/Additional District Magistrate, or Project Director District Rural Development Agency, or Chief Executive Officer Zila Parishad. In other States the coveted district assignment as District Collector (also referred to as Deputy Commissioner or District Magistrate in some States) accrues along with the first promotion. Some go to the Secretariat as Deputy Secretary to the State Government upon promotion.

Then follows a period of rotating between being District Collector, Deputy Secretary to the State Government in the State Secretariat, and a Director or Head of Department (HOD) in an executive State level department in the State capital. Some get assignments as Executive Director or Managing Director in State Government Public Sector Undertakings or 'State Enterprises'. A District Collector posting, like that of HOD or Deputy Secretary can come more than once to an IAS officer. Most IAS officers prefer a District Collector posting to that of a Deputy Secretary to State government because of the greater importance accorded to a Collector by both government and by society, as also because of the perks available as a Collector in the field. Later, as seniority brings further promotions, the officer may become a Special Secretary to State Government—but still rotates between that, being District Collector in a larger, more important, district, and being an HOD.

Then comes a major milestone—promotion to the Supertime Scale of the IAS and posting as a Secretary to government heading an administrative department in the State Secretariat. Equivalent postings may be Divisional Commissioner coordinating a number of districts (or an Area Development Commissioner) or being HOD of a more important executive department with the designation becoming Commissioner instead of Director, or Chairman and Managing Director of a State Enterprise. There are also some not so popular postings like being made Member of the Board of Revenue or Commissioner for Departmental Enquires. Till the late 1980s or early 1990s most IAS officers retired in the Supertime Scale with only one or two rising higher to become the State's Chief Secretary or the Chairman of the Board of Revenue. Now, however, a level of Principal Secretary to State Government above the Supertime Scale exists and most officers reach that level. The erstwhile posts of Secretary to Chief Minister and Secretary to Governor have also now got upgraded to the level of Principal Secretary. Such officers also get to head important State Enterprises. A handful of officers (not all the officers in any batch because many retire as Principal Secretaries) attain the grade of the Chief Secretary and are designated as

Additional Chief Secretaries or Chairman, Board of Revenue—and of course a select few become Chief Secretaries in the State Government. The contributors to this volume include more than one officer who served as Chief Secretary.

This is the normal pattern within the state, but other assignments which do not from part of the cadre posts designated for IAS in the State Government are also possible. Two of the reminiscences in this section allude to assignments as Vice-Chancellors of Universities, and one to being a visiting faculty at Indian Institute of Management, Ahmedabad.

The IAS being an All-India Service, its officers can also rotate between the State of their allotment and the Central Government. But for that, not only does the officer have to give his option or desire for a deputation to the Government of India, but the State Government has to agree to permit such a move, and the Government of India to accept the officer after reviewing his/her service record—whereby he/she is 'empanelled' and accepted on the offer list for central deputation. Thereafter, the officer has to be accepted by a specific Central Ministry for a specific job in Delhi or elsewhere in the country, and this has to be cleared by the appointments Sub Committee of Cabinet which includes approval by the Prime Minister.

Officers who have yet to attain the supertime scale go to the Government of India as Deputy Secretary or Director to Government of India. Those at the level of supertime scale go as Joint Secretary which is a key assignment in Government of India. The Principal Secretary to State Government corresponds to Additional Secretary in Government of India, and Additional Chief Secretary or Chief Secretary to State Government to the post of Secretary in Government of India. In the last couple of decades a number of Central assignments equal in status and pay to that a Secretary to Government of India have also emerged—many as Secretary to various national Commissions.

The first time an officer goes to Government of India there is an initial struggle to adjust to both living and working in a different and more impersonal environment. However, soon the all-India nature of issues involved in Central Government postings and the various attractions of metropolitan life in Delhi become more than acceptable to many an officer and his family.

The system calls for rotation between postings in Central Government and in State Government. A Deputy Secretary gets a 3-year tenure at the Centre, a Director a 4-year tenure and a Joint Secretary a 5-year tenure. After a Central tenure an IAS officer has to serve a minimum mandatory 3-year 'cooling off' period in the State Government. In this way, the Central Government gets the benefit of persons experienced of having worked at the district and state levels, and a State Government has available to it persons who have dealt with all-India and international issues while working in the Central Government.

However, a tendency has developed amongst some officers, either because their families decide to permanently settle in Delhi, or because they have not been allotted to their home states and feel that they are 'outsiders' in their state cadre, or because they fall afoul of the politicians in their cadre state, for officers to try to get their Central deputation extended or to get their 'cooling off' period in the State Government reduced, so that they can spend much of their service career in Delhi. This often involves seeking political pressure and patronage and developing links with politicians and senior IAS colleagues who can then act a 'godfathers'.

Opportunities for IAS officers, particularly those who have served in Government of India to serve in multilateral (UN etc., agencies) at foreign locations have gone up in recent years, though they were not totally unheard of in the 1950s and 1960s.

Since the 1970s there has been a lot of emphasis on training and capacity building for the IAS. Attending of one short course every year or once in two years at selected institutes in the country became compulsory. Opportunities for very short, or three months, or one year training at Universities abroad also increased significantly. From the 1970s to 1990s many opportunities existed in Commonwealth countries and especially in Britain and many IAS officers obtained a second Master's degree from a University in Britain on scholarships earmarked for government servants. Later the IAS officers have had to compete with people from outside government and a number of IAS officers have now been going especially to USA for long trainings.

Opportunities for further government assignments after retirement have also increased over the last decade or so—particularly for those who retire from Government of India. The reminiscences in this volume include one (in the second section of the book) from an officer initially recruited in the early 1950s who retired from Government of India and eventually rose to be Governor of an Indian State, as also those by officers who retired from the State Government yet obtained further government assignments.

Earlier, very few IAS officers took up a private sector job after retirement. Now, many have started doing so. In fact, gradually some IAS officers have also started opting for voluntary retirement to join the private sector, something virtually unknown till 20 years ago.

The above is a simplified and generalized depiction of the career progression and life pattern of members of the IAS.

However, within this overall framework the postings or assignments of IAS officers can be extremely varied.

The Annual Performance Appraisal Report (APAR) form asks the reporting officer to suggest for very senior IAS officers as to which out of twelve domains would be most appropriate for the particular officer to be posted in. Not every officer in these domains is from the IAS, but some members of the IAS may be found working in each of these domains.

These domains cover virtually every ministry, department or agency in Government of India as indicated in the following table:

I. Agriculture and Rural Development			
1.	Department of Agriculture and Cooperation	2.	Department of Agricultural Research and Education
3.	Department of Animal Husbandry, Dairying and Fisheries	4.	Ministry of Agro and Rural Industries
5.	Department of Rural Development	6.	Ministry of Panchayati Raj
7.	Department of Land Resources	8.	Department of Drinking Water Supply
9.	Department of Food and Public Distribution	10.	Department of Consumer Affairs
11.	Ministry of Food Processing Industries		
II. Social Development			
1.	Department of Health	2.	Department of Family Welfare
3.	Department of Ayurveda, Yoga and Naturopathy, Unani, Siddha and Homeopathy (AYUSH)	4.	Department of Secondary and Higher Education.
5.	Department of Elementary Education and Literacy.	6.	Department of Women and Child Development
7.	Ministry of Social Justice and Empowerment.	8.	Department of Urban Employment and Poverty Alleviation.
9.	Ministry of Overseas Indian Affairs		
III. Culture and Information			
1.	Ministry of Information and Broadcasting	2.	Ministry of Culture
3.	Ministry of Tourism	4.	Ministry of Tribal Affairs
5.	Ministry of Youth Affairs and Sports		
IV. Natural Resources Management			
1.	Ministry of Environment and Forests	2.	Ministry of Water Resources
3	Department of Ocean Development	4.	Ministry of Mines
V. Energy and Environment			
1.	Department of Atomic Energy	2.	Ministry of Non-Conventional Energy Sources
3.	Department of Coal	4.	Ministry of Petroleum and Natural Gas
5.	Ministry of Power		
VI. Communication Systems and Connectivity Infrastructure			
1.	Ministry of Civil Aviation	2.	Department of Information Technology
3.	Department of Telecommunication	4.	Department of Posts
5.	Ministry of Road Transport and Highways	6.	Department of Shipping

VII. Public Finance and Financial Management			
1.	Department of Disinvestment	2.	Department of Expenditure
3.	Department of Economic Affairs	4.	Department of Revenue
5.	Ministry of Company Affairs	6.	Planning Commission
7.	Ministry of Statistics and Programme Implementation		
VIII. Industry and Trade			
1.	Department of Industrial Policy and Promotion	2.	Department of Chemicals and Petrochemicals
3.	Department of Commerce	4.	Department of Heavy Industries
5.	Department of Fertilizers	6.	Ministry of Textiles
7.	Department of Public Enterprises	8.	Ministry of Small Scale Industries
IX. Internal Affairs and Defence			
1.	Department of Defence	2.	Department of Defence Production
3.	Department of Defence Research and Development	4.	Department of Ex-Servicemen Welfare
5.	Department of Internal Security	6.	Department of States
7.	Department of Official Languages	8.	Department of Home
9.	Department of Jammu & Kashmir Affairs	10.	Department of Border Management
11.	Ministry of Development of North Eastern Region		
X. Housing and Urban Affairs			
1.	Ministry of Urban Development		
XI. Personnel and General Administration, Governance Reform, Regulatory Systems			
1.	Department of Personnel and Training	2.	Department of Administrative Reforms and Public Grievances
3.	Department of Pensions and Pensioners Welfare	4.	Department of Legal Affairs
5.	Legislative Department	6.	Department of Justice
7.	Cabinet Secretariat	8.	Ministry of Labour and Employment
9.	President's Secretariat	10.	Ministry of Parliamentary Affairs
11.	Prime Minister's Office	12.	UPSC
13.	Election Commission		
XII. Science and Technology			
1.	Department of Science and Technology	2.	Department of Scientific and Industrial Research
3.	Department of Bio-Technology	4.	Department of Space

A similar listing done at the State Government level would also show that IAS officers can be posted in any domain of government. Almost all Secretaries and Principal Secretaries heading all Secretariat or administrative departments in State Governments are IAS officers. Well over seventy per cent of all HODs of executive departments are from the IAS. Virtually all State level public sector utilities or state enterprises are headed by IAS officers. All Collectors are members of the IAS. Thus, each officer works in an extremely wide variety of fields or sectors/sub sectors during his/her career.

This is reflected in the seven pieces in this section (one written in the late 1980s and all the rest after the turn of the Century) wherein the IAS memories of the seven officers now retired or dead cover the 60 years from independence and the days following partition till today when the first decade of the 21st century is more than half gone.

1 R.D. THAPAR

Reminiscences of My Service Career

Prelude

The Year 1949

One early September morning, Sarla and I were still asleep on charpoys spread out in the back street of our house in Rehgharpura, Delhi, when we were woken up by someone banging on the front door and shouting my name. Hurriedly I got up and on opening the door found standing there and gesticulating wildly my friend and colleague D.N. Sethi. He had a newspaper in his hand and conveyed to us the happy news that I had been selected for appointment to the IAS through the Emergency Recruitment Scheme.

This once again supported the truth of the repeated cliche that divine justice though sometime delayed is seldom denied. Eight years earlier I had topped the University at MA examination but due to wartime restrictions on recruitment and certain other factors had to spend the next six years in a Class II service under the Central Government. In between had intervened the trauma of the country's partition when my family (alongwith million others) had to leave its home and move to Delhi to set up a new home in an unelectrified house situated in a locality where you breathed the smells of hides being treated. All this was now to change.

District Administration

I joined Metcalfe House, New Delhi on 15th October, 1949 and stayed there till the year end, undergoing a compressed (not abridged) training programme. Our part-time Principal was S.B. Bapat of the ICS, who later on chose to take premature retirement. He took no formal teaching course but shared with us gems based on his personal experiences. Out of many of these, I recall two: do not speak ill of a subordinate in the presence of his colleagues and do not criticize your boss before your colleagues as certainly this will reach your boss. He cautioned against (a) a relative (e.g., father) staying with you becoming overtly intimate with any person of the locality (this could supposedly give rise to a conduit to your developing); and (b) meeting self-styled intermediaries in private who could cash in on their contact with you without bothering even to mention any specific grievances. I must mention here a humane aspect of Bapat who when informed of my (and S.L. Khurana's) allotment to Assam, which would have largely materialized the prospect of emotional rehabilitation (for our parents) dictated out representations and brought back next day revised orders allotting both of us to Rajasthan. We were overage recruits between 27 to 45 years old. With our diverse backgrounds, it took some time before we felt settled down to class room routines. Initially, there was a marked lack of rapport with the Vice Principal who was keen to enforce discipline like no smoking etc., but as days passed and with most of us having our first brush with the structure aspects of district administration and criminal and civil law, supplemented by very interesting talks from a galaxy of guest speakers, the atmosphere became more congenial for training routine.

The emergency intake (including the war service and the special recruits of 1956–57) seems to have been discarded as a source of recruitment to the country's top civil services. To me it seems that reasons for this decision are insufficient. On the other hand, there are many positive factors which would favour a continuing resort to this source. It would provide an opportunity to: (a) the late flowering (as also those who initially chose a different career and later on decide to join the civil services) material; (b) the officers of other services at the Centre who could bring in their rich backgrounds after say up to 8–12 years in different fields; (c) the outstanding state civil service officers who in most northern and eastern states (where recruitment is 75% directly through the PSCs) have to wait for nearly 20 years before they reach the consideration range for promotion to the IAS; and finally (d) supplement the direct recruitment which at one stage was 30 per annum and has now exceeded 150 per annum. A ceiling of 100 per annum could operate for direct recruitment and balance requirement could be met through this special source. This should, however, not be done on an ad hoc basis but become a regular source to be resorted to say once in two years. Being overage, these recruits will not dilute the promotion prospects of the direct recruits. As regards quality I need only mention that in my batch of four allotted to

Rajasthan, two ended up as Secretaries to Government of India and one as a State Chief Secretary. Two of them were after retirement appointed as Advisors to the Governor (and one, S.L. Khurana has become a Governor) not a bad record, I should say.

On 5th January, 1950 I travelled from Delhi to Mathura by Frontier Mail, an elite train those days. Late Sushital Banerjee was at the platform to meet me. He took me home where I stayed till he found a separate accommodation for me and my family. This was to by my home for the next 27 months. Those days a Joint Magistrate (which was my designation) had the prestige which went with a Collector designate. The district was irrigated by two canal systems, as also being as important pilgrim centre had a satisfactory district roads coverage. These made touring both comfortable and enjoyable.

At that time an SDO (Sub-Divisional Officer) had to spend a fixed number of nights out every year and the precise villages to be inspected were specified by the Board of Revenue. This system assured that every village was visited by the SDO at least once every five years. The need for such an intensive touring has decreased due to most of the districts opening up, spread of awareness with growing education and a significant rise of the local leadership. Even then as India still lives in its villages, it will be to mutual advantage of the administration as also of the villagers if Jeep culture could be curbed and sub divisional and district officers are required to camp deep in the interior away from roadside villages, for a minimum number of nights out, every year. It may not generally be necessary to camp in tents (as I did during two winters) as schools or panchayat buildings have since become available for the purpose.

As a probationer, I had the opportunity of coming very close to my Collector. This was a time honoured tradition as the probationer learnt quite a lot by observing how his Collector functioned on files, with the district officers, during interviews with the public and while dealing with grievances orally presented to him while on tour. He, on occasions, accompanied his Collector on district tours and again watched how various matters were attended to or how the Collector carried out inspection of tehsils, sub-treasuries and police station. Socially, he was a permanent invitee to all parties given by the Collector and was thus made aware of the social obligations of the district officer. Later on, during my 4-year term as a Collector I had three IAS probationers attached to me and I took this responsibility somewhat seriously. I saw the probationers through their difficult district training and can recall with satisfaction the subsequent record of at least two of them. I think this phase of training is important enough for the government to attach probationers with experienced Collectors who can be expected to realize their responsibility in this regard.

My Collector at Mathura was an able and hard working officer. But these qualities got largely neutralized by the generally poor view that he took of the capability of his colleagues including the SP, his SDOs and the political and civic leaders. Very early in my career I thus witnessed the relative ineffectiveness of a highly competent officer who depended far too much on his own individual efforts. Later on also I found a somewhat similar attitude repeated again and again. The number two officer in an organization was more often than not sidelined and not kept involved with the mainstream functions of the department. This attitude was born out of a reluctance to broad base the decision-making level. The head of the organization perhaps found it easier to issue instructions to his subordinates rather than try to reach 'joint decision' in full consultation with his next junior level, who had the seniority and experience to occasionally present a differing point of view, after which it might be inconvenient to issue ill-considered or biassed orders.

There were no doubt exceptions also. I had, however, the good fortune to work closely with late B. Mehta who was Chief Secretary of Rajasthan for nearly a decade. He was an officer of average competence but he succeeded largely by leading an efficient team. He had the quality of picking officers to work in key positions, making wide delegation and then completely trusting them. The result was that he got total loyalty and optimum output from his selected team. Obviously the output of a trusted team was much more than that of a single individual, however capable he may have been. He was one of the few Chief Secretaries whose contribution to development of the state was recognized by conferment of a Padma Shri Award.

Towards the end of my stay at Mathura, the first general election was held and I got rich experience in my capacity as a returning officer of two assembly constituencies. For an administrative officer, the total output of experience in organizing a general election or a census or during a natural calamity far exceeds that obtained during months of routine administration. This decision-making and supervisory faculties get fully extended and the confidence gained in successfully organizing, controlling in an effective manner a large scale machinery to cope with a massive situation helps in his total growth. The first elections were organized on the basis of rudimentary polling facilities. This situation further compounded because of the difficulties created by the inability of an illiterate rural voter to correctly identify the favoured candidates box from a large number of boxes arranged in a dingy corner of an ill-lit room. Those days, each candidate was allotted a separate box and a double-member constituency could have as many as twenty boxes. The general feeling in such circumstances was that God's hand was directing the polling of votes in favour of the most suitable candidates.

Late March, 1952, I reached Kota in Rajasthan where I had been transferred as SDO (subsequently also as Additional Collector). The district set-up was at that time a recent phenomenon in Rajasthan. Kota had 19 tehsils and my sub-division had 5 as against 4 and 1 respectively in Mathura. It was agriculturally a very rich district but most holdings were large sized and cultivators were generally lazy and not overtly aware of, not keen on, applying modern techniques to agriculture. Chambal project was still under consideration, the negative voices claiming that electricity will be surplus and irrigation would cause waterlogging and salinity.

The latter apprehension had some basis as the top soil in the district was hardly 6 feet deep and initial neglect in ensuring adequate drainage did cause these problems. However, the fear that electricity would be surplus was not new to Chambal only. Starting with Bhakra right bank, on to Rihand and then Shravarthy, this fear was repeated and contributed much to the damage subsequently caused by acute shortage of power. These projects were not only delayed in implementation, but as Nangal, Kota and Rihand led to allocation of temporarily surplus large quantities of power at very cheap rates for industries which used electricity as raw material. As the commitments both as regards quantities and rates were on long-term basis, the damage could not be undone when the purely temporary surplus disappeared.

Diametrically opposed to this is the culture among the irrigation engineers whose estimates as regards project viability are generally unduly optimistic. As Finance Secretary I had statistics compiled of minor and medium irrigation projects completed by then. These disclosed that while cost over runs were substantial not only in terms of money spent but also the time actually taken to complete the project, the actual command area irrigated and the revenue income were grossly below those included in the project reports.

Rajasthan was (and may still continue to be) a typical example of what Gunnar Myrdal called a 'Soft State'. In its case, the softness got compounded by an innate all pervading attitude of courtesy to be shown not only to one's superior but also to one's subordinates (drivers and peons were addressed with the suffix 'ji' added invariably). This approach in administration got translated into a clinical inability to be firm, not to speak of being harsh. The Minister incharge was appalled at the suggestion that prosecution should be continued even when the embezzled amount had been made good (the lonely secretariat officer reacted by noting that such a view would make embezzlement a risk-free operation, as if you got caught you refunded the amount, otherwise you could retain it with impunity). Late coming to offices was the norm and 'recommendation' was an accepted way of handling personnel matters. Half seriously, transfer orders were labelled merely as show cause notices, and affected persons fully availed of this attitude in getting these orders modified. Despite comparable delegation of powers, it was not unusual for direct government interference within the delegated authority. This rarely gave rise to protests, however, with some exceptions. Government orders transferring some overseers were challenged by an outstanding CE (Chief Engineer) on the plea that such orders should be passed after the government withdrew the authority regarding transfer of overseers delegated to him. When I was Director of Education, I received regularly letters from the Education Secretary concerning individual teachers. To each such letter my reply was on the line taken by the CE. There was never a come back to such a response but further cases of this type continued. Transfers of SHOs and Tehsildars were more frequently made (although these powers stood delegated to SPs and Board of Revenue). In a particular district, the average stay of an SHO at a Police Station was a month. I am not sure whether most of the DMs were aware of a requirement in the Police Regulations that SHOs could be transferred only on consultation with DMs. There in another important provision in the Police Regulations which directs that firing by police should not be in the air but at the legs so that its effect is visible. When I mentioned this to a highly successful Police Officer, his reply was typical: there are seldom any instances of enquiries ordered by the government when police has not fired or fired in the air. On the other hand, there is invariably a judicial enquiry ordered whenever police has ordered firing on the lines indicated in the Policy Regulations. One could add a post script by mentioning that while there may be enquiries against wrong decisions made by an officer in a bonafide manner, there are no cases in my knowledge when enquiries were ordered against the conduct of an officer who for long periods had not taken a decision. In fact, a senior officer had once advised me that one should not be in a hurry to take decision as most cases would get resolved automatically and would not require any decision if a matter was kept pending for long.

Much is said about interference from the politicians. I can categorically say this about this my personal experience in Rajasthan, that neither at district level nor within the Secretariat was there any large scale attempt at recommended actions from the political leaders. As Director of Education, a colleague and I were members of a 3-men committee charged with making selections of Head Master. We used to joke that none from among the very large number of candidates had 'flattered' us by bringing any political pressures in their favour. It seems to me that one makes one's reputation in this regard by saying no in the first dozen cases or so and thereafter the inflow of recommendations automatically dries up. There are three facets of this culture which I would like to briefly refer to:

(a) In quite a few cases, officers give a clear hint that they are susceptible to such pressures, the quid pro they expect is gaining of favours from the political leaders in postings/promotions. In such cases the number of recommendations made, accepted and favour gained in return are significant in number.

(b) While those who give way to pressure from political leader do gain favour (specially in comfortable or lucrative postings), I cannot recall cases where due rights were denied to those who chose not to give in. It was mostly the less important political leader or the weak Minister who interpreted rejection of his recommendation as a personal slight. An important leader or a strong Minister had full confidence in his intrinsic importance or strength. Nathu Ram Mirdha, one of the strongest Ministers in his time, had very good relations with his top level aids as he gave freedom to them to examine cases as they thought fit as he had the strength to overrule them wherever he felt so inclined. In fact, we tend to unduly malign the politician for interference while many more wrong decisions are taken on the intervention of an interested colleague. The 'son-in-law' syndrome largely confirms this view.

(c) We need not be unduly harsh on local officers who have wider contacts and thus have to withstand more widespread network of recommendations. It is easier for an outsider to feel superior in this regard but the truth of the matter is that their ability to resist gets an underpinning from a much narrower circle of those who can make recommendation to them.

On this subject I felt free to advise my probationers that they had the choice only at the start of their career to become 'convenient' officers. However, if they decided not to follow this path, then they should not feel bitter in case their colleagues who decided otherwise, had a more comfortable career progression; secondly, that in a democracy the political leaders had a useful role to play, e.g., by bringing to the notice of administration public grievances or reaction to government policies etc., and it would be wrong to react negatively to any suggestion or recommendation which emanated from them. These deserved as careful an attention as those coming from any other sources.

I worked as a Collector for nearly four years (somewhat unusual these days). Having personally benefited from this experience, I strongly subscribe to the view that this is perhaps the most important input in the process of developing in an IAS officer the qualities of confidence and capacity to take quick decisions. Government of India has repeatedly stressed the need for providing to IAS officer adequate experience in this post. The cadre structure has however got greatly distorted by the number of districts remaining virtually static and a relentless growth in non-district posts. One way to correct this growing imbalance would be by increasing the number of districts. This can be justified on grounds of increase in population and a need for more intensive district administration. Results of such an approach can be seen in Haryana, Punjab and to a lesser degree in Bihar. I believe a suggestion was made in the Second Plan that gradually each such division should be upgraded into a district. In view of the cost involved, this can be achieved in a phased manner.

Some of the district in each state are important because of the size (area or population) or have a history of communal troubles or are prone to natural calamities. Such districts in particular need to have more experienced officers. In my state, a short-lived decision was taken in early 1960s to post all selection grade officers to such districts. This approach not only served the purpose of posting senior officers to important districts but also provided a last opportunity, before they got promoted to super time scale, to an IAS officer to renew his experience of district administration. I think this requirement needs to be built into IAS pay structure which will permit availability of selection grade only on the post of Collector. As a corollary to this, the post of Director in the Central Government would stand abolished.

This seems to be an appropriate stage to record my experiences relating to some of the other important aspects of the district administration:

(a) I found that many district judges were inclined to generally pass order of acquittal. One particular judge passed such order in 27 out of 29 cases decided by him. It is quite possible that the fault lay with defective investigation or incompetent prosecution. I recall the informal comments made by an inspecting Chief Justice that the prosecution was always at a disadvantage as against the defence because the latter not only had personal interest in the case but that within his means the defence could hire the best available legal aid. He went on to remark that in this context, the Magistrates did succeed by their somewhat executive approach in evening out the inherent imbalance.

Prosecutions launched on the basis of defective investigation or acquittal that result from incompetent prosecution of cases in courts must be avoided to the extent possible, as in addition to causing unnecessary harassment to a member of the public, these involve waste of public money. I remember that when I had just joined service, for each case which resulted in acquittal it was mandatory for the prosecutor to propose an acquittal note giving reasons that had led to acquittal. These notes were submitted to the SP and the DM who could thus take suitable action in the cases of negligence or incompetence. I hope this practice has continued or been revived. A connected aspect is the filing of appeals on behalf of the government. It was my experience that in almost all cases where government lost in lower courts the government counsel recommended filing of appeals and the legal department sanctioned these as part of a defensive mechanism. As State Finance Secretary I had suggested that data be collected of appeals filed and accepted out to those for a given period to examine this problem in depth. Such a review undertaken periodically can help reduce filing of government appeals as a matter of routine. It will thereby reduce harassment, save public expenditure and to an extent bring down appellate work load in the higher courts.

(b) In the past, the Collector's position as a Captain of the team at the district level (virtually representing the total government at that level e.g., Section 80 CPC notice continued to be served on him) was never questioned. Times have changed since then but still a Collector is able to secure acceptance of this position not always by virtue of his post but because he alone at that level can directly approach the government even the Chief Secretary. If he uses this tool to help sort out problems at the district level, he gets from his colleagues a more willing acceptance of his leadership. Difficulties have arisen when an individual Collector has not only been unhelpful but has compounded this default by assuming a position of arrogance verging on rudeness.

(c) Democratic decentralization was introduced in 1957 with a lot of fanfare. Great hopes were raised that this was a right step towards what C.M. Trivedi (an eminent civilian) termed as 'decentralization of democracy'. Democracy will not develop into a culture if it remains confined only to the central and state levels. It must come down to district, panchayat samiti and panchayat level. A lot of benefits had flowed from this programme in the early stages, more importantly in the sphere of generating local leadership which helped articulate local felt needs. However, interest has of late waned as would be evident from almost complete absence of public debates on these institutions. The State Governments have contributed to this trend by refusing to make any further delegation of function to these bodies. Another factor which has been responsible for this development is the irregular elections being organized for these bodies. In my state of Rajasthan, elections were not held for more than a decade. This seems to be an attitude to local bodies *per se*. Wholesale super-cessions have been ordered and administrators instead (State Government officers) continue for prolonged periods. During the British regime, our leaders were vocally critical of lack of importance which the government then gave to the development of local bodies. Even then, Allahabad Municipal Board (and elsewhere) succeeded in electing a person of the calibre of Pandit Moti Lal Nehru as its chairman. Since independence large scale supercessions of local bodies delayed elections and inadequate delegation of functions to them (in some cases, these are even less than what was the position during British period when District Boards, e.g., controlled secondary schools, dispensaries and district roads) have stifled the development of local bodies, both urban and rural. A stage seems to have been reached when public interest in this level of government has totally waned. I think this to be an unhealthy trend for growth of democratic culture in the country and our political leadership should seriously consider whether as in the case of imposition of President's Rule, a statutory limit should be placed on the maximum period for which a local body can remain superceded. Further, periodical commissions, say once every five years, should study and review the development of local bodies and make recommendation for suitable devolution of administrative functions and finances to them.

Functions which are easier to delegate are at least those which were being exercised even during the British period, i.e., secondary education, dispensaries (including veterinary), internal roads, domestic electric and water connections, metre reading, billing and cash collections. Otherwise over time electricity and water boards would be completely overwhelmed by these elementary functions and the non-technical staff would come to have a disproportionately large claim to the care and attention of these boards and their officers, much to the neglect and detriment of these intrinsic functions, viz., of generating electricity and developing sources of potable water supply, maintaining them at optimum efficiency levels and laying down loss saving distribution system. Apprehensive note is often voiced that funds so collected by local bodies would be diverted to meet routine expenses and that payment of dues of the state electricity and water boards would suffer in the result. This could be avoided by stipulating requirement that such funds would be banked in closed accounts which carry a first charge of meeting the bills of the electricity and water boards. A healthy local government structure not only helps provide a base for training local leadership, a pool for future leaders at the state and central levels, but is also a safeguard against emergence of totalitarian culture in the country. On the other hand, one cannot always hope for growth of democratic traditions at the central and state levels while continuing with the policy of suppressing their development at the local levels.

(d) Rajasthan is geographically the second largest state in the country. It had five posts of Divisional Commissioners till 1960, when it was suddenly decided to abolish all of them. The ostensible reasons given at that time were that expenditure on these posts was disproportionate to their utility in the administration structure. As regards expenses, I do not think much has been saved because at one time or another Rajasthan has had, proportionate to its cadre strength, perhaps the highest number of super time posts. A case for the posts of commissioners rests on a number of factors. UP, which after independence brought down the number of commissioners to perhaps three has gone back to the original number. Barring a couple of South Indian states, which never had these posts, all other states have continued with them.

The commissioners are useful as eyes and ears of the government in outlying areas, in coordinating varied governmental activities at their level, in overseeing the work of collectors in administrative and development fields, in conducting informal enquiries into any serious complaints reaching the government and above all in organizing the large scale efforts required to meet natural calamities or events of similar magnitude. It has always intrigued me as to how the Chief Secretary found it possible to keep such an intimate contact with 27 collectors, on their work the year round, so as to feel competent to initiate and write confidential reports on them (Rajasthan has since reintroduced the system).

Services

Out of my 29 years in the IAS, I spent eight in the district and for nearly 15 years a major part of my responsibility involved dealing with service matters within the state and at the Centre.

The responsibility for dealing with service related matters is in the nature of a sacred trust reposed in you both by the government as also by the members of the concerned services. Early in my career I had in routine endorsed a recommendation that the senior-most officer may be superceded and next officer may be promoted. I was then advised by my first Under Secretary, C.D. Sharma, that each such case, general or particular, must be examined as if the case in question was your own case, Unfortunately, there is a generally accepted view that 'the constitutional guarantee of equality before law' does not apply to service matters dealt with at government level and hence the widespread repetition of the snide remark "show me the man and I will show you the rule". This absence of confidence in the impartiality of government has given rise to the tendency to seek relief from the courts. I hope the recently constituted administrative tribunals are a step in the right direction and their overall utility will not get limited merely to reduction of work load in the courts but that their decisions will help revise the trend of a growing feeling of loss of faith by the generality of employees in government Adoption of uniform principles while dealing with service matter is a sine qua non. This should no longer be merely a principle to be enforced by courts but be seen by the employees an emerging from the generality of government decisions.

My long experience in dealing with service matters has highlighted another aspect. There is seldom a finality to a government decision on such matters until a favourable decision has been secured. The affected person persists in making repeated representations in the hope that at some stage, circumstances will favour him. There might be genuine change of attitude at the (new) decision-making level, a more sympathetic political boss or a favourable court decision in a parallel case. Take for example the case of a Chief Engineer who was continued as an Additional Chief, functioning as such under a Chief Engineer. Almost four years later, on his representation a decision was taken, the Accountant General's protest not withstanding, that this officer should be deemed to have been promoted as a Chief Engineer retrospectively (and remunerated as such) even though at that time a conscious decision had been taken to grant extension in service to the Chief Engineer and that particular Engineer had functioned and discharged the responsibilities of an Additional Chief Engineer.

During the four years that I was responsible in the Home Ministry for processing requests for changes in cadre of IAS/IPS officers, the only ground on which such request were granted was the bringing together to one cadre of husband and wife. However, during this period, four officers succeeded in getting their requests accepted on grounds other than this (in three cases the ground given was that they had remained away from the parent cadre for long periods, which initially was itself an extraordinary step. Their representations for change of cadre were rejected repeatedly. However, their persistence got them success and finally their requests were accepted and cadre transfers were allowed.

I strongly believe that individual officers are willing to accept hardships in the matter of postings and transfers provided these result from application of accepted principles and favours are not shown in individual cases. Again during the period that I was dealing with IAS/IPS in the Home Ministry, allotment of individuals to various state cadres was made strictly in accordance with an approved formula. In one or two cases when any probationer succeeded in being given an insight into the precise process adopted in making such allocations their response was that not only the formula was being fairly implemented but that it was being ruthlessly applied. The result was that most of the probationers by and large willingly accepted allocation to far off States. Similarly, when in early 1960s, Rajasthan Government decided (I was at that time Secretary, Services) that an officer must work as a Block Development Officer for two years before he would be considered for appointment as Sub-Divisional Officer for two years before he would be considered for appointment as Sub-Divisional Officer, the decision was easily implemented as it was uniformly applied to all including the (then) Chief Minister's son-in-law and the (then) Home Minister's son. The result was that all officers willingly moved to interior places where most of the headquarters of the BDOs were located. This decision had to be scrapped subsequently as exemptions came to be made which in due course made implementation of the general decision a difficult matter.

Based on my own experience as also while dealing with service matters, it seemed to me that government employees feel most concerned about the level of their emoluments, promotion prospects, seniority and postings/transfers.

(a) Emoluments are generally determined on the basis of recommendations periodically made by Pay Commissions. I was Joint Secretary in the Third Pay Commission and had then hoped that it might be the last occasion a Pay Commission with wide ranging terms of references would be appointed. There is no doubt a lot of advantage in asking a Pay Commission to review pay scales and service conditions. But I found the relativities *inter se* were so well entrenched that basically a Pay Commission only determined a few model (bench-mark posts) scales and fixation of pay scales for the remaining posts was mostly a clerical exercise. However, an employee attaches importance not only to his own emoluments in absolute terms but also relative to what others are being paid. This belief gets strengthened by the general experience that while all Pay Commissions recommended a much fewer number of scales, it became difficult for the government to resists demands for upgradation on the basis of pre-existing differences that finally (during the intervals between any two Pay Commissions) most of the abolished pay scale had to be restored.

Over the years pay scales have gradually improved significantly. However, compared to rewards in the private and even the public sector, there is still room for further improvement, but there are important constraints also. One is the question of numbers. It is an admitted fact that government offices are scandalously overstaffed. In fact, an experienced Chief Minister felt frustrated enough to burst out saying: whatever additional revenue we raise, goes into defraying the increase of pay/allowances which becomes available to government employees. I felt similarly affected when I learnt that a marginal interim relief recommended by the Third Pay Commission to the low-paid employees would cost Rs 45 crore. Earlier, as Finance Secretary, Rajasthan, I could not secure from the Central Government, additional provision of Rs 2 crore for the nationally crucial Rajasthan Canal Project, on which construction work started in late fifties and it may be another decade before it is completed in all respects.

There is very little scope for savings unless there is a drastic change in the structure of government offices. Government work has become more complex and there is minimum scope for clerical examination of proposals which reach the higher echelons of government offices. In my State, an officer-oriented system was introduced in the services and Finance Department in 1960. I was then Secretary, Services and later on became Finance Secretary. So from personal experience I can vouchsafe for the benefits which flowed from this system. Government of India too has in a half-hearted manner introduced the desk officer system in a few offices. However, this has been continued as an exception rather than a rule. Expansion in this direction should effect savings on staff and infrastructure by reducing overall number and improve efficiency.

Quite a few of government programmes have ceased to be relevant with passage of time. This became apparent to me when I had an overview of the Central Government administrative machinery from the vantage point of being Joint Secretary in the Pay Commission. Finance Minister has recently directed the introduction of zero budgetary concept which will bring up for periodical reviews the continuing relevance of ongoing programmes. This, if fully implemented, should result in sizeable economy.

Expenditure on payment of overtime allowances has been showing an upward trend. This linked with the widespread practice of working late hours. In most government organizations overstaffing and overtime payment at the same time are two phenomena which are difficult to explain except on the basis of lack of proper supervision. When I was in the Pay Commission I found it difficult to retain a PA who made a grievance of the fact that I was not regularly sitting late nor asking him to sit late. I took permission of the secretary and successfully persuaded the Commission to recommend against payment of overtime specially when none of the State Government had felt the need to adopt the practice of paying overtime. This recommendation was subsequently not accepted by the government. In this context I recall one of the earliest directives issued by the Late Prime Minister Lal Bahadur Shastri against the practice of sitting late in offices. He said that if people worked late on a regular basis it showed that working hours were not being properly utilized. However (like the cabinet decision on closing down of public sector guest houses), this direction was ignored as it was against the prevalent culture where a very important secretary, who regularly kept late hours himself, when he gave higher praise to any of his officers who was always available in office at late hours and on holidays.

Within these constraints, government has to recognize that for securing total loyalty and unquestioned integrity, the civil servants manning posts in the higher levels have to be assured certain levels of remuneration. Much has been done in the past few years but unlike my earlier years in service, bureaucrats no longer live a segmented social existence (I purchased my refrigerator 11 years and transistor radio/desert cooler 19 years after joining the IAS). They are today as much a part of the consumeristic social milieu as the rest of the middle classes. They have by and large lost two additional sources of funds available to us earlier and which taken together helped us to keep our heads above the water level, despite denial of dearness allowance (to me after 1954, i.e., for nearly a quarter of century). A car cost Rs 9,000 and one could sell it after few years without any depreciation. Thus, loan instalments were low and there was no loss on resale. Secondly, a house could be constructed with an investment of less than Rs 1 lakh and the rental income therefrom was generally enough to meet the monthly repayment instalment. Now a house costs much more, would perhaps require additional sources of finance and its servicing may pose difficulties. Some serious thought should be given as to how the benefits under those two heads which were earlier available (and not only provided additional source of income but the provident fund and gratuity remain untouched) could be continued without imposing unacceptable burdens on government.

(b) Promotion prospects are in some ways more important to the government employees than the scales of pay. IAS is the most attractive service not merely because of the small edge in emoluments but because of the availability of very attractive promotion prospects. The recommendation of the Third Pay Commission for periodical review of cadre structures of all the services was a right step in this direction. I would like to highlight here some of the important aspects relating to promotions.

There is a general reluctance to adopt merit as a basis for promotions. This results in denial of one reward that can be given for really meritorious performance. There are no doubt inherent difficulties involved in judging merit. The confidential reports are not totally reliable and at best include some proportion of value judgments. Those adversely affected by operation of merit system impute motives and shout foul. In fact, those who are left out do not accept their supercession as a fair judgment and then their performance deteriorates even further. Despite all these handicaps it seems necessary to pursue a policy of promotions based on merit at least at two stages: promotion from one service to another and promotion to top levels within the services.

To illustrate: promotion from State Services to All India Services (or for that matter from subordinate services to gazetted or from Class II to I services) should not be treated as rewards to be given for average performance together with length of service. On the other hand, these should be considered as quantum jumps stages. The relevant rules provide that those with eight years service are eligible for being considered for promotion from State Services to the corresponding AIS. However, as promotions are being made on the basis of seniority-cum-merit, in the states when direct recruitment to State Services has been kept at a very high level, those actually considered for promotion to All India Services have generally put in nearly 20 year of service. This does not normally leave much scope for rewarding proven merit nor does it provide the concerned officer with enough incentive to try to perform above the average. As against this during the pre-independence days only really outstanding officers, got rewarded by appointment to coveted posts. It is because of there being a significant rise in one's career level that more than the usual raise in emoluments is given on such promotion. Incidentally, it has always intrigued me as to why while in All India Services and Central Engineering Services, promotions are straightway to the senior scale with corresponding weightage given in seniority, in the Central Revenue and Accounts Services promotions are to the junior scale only with no weightage given in seniority. The sooner this oddity is removed the more attraction will be these promotions and therefore stricter should be the criteria adopted for granting them.

Similar appears to be the case for promotion to higher levels within a service. In a landmark judgment, S.R. Sharma vs. the Union of India, the Supreme Court affirmed that higher one went the greater the need to give merit a bigger place in promotion. At these levels, the principle of seniority is fair only to the average performers, and the interests of government work as also those of the people at large receive a back seat. In actual practice there are hardly any supercessions in the All India Services on promotion to the first level in the super time scale. Those who are not selected for such posts at the Centre are given corresponding positions in the states. Thus, once the entrance examination for recruitment to these services has been cleared one is assured of rising to a super time scale post (with corresponding promotions in the defence services where strict screening takes place for promotion beyond the Colonel's rank). Such an approach creates a feeling of resentment in members of other services when they find average AIS officers reaching such high positions. It also leaves no incentives for continued efforts at achieving excellence but on the other hand breeds an attitude of complacence. It kills a spirit of healthy competition. It is for serious consideration whether the select lists now being prepared for posts at Joint Secretary level under the Central Government should be a joint exercise in collaboration with the concerned State Government and even with a member of the UPSC also associated so that it should not be seen that super time scale posts in the states could be adequately manned by officers found not suitable for holding corresponding posts at the Centre. Those found unfit at three successive reviews could then be considered for premature retirement; otherwise they will be a burden on the administrative machinery in the States.

Here I should like to sound a cautionary note that whatever criteria is adopted for promotions, it should be a stable one and operated on a long-term basis otherwise there may be pulls and pressures from the affected interests and the whole exercise may become counter productive.

(c) Normally seniority is determined on the basis of statutory rules and therefore causes very few problems. However, there have been a series of instances when seniority remained disputed over prolonged periods and the disputes were finally settled by the Supreme Court. Then disputes create intra-department friction and bad blood leading to formation of cliques and loss of a spirit of comradaire within the same cadre, It can affect the efficiency of the concerned department and in any case a continued feeling of uncertainty has to be avoided in public interest. It is not possible to avoid bonafide mistakes in determination of inter-seniority which may finally give rise to court cases. However, all efforts should be made to restore stability by seeking early settlement of all such cases and not allow these to be dragged on for an unduly prolonged period to time.

(d) All postings/transfers are ordered in public interest. It is on the basis of experience gained in various types of jobs—staff and line—that an individual matures to a stage when he is considered for posting to higher jobs, carrying much higher responsibility. However, in practice, this concept has got largely distorted due to interference by external factors. As I said earlier, most of the officers are willing to accept transfers which would cause them inconvenience, provided these flowed from an accepted policy which is applied to all uniformly. Such an approach would constitute the single most important factor in removing a major source of discontent among the rank and file of the services. The different components of such a policy would be: rotation as between attractive and not so attractive place, e.g., at capital and outlying stations; secretarial (with special pay) and field postings; a reasonable tenure at each station; avoidance of external pressure is exercised at the insistence of the concerned officers). Sometimes, the usefulness of an individual officer become the reason for his continued posting in a particular job. Even in such cases it would be to mutual advantage if long tenures at one station were avoided. The only one of my batch of four officers who did not reach the level of Chief Secretary was retained at one place for nearly two decades. Intellectually he was the best equipped of the four (a doctorate and author of a number of academic books) and he made significant contribution to the laying of infrastructure for the industrialization of the state. However, when his turn came for being appointed as a Chief Secretary, he was passed over because of an unsubstantiated suspicion, perhaps based on prolonged tenure at one station, that he was close to the earlier regime.

This would seem to be an appropriate place for discussing the operation of central deputation quota for All India Services and Central Secretariat postings for Central Service Officers. In the federal structure that we have given ourselves, the All India Services were conceived of as one of the tools to strengthen the Centre-State relationship. It was expected that these officers will bring to the central offices an intimate knowledge about the conditions in their respective states and carry back with them the knowledge and all-India outlook developed at the Centre. This concept has got distorted by the fact that in actual practice the same set of officers come on deputation to the Centre again and again. Thus, it is not unusual to find many such officers virtually spend most of their service career at the Centre, and occasionally go back to their states in a sort of reverse deputation and that too for short spells only. Not only this (till recently), grant of extension in tenure was not an uncommon feature. The large bulk of the State Service officers promoted to All India Services choose not to volunteer for such deputation. To correct this state of affairs and to expose the largest number of IAS officers to deputation at the Centre, steps need to be taken to enforce a turnover of officers being brought to the Centre, in some cases even against their expressed wishes; to be ruthless in regard to the length of tenure; and to increase the cooling off period to at least five years so that it brings in the net of central deputation quota as many officers as possible.

I have now virtually reached the end of this personal journey down the memory lane. It only remains to record reflections on only three other service matters: new All India Services; State Public Service Commissions; and training of officers.

New All India Services: On 1 January 1966, I took charge as Joint Secretary in the Ministry of Home Affairs with the responsibility *inter alia* of giving effect to the statutory resolution already passed by the Rajya Sabha in this behalf for the creation of certain new All India Services, viz., Indian Forest Service, Indian Service of Engineers, Indian Education Service and Indian Medical and Health Service. Of these it was possible to constitute only the Indian Forest Service modelled on the lines of the existing All India Services. The main hurdles in the way of creating the Indian Service of Engineers was the insistence of the Ministry of Works to have, in addition to the various State cadres, a separate central cadre. Their arguments in support of this plea was their large scale requirement of Engineers for the CPWD and thus their need for continuity of a core of Engineers. The states, on the other hand, were suspicious of any move to have a central cadre which they felt would come to have an elite status as was the case earlier with the central pools of ICS/IAS (since abolished). Later on, regionals sentiments came to the forefront and most of the states developed an attitude of opposing the creation of new AIS on the ground that it was not necessary to do so. The states do lose some control over member of the AIS and do have to receive a significant number of outsiders, centrally recruited through the UPSC.

It is not necessary to argue in favour of the merits of the resolution passed by the Rajya Sabha. All India Services do make an important contribution towards strengthening the federal structure. At an appropriate time, the central leadership should throw their weight behind this proposal/and past experience has shown that once the process of implementation begins, pressures are generated by members of those participating in the new services. I would however like to add here that AIS in the field of Medical and Health, and Education cannot be modelled on the pattern of the existing All India Services. These functional areas are of a diverse nature, covering different specializations and sub-specializations. The easy inter-changeability among members which is essential for constituting a service should be the old IES and IMS where there was no concept of cadre posts but that of encadred members who carried their status to whichever posts they held for the time being.

While on this subject, I should like to add that the role of IAS has to keep changing in a fast changing milieu. Long ago, posts of even Post Master General, Commissioner, Income Tax and Chairman of the Central Board were held by members of ICS. With the constitution of Class I Service in these departments these posts are now rightly being held by the officers belonging to the respective specialized services.

Anomalies in pay scales however continued till these were largely removed or toned down by the Third Pay Commission. I hope the Fourth Pay Commission completes the process and the highest posts in these departments are given the highest pay scale available under the government.

This process has to be extended to all the remaining areas of major activity which are of natural importance whether under the State or the Central Government, viz., agriculture, education, co-operatives and animal husbandry. I was appointed as Director of Education in 1956 and even three decades later that post is still held by an IAS officer. In some of the states the post of Director of Agriculture, Director of Animal Husbandry, Director of Fisheries and Director of Sheep and Wool are held by IAS officers. In almost all the states the posts of Registrar of Co-operative Societies are also held by IAS officers. The specialized services in these areas have an equally important contribution to make and it does show administrative or personnel policies that during all this while it has not been found necessary or possible to fill in these posts by appointing officers drawn from the specialized services. All these sectors pertain to development of rural areas and uplift of the economic status of the vast majority is a limit beyond which the successful implementation of vital programmes in these fields require much more than mainly administrative inputs. Efficient administration is no doubt vital for the successful implementation of all developmental programmes but development cannot continue to be merely confined to good administration. The specialized services in these areas should be allowed to make more important contribution. And it would be wrong to continue to hold that specialized officers are not capable of ensuring efficient administration. In vast areas, in the states, posts at all levels are held by engineers and doctors and if they can be depended upon for administering crucial development programmes, there is no reason to continue to show lack of similar confidence in members of other services. Four steps need to be taken in this regard straightway. These are as under:

(1) Remove the mental block that there are dangers involved in allowing the top posts in these areas to be held by officers of these specializations, and all steps should be initiated to effect the change over in a given time frame.

(2) Improve their scales of pay and cadre structures to the level equivalent to those of comparable administrative posts so that persons of requisite calibre could be attracted to these department also.

(3) Start recruitment at sufficiently high levels in these departments (recruitment to education and agriculture departments) continues to be made very largely at non-gazetted levels only.

(4) To the extent necessary organize training programmes for providing an administration underpinning to the specialized officers in these fields.

To this context, I would like to add that greater use needs to be made of the existing provision in the IAS (promotion) and regulation for promoting to IAS, officers drawn from other States Services also. In my state, an educationist, an engineer, a secretariat service officer and an animal husbandry officer were promoted to the IAS and their subsequent performance justified this fully.

The administrative tasks are huge and it will be well nigh impractical to continue to depend for this almost totally on the administrative services for effective implementation of complex developmental plans being considered for raising the living standards of the million of people who are still living below the poverty line. And for the success of such an interdisciplinary effort, a feeling of equality among the various constituents of the development term is a *sin qua non*.

Training: We are a large country but the size of the bureaucracy has become disproportionately large. To motivate this large mass to discharge their allotted functions even in a reasonably efficient manner, they have to be led and inspired effectively. This role naturally falls on the shoulders of the member of various All India and Class I Services, who cannot expect to have their leadership role accepted by their subordinates only because the organizational relationship is that of officers and subordinates. The leaders have to display on a continuous basis, qualities which will show that they can lead successfully. This will, at the minimum, require better knowledge of the work being conducted in a particular organization; the role this organization play as part of the whole development/government; and, now more than in the earlier years, developed qualities of man management. To achieve these characteristics, in a fast changing world where fresh frontiers of knowledge in every field are being reached, it is necessary to finally discard training on the job concept and replace it with a finely tuned institutional training programme concerning various stages in a career span. In most of the states, administrative training institutions have been set up but they mostly devote their energies to the training of administrative personnel and that also at the entry stage only. The need (and benefits) of a refresher course at 6–10 years and a senior course (16–20 years) of interdisciplinary groups have been in theory accepted. However, in actual practice, neither the trainers nor the trainees have the incentives available to both, in the Defence Services. It is necessary to build a culture where the trainers and trainees accept that both positions are recognition of their merits and are an indication of their expected advancement to higher levels. Conversely, those bypassed for this, should be denied advantages of advancement beyond certain levels. The heads of these training institutions should get promotion much ahead of their peer groups so that postings on these positions go to specially selected officers (and not to those for whom alternative postings are not available for the time being).

Personnel management now does involve a move away from display of authoritarian attitudes, an impatience with country views, insensitiveness to human frailties and aloofness verging on rudeness. A leader of the team, to be effective, has to earn the loyalty of his colleagues, motivate them and carry them along. Dharam Vira, L.K. Jha and Sivaraman certainly lost nothing in being effective, by adopting non-human postures in personnel matters.

Public Service Commissions: These institutions have been assigned a very important role in our constitutional framework. They are intended to ensure merit as the basis of selection for appointment to certain levels of posts under the government as also to protect employees from any capricious disciplinary action. There has however been an erosion of some confidence in these august bodies. It was disconcerting to be approached by a government servant with the request that the PSC had agreed to consider his case favourably on further references being made to them. This attitude partly flowed out of two developments.

Members of the PSC are banned from accepting any further employment under the government, this restriction has however been very narrowly interpreted and retired members have in the past been appointed as Chairman of Improvement Trusts, Chairman of State Board of Secondary Education, Vice Chancellor and Advocate General and even a State Governor. Legally, none of these posts are under the government. However, appointments to all these positions are made by the government and it is difficult to believe that the impartial conduct which was sought to be protected by a ban on the possible lure of a post under the government will remain unaffected by the prospect of offer of an appointment by the government. Justice M.L. Jain (then Deputy Legal Adviser in my state) had recorded a well documented note to argue that the framers of the Constitution had even frowned upon the offer of an honorary appointment to a retired member of the PSC on the ground that even honorary appointments carried perks including exercise of certain extent of patronage. Of late there is also a trend in the direction of appointing politicians who after ceasing to the member of the PSC take up active politics over again. Both these trends need to be reversed in order to reaffirm the confidence of the candidates and of the government employees in the total impartiality of the member of the PSC in all the matters which come within their purview. The matter is important enough to be considered by a suitable all-India forum whether like the recent decision in regard to the Chief Justices of the High Courts, the Chairman of the PSC should be a person brought in from outside the state. In fact, it would perhaps be desirable to adopt a convention under which half the members are appointed from outside the state. This is not intended to challenge the integrity of the insiders but to protect the institutions from any further erosion of faith in their impartiality.

Post Script

By the end of 1976, some officers of the batch just next below to me were appointed as Secretaries to the Government. It was virtually clear to me at that stage that I would retire as Additional Secretary. But certain developments (in which I had no role whatsoever) led to my appointment as Chief Secretary of my State, Secretary to Government of India, Civil Supplies and Cooperation and finally as Commerce Secretary from which position I retired on 1 July, 1978. The wheel had thus turned full circle and re-established once again that divine justice could sometimes be delayed but seldom denied.

2

V.I. RAJAGOPAL

Administration, Administered and Administrator

I have been loath to writing anything like my memoirs for a variety of reasons:

- They tend to be self-adulatory. It would be more appropriate for others to speak of your achievements.
- It would be presumptuous to assume that one could be a role-model.
- Every generation has its own goals, aspirations and a road map to determine their course.
- Every generation lives in a different milieu, which has an impact on its behaviour, attitude and responses. E-governance has now become a reality and has thrown open the door for constructive opportunities, undreamt of during my generation. At the same time, political contradictions and chaos seem to be threatening the very fundamentals of governance. Nature has given a wake-up call through the Mumbai floods.
- Administration is team effort; the contribution of the team is as crucial as the leadership capabilities.

Nevertheless I also believe that there are certain fundamentals which do not change and should constitute the bedrock for any administration:

- A high sense of and adherence to righteousness.
- Reaching out to people, being godfather to those who have none, being voice of the voiceless.
- Law should protect, not punish only.
- *Swasti prajabyah paripalayantam, nyayena margena mahim mahisah.*
- *Sham no astu divipadeh sham chathuspade.*

- *Yatra Yogeshwarah krishno yarta partho dhanurdhara tatra srir vijayo bhoteer dhruvanitir matir mama.*
- *Yoga karmasu kaushalam.*

The last extracted from the *Bhagwad Gita* is the motto of the IAS engraved in its emblem. You pledge to give out your best. The earlier quotation, again from the *Bhagwad Gita,* emphasizes that where there is action, coupled with divine benevolence, positive results are bound to follow. The quotation preceding the last two, from the *Vedas,* emphasizes that the administration (ruler) should be just not only towards humankind but also to animals and birds.

Many more from the ancient lore could be added but suffice it to say that from time immemorial, the emphasis has been on righteousness and justice. Recently, President Abdul Kalam was also eloquent on the theme, while addressing the Governors' Conference.

I view my brush with administration in three contexts:

- First as an outsider
- Then as an insider
- Again as an outsider but with an insider's knowledge and experience.

The Outsider

The very early impression about administration dates back to the days when I was in my primary school in Rangoon (now Yangon) when our school bus used to be stopped by traffic policemen. There would be an altercation between the policemen and the bus driver and then the bus would move on. Your sympathies would be naturally with the bus driver and you would give a cold stare at the receding backs of the policemen.

The years in the secondary school at Nemmara, my hometown in the then Cochin State, more or less coincided with World War II. Cochin State, in size small like Bundi in Rajasthan, was one of the most progressive states in the south, as could be discerned from the fact that even as early as in the 1930s it had a well-penetrated health care system and educational infrastructure. The house opposite to our's in the village belonged to a Revenue Inspector and one would envy him for the regular delivery of vegetables and other goodies at his house. The war effort had its impact on everybody, with every small minion of the government playing his role as a petty tyrant. You would only writhe in impotent anger.

In the early years of World War II, defeat of the British forces always sent a thrill through the adolescent spines. The German and Japanese victory was incidental. It was the defeat of the British that provided the vicarious and perhaps patriotic pleasure. The Quit India Movement coincided with my Intermediate Studies in Annamalai University. There were the usual student protests and strikes. The police would look menacing while confronting the students, but nothing like Gurgaon ensued. The University remained closed for a long spell!

World War II, particularly after it engulfed the East, had an immediate impact on my family. My father who was in Burma (now Myanmar) Railways had returned to India and passed away in 1940. Other Burma-based relatives also returned to India, shattered and impecunious. Only one brother continued in the Burma Medical Service. The World War II tumults and my father's demise, coupled with the collapse of the joint family system, resulted in my studies being interrupted during 1944–48. I found myself part of the war effort during these war and post-war years, before I resumed my studies in 1948 at the Andhra University, Waltair. One came across a number of British soldiers and Italian prisoners of war during this period, some arrogant, some noble. India became independent in August 1947, Gandhiji was assassinated in January 1948. I resumed my interrupted studies in June 1948. I was in my second year in the University when India became a Republic. There was nothing much by way of contact with general administration during these years, even though I happened to be a student leader.

After I left the University in 1951 and throughout the period I was a lecturer in the Vivekanand College, Madras, the same situation continued.

I was 31 when I entered the IAS in 1958. Till then I was an outsider to the administration. Like a large majority of our countrymen, one would not know how to distinguish between an Inspector or a Deputy SP or an SP. All were khaki clad men, the more you kept away from them the better. An apocryphal story that must be doing the rounds even today in the IAS Training Academy is about an old woman blessing an SP, "May God make you a thanedar". Everyone would laugh, partly derisively at the woman's ignorance. But, the moral is that the ordinary people's lives and administration ran parallel to each other.

Lesson: In narrating the course of events upto 1958 my purpose is only to highlight the fact that, by and large, a majority of people do not have any day-to-day interaction with the administration. They would like to be left alone to pursue their avocation and livelihood activities without any hindrance. They would also like the administration to ensure peace without intruding into people's lives. This I believe is valid even today.

The Insider

I entered the IAS through special recruitment, for which examinations were conducted in 1956 and interviews held in 1957. April 1958 saw a group of people heading on to Simla to join the IAS Staff College, travelling in the Kalka-Simla rail car. There was total silence inside the car, each of its occupants savouring his self-importance, till someone chose to break the monotony of silence!

Way back in 1953, an astrologer had predicted that by 1961 I was destined to be a ruler, which, in modern terms, meant that I would be Collector of a district. He had also predicted that my elevation would coincide with a bereavement in the family. I had pooh-poohed the idea, as I was then 27 having crossed the maximum age limit for entry into the All India Services. When a couple of years later there was an announcement in the Lok Sabha about special recruitment, I remembered the astrologer. When the details of the recruitment plan became available, a pall of gloom descended on me as I was not fulfilling one of the criteria relating to minimum income as a pre-condition for eligibility for sitting in the examination. There was a furore in the Lok Sabha created by the MPs from the South who successfully argued that since the pay structure in the South was generally lower than what was obtaining in the North, the eligibility criteria relating to income should be revised. The revision, which followed, brought me within the zone of eligibility and I could see the astrologer smiling encouragingly. I qualified for the interview whose venue was the Vidhan Saudha, Bangalore. When I went for the interview, I was staying with a relative in Bangalore. After having got dressed up, I was waiting for my host to get ready. He was to drop me at the place of interview. In his drawing room on a table was lying a paper that had served, perhaps, as a wrapper for some grocery items bought. The printed matter on the wrapper related to bee-keeping. I had time to go through the entire write up, which was fascinating and informative.

The first question that the Chairman of the three-member Interviewing Board shot at me was something along these lines:

> Well, Rajagopal, you must be knowing a lot about book-keeping as you have been a student of Commerce. Tell us something about bee-keeping.

What followed can be visualized. The answer set the tone for the rest of the interview. When the results came on Good Friday 1958, my name was within the first twenty.

Lesson: It can be debated whether you carve out your own destiny or whether destiny casts you in a preordained mould. I need not be apologetic for believing in the latter.

The six months in the IAS Staff College located in the Grand Hotel, Simla were marked by exposure to serious discussions and light hearted banter. On the whole, it was great going. All the members in our batch were middle-aged and married (some were at Simla with their spouses and children). George Jacob, the Principal, instilled in us a sense of pride for being in the IAS; Dr Jalota thundered on equality before law and equal protection of laws. Prof. Ramaswamy's eloquence on the vagaries of big dams has its echo even today. He had also a dry sense of humour. Dr Rao introduced us to Dr Schumpeter, even before we could learn to spell the latter name correctly. There was also Dr Pathak, who reduced criminal laws into formulae for easy memorizing.

When we had our final exams, there was in the Hindi paper a question: Use in sentences—the word was *Chal basa.* I did not know the meaning of it. So I wrote something like *'Hum sab ek na ek din chal basenge'.* Only later did I get to know the meaning of the word, but my answer was not only correct but, also unintentionally philosophical.

It was during the Simla stay that one got to know about the state, which one had been allotted to. In view of my ranking in the select list, I was originally allotted to Kerala, my home state. Now enter my friend Ramunni Menon. His allotment was to Bihar cadre. He had a problem. His wife Malati was in the Kerala Medical Service. Before he qualified for the IAS, Ramuni was in politics having contested (unsuccessfully) for a Kerala Assembly seat from Thrissur. He knew the ropes and he also personally knew the CM, Kerala. Rest was easy for him. A few phone calls and a letter from the CM saw Ramunni being allotted to Kerala in my place. In my original application for IAS, I had stated that I would serve 'Anywhere in India'. This was not because of any claims to being pan-Indian. At that time, you were not sure whether you would get selected and so what was the point in naming a child before it was even conceived. I was allotted to Rajasthan and someone else keen to go to Bihar replaced Ramunni.

In the event, I must say, I do not regret, in the least, my allotment to Rajasthan. Destiny again played its role.

On our return from Simla, while at Delhi, we had a late evening meeting with Pandit Jawaharlal Nehru at the Teen Murti Bhavan. He talked to us extempore for an hour or more and what he said only he could say. I was overwhelmed. Returning to Metcalfe House where we were staying, I reduced to writing what Panditji had spoken to us about. I had passed on what I had written to someone who was keen to read it. He never returned it. If it had remained with me, it would have been one of my precious possessions.

The Rajasthan Odyssey had an auspicious start. Kailash Ujwal and I had arrived at Jaipur by an early morning train in January 1959 and checked in at the Government Hostel. Later we got in touch with Shri R.D. Mathur, the then Special Secretary (Appointments). He invited us for breakfast at his place located proximate to the Hostel. He later took us to the Secretariat and introduced us to the CS and made us very comfortable. Shri R.D. Mathur was one of those rare types amongst officers hard to find and he left an indelible impression on me.

In continuation of the institutional training at Simla, the field training followed at Kota. Two other IAS officers and one IPS officer also were allotted to Kota for training at the same time. One began to get the first taste of what exercising power meant. During settlement training we learnt how the *jareeb* was used for making actual field measurements. The patwari also explained how with a deft sleight of hand the measurement can be manipulated to achieve any desired result! One can recall a number of light moments. One such is as follows:

- The Settlement Officer said that the Malhan Settlement Report is a must for any one to know all about settlement. For quite sometime, I was under the impression that Malhan was the name of a tehsil. Only later I learnt that the reference was to Baij Nath Malhan who, in due course, became a good friend and well wisher. Baij was God's own man, so God embraced him to his bosom early.

I was holding my first court as Magistrate Class I. The IPS trainee D.P.N. Singh (Gagan) (he retired in good time as DG, CRPF) was doing his training phase as Prosecuting Inspector. He appeared before me in this capacity. The defence lawyer thought that this was a good opportunity for him to put an apprentice under him to represent him. The serious and comic sides can be imagined. I am sure what must have passed through Gagan's mind must have been something like this. Should he address the court as 'Your honour, I have a submission to make…' or 'Well, Raja, listen, that chap is talking tommy rot'.

Derrick Joseph, Vinay Vyas and I were the three IAS trainees at Kota. At some stage in the course of our training, all three of us were in one room holding our courts with one prosecuting inspector rushing from one table to another much to our chagrin.

Small incidents, providing momentary mirth or irritation, but they did leave behind certain impressions about how the system functioned or malfunctioned.

The field training got rounded off with a short spell at OTS, Jodhpur and a written examination.

My first regular posting was as an OSD in the Appointments Department. R.D. Thapar succeeded R.D. Mathur as Special Secretary. R.D. Thapar was also a great officer, strict but very encouraging. If the noting on file going before him was good, he was quite generous with his appreciation—which was a source of great encouragement to a beginner. As OSD, I came in contact with quite a number of Rajasthan officers and some mutual regard developed with most of them.

The various posts that I held during my service career provided me with a lot of job satisfaction and I could not have asked for more.

I was:

- Collector of three districts Banswara, Jhunjhunu and Kota.
- HoD as Director of Industries, Registrar, Cooperatives Societies, Transport Commissioner and Chairman, RSEB.
- Special Secretary to Government in the Departments of Agriculture, Animal Husbandry and Cooperation.
- Administrator of Rajasthan State Cooperative Bank and Rajasthan Rajya Bhoomi Vikas Bank.
- Commissioner and Secretary to Government in different departments like Cooperation, Industries, Medical and Health, PHED and lastly Home.
- Regional Director, National Savings Organization.
- Under Secretary in the Department of Defence Production at the Centre.
- Deputy Secretary in the Department of Community Development at the Centre.
- Vice Chancellor, University of Rajasthan, some 13 years after retirement.

In all the jobs that came my way, I used to take 3–4 months to know all about the department, its key personnel, their first names etc. Then, a plan as necessary would emerge to galvanize the entire set-up to rise up to its full potential. Many milestones were crossed, new benchmarks were established, but that is what is expected of any administrator. It should be recognized that every person has his own perspective and he would concentrate on his job accordingly. Each posting/placement provided opportunities for innovative administrative interaction. What, however, stood out was the response of the employees, when they got motivated.

Banswara was my first district posting as Collector. When the posting orders came, many also came to commiserate with me. But I told them that the southern-most district of Rajasthan was the nearest to my home state. Within a month of my taking over at Banswara my mother passed away. The astrological predication came true.

The first ever Panchayati Raj elections in the state were held when I was at Banswara. A few memories linger.

- For the panachayat elections, the names of the polling booths and the officials were listed in an alphabetical order and the names and polling booths were matched. There were no complaints about the posting of officials.
- Shri Hardev Joshi was an important Congress leader of Banswara and Dungarpur districts. Somehow he did not seem to feel comfortable with me and within one year I was transferred out of Banswara. Years later in 1971, I was transferred as Director of Industries from the post of Collector, Kota which I had held for more than two years. Shri Joshi was then the Minister of Industries in the Sukhadia Cabinet. He phoned me up in Kota to say that I should not have any misapprehension that he had sought me out for the post of Director of Industries to settle any old score with me. He wanted someone like me to be the Director. During the two years plus I was on that post, I do not remember to his ever having interfered with my work. Later Shri Joshi became CM, more than once. We were on the best of terms and I had the privilege of enjoying his total confidence.

After Banswara it was Jhunjhunu. It was while I was in Jhunjhunu that the 1962 General Elections took place. During those years, the elections to the Lok Sabha and State Legislative Assembly were simultaneous. There was an election petition filed against the winning Lok Sabha candidate. As District Election Officer I had to give evidence before the District and Sessions Judge in Jhunjhunu. During the course of the proceedings, the counsel for the petitioner had focussed his question in such a way as to imply that I had colluded with the winning candidate to make him win. I had responded, while giving evidence, that the implied allegation was a 'canard'. The matter later went on appeal to the High Court where the counsel for the appellant, I learnt later, was harping on the word 'canard' to emphasize that I not only colluded but was arrogant also. Chief Justice Beri took upon himself to read my entire evidence in the open court and concluded that the evidence taken as a whole was candid and any allegation of collusion against the District Election Officer was not sustainable. Having lost in the High court, the appellant moved the Supreme Court.

I had by then taken over as Under Secretary in the Department of Defence Production at the Centre and my evidence was taken on commission with the lawyers of the appellant and the non-petitioner being present. After the official recording of evidence, the lawyer for the non-petitioner, an elderly gentleman, courtesy and kindness personified, asked me whether he could take some liberties with me. He advised me that whenever any question is answered in a court, simple words would be adequate. If I had said 'no' instead of using the word 'canard', I would have answered equally effectively. He said lawyers tend to prejudice the judges by picking up some expression or the other used during evidence. I had always remembered this sound advice. The appeal was rejected by the Supreme Court also.

The next district posting was to Kota. For me it was almost a return of the native. Between Kota and Jhunjhunu a spell of deputation to Government of India, first as Regional Director, National Savings Organisation with headquarters at Jaipur followed by posting as Under Secretary in the Department of Defence Production and thereafter as Deputy Secretary in the Department of Community Development deepened and broadened the experience which can be gained only by a spell of assignments in GoI.

I had the advantage of this experience when I joined as Collector at Kota in the late 1960s. 1969 was Mahatmaji's centenary year and the Government of Rajasthan had decided on a programme of allotment of land to landless SCs/STs to commemorate the occasion. It was a satisfying though tiring experience in making allotments all over the district. The plan of action included making appropriate simultaneous entries in revenue records so that no doubts could arise later. I had also undertaken test checking to find out whether the instructions were implemented. I thought to myself that the revenue hierarchy had risen to the occasion and all available surplus land had been allotted.

Lo and behold, ten years later, a similar campaign was launched and similarly land allotments were made. Where did the land come from? In retrospect there was a remorse that there were perhaps loopholes in the campaign undertaken by me in 1969.

It was PM Indira Gandhi's first official visit to any state after the Congress split and birth of Congress (I) and she chose Kota for such a visit. There was an inauguration programme in Shriram Fertilizers in which she was to participate. In the political sense the importance arose because of two reasons. One, for her it was a triumphant post-election visit to a state whose CM was on the other side of the Congress fence. Shri Sukhadia had identified himself with Congress(O) and so, for him also, the visit was important. Secondly, the Jan Sangh, a dominant political force in Kota, had announced black flag demonstration during the PM's visit. The atmosphere was surcharged with tension and anticipation. For the administration at Kota as well as for the CM, it was important that the situation got defused. I had cut out a role for myself. I got information through my sources that the black flag demonstration was likely to be called off if the CM were to hold a formal discussion with the MLAs from Kota who were in the main, from the Opposition. Accordingly, a meeting was arranged at Jaipur, after the CM had talked to me personally. I was also asked to be present at Jaipur by the Chief Secretary. The time for commencement of the meeting 10 a.m. was nearing and no MLA was in sight. If none turned up, I would have cut a sorry figure. But exactly at 10 a.m., all the MLAs trooped into the CM's chamber and the CS and I heaved a sigh of relief. The PM's visit went off without any untoward incident and the CM was gracious enough to thank me copiously.

There was a sideshow during the time that we were busy with preparations for the PM's visit. A Judge of the High Court landed up at Kota a day or two prior to the PM's visit. Accommodation was arranged for him in the Circuit House Annex. In the Kota Circuit House, then, there were two identical structures, one was called Main and the other, the Annexe. I had gone to pay a courtesy call on the Judge. He was in a bad temper with the Manager of the Circuit House, for his being assigned a room in Annexe. I tried to explain to him that if the buildings had been referred to as Block A and Block B, there would have been no problem but, somehow, right from the State times the buildings had been referred to as Main and Annexe. In the course of conversation I just happened to mention that there was pressure on accommodation in view of the impending visit of PM and that even the CS and IGP had to share a room. The Judge got infuriated and asked me whether I knew that the High Court Judge was above CS and IGP in the order of precedence. He also expressed a desire to leave immediately for Jhalawar, rather than stay at Kota. I left him to his pleasure with an offer of any help that he needed to move to Jhalawar.

After reaching Jhalawar, he called me up to express regrets for losing his temper with the Manager of the Circuit House, further reassuring me that he was aware of the pressure that came on the Collector and the district administration when the PM was to visit. I also reciprocated by trying to mollify him for the inconvenience caused to him due to a concatenation of circumstances. Incidentally, after the merger of the princely states in Rajasthan, he was initially assigned to the IAS. After sometime, he opted for the judiciary!

There was pressure on government accommodation in Kota and the officers of the lower judiciary had a genuine grievance that they were having a raw deal compared to the Executive Magistrates. A mutually agreed implementable formula got worked out which was to the satisfaction of the aggrieved officers. I was also clear in my mind that judicial officers should not be exposed to the embarrassment of having to hire private accommodation. There were also inherent dangers. The satisfactory arrangement worked out had reached the ears of the Chief Justice also.

Years later, the Chief Justice who had retired was the presiding officer of the committee constituted under the NSA to review cases of detention. I was then Home Secretary. Justice Changani had an occasion to remark that if the cases which came up for review had passed through my hands, he could be certain that they could not be faulted in law or on grounds of non-application of mind. In fact, not a single case of detention was set aside in review!

Lesson: Right action is its own reward. It can also fetch long-term dividends.

While recalling the Kota days I surely miss Vinay Vyas, who was a trainee along with me and Ajay Dube who was a trainee under me. Both of them succumbed to heart attacks at a young age. Both would have scaled great administrative heights had they lived.

One sunny morning while driving back from Delhi, at the Gurgaon intersection, I took a decision, on the spur of the moment, to surprise R. Ramakrishna, who was Collector at Alwar. I was also on a quest, as Director of Industries, for land at Alwar for industrial purposes.

RR was sitting deeply immersed in thought in his office at his residence. When I broached the subject of Industrial Area with him, he said that I had come at the right moment; there was an area, which would serve my purpose. If the land was found fit for industrial use, he would be saved from the embarrassment of having to allot banjar land unfit for cultivation to the landless, for which local political pressure groups were clamouring. The patwari concerned was also present in his office. After a quick look of the area, I told RR that I would get back to him after reaching

Jaipur as I would like to consult B. Mehta, the erstwhile CS, who was heading RIMDC (predecessor to RIICO) as its Chairman. I wanted Shri Mehta also to see the area. But, Shri Mehta was emphatic that my satisfaction amounted to his approval. I duly communicated on phone Shri Mehta's reaction to RR, who immediately issued appropriate orders and promptly asked the local representative of RIMDC to take possession of the land. Thus, Matsya Industrial Area was born!

When the Indraprastha Industrial Area of Kota was getting carved out, I was Collector there. By the time the acquisition formalities, which included negotiations with private parties whose land in small patches, were also involved, I had moved out as Director, Industries. RIMDC had promptly issued cheques to all those whose land had been acquired, and one of them who received the cheque was an elderly Sikh gentleman, an epitome of old world courtesy. He could never imagine that a cheque would land upon him without his having to make any special effort. He along with his Sardarni and children called at my residence at Jaipur to thank me. While taking leave of me, he asked me with a lot of hesitation, whether he could give my family a jar of Amla Morabba—a pure gesture, which merited a reciprocal acceptance with thanks!

It was in 1971 that there was a government servants' strike when Shri S.L. Khurana was the CS. He was a no-nonsense officer, soft at heart, at the same time, tough in his demeanour. As part of the administration strategy not to be cowed down by the strike, the Government empowered all HoDs to make direct recruitment of clerical staff—post-graduates as UDCs and graduates, as LDCs. I was then Registrar, Cooperative Societies. In the recruitment made in the Cooperative Department, more than 90 per cent were girls! One aspirant who appeared before me was a Ph.D. I told her that the job of UDC was hers for the asking but I would be happy if I could be saved from the embarrassment of having to give her a letter of appointment. Fortunately, for me, she got the job of a lecturer and she thanked me for the consideration I showed her.

The induction of the girls had an electrifying effect in the office. There was greater punctuality, the men started coming well-attired and neatly-groomed. There was much less of shouting in the office. On the whole, efficiency improved.

Years later, after retirement, when I attended a function at the Sahakar Bhawan, a group of women surrounded me and said that they had been recruited by me and that they were all well-settled in life. The moment was nostalgic and touching.

I remember the difference of opinion I had with the Minister of Health when he wanted that the government should sponsor a girl from Tonk as a nominee for admission to the Medical College at Jammu. There was and is still a reciprocal arrangement between the two state governments regarding nomination. I said it was necessary to verify her antecedents, with which he did not initially agree, but later reluctantly agreed. On verification it was found that the girl had arrived from Pakistan only recently on a temporary visa. I politely refused to be party to her being sponsored and said I would oppose it. I could persuade the CM to agree that the candidates to be sponsored from Rajasthan should be from the list of successful candidates in the PMT, who were at the tail end, in order of precedence. This policy was in vogue till the then government lasted. Later, the policy was thrown overboard with the Minister of Health in the next government holding out an argument that the state nominees were the ambassadors from our state to J&K and should be at the government's discretion.

Mr S. of the Central Scientific Instruments Organisation walked into my office one fine morning when I was Secretary, Health. Anyone from the central set-up would always have his nose up when dealing with a State Government functionary. Mr S. came with a loud complaint that his request for some space for establishing a branch of his organization in Jaipur was gathering dust for quite some years and he was keen to be updated on the matter. A small chat, a cup of tea and he calmed down and he said that he would be happy to be allotted a plot or a constructed building. Immediately I spoke to T.N. Chaturvedi, who was Chairman of RIICO and within a matter of few seconds, Galundia, a manager in RIICO, arrived in my office to take Mr S. around to show him the available facilities. Mr S. returned saying that a constructed building he saw in the Malaviya Industrial Area would do. Then, he suddenly changed his mind and said that he would prefer a building close to the SMS Hospital. A brief telephonic conversation with Dr G.C. Sharma, Principal of SMS Medical College resulted in Mr S. being shown what was available near SMS Hospital/Medical College. Mr S. finally exercised his preference for a structure not far away from the swimming pool in the Medical College Hostel for boys. Post-lunch Mr S. was back in my office to say that there was only a token budget provision for the Jaipur branch. I spoke to Anil Vaish, who was then DS, Finance and he agreed on an immediate payment commensurate with the budget provision, the rest of the amount to be paid by CSIO the next year after appropriate budget sanction.

Finally, exhausted, Mr S. blurted out that he had not anticipated that things would move so fast. He had not come prepared for this eventuality. He said that he had come primarily to attend a marriage function and wanted to avail of the opportunity to have an official discussion!

My name always gets associated with the comprehensive failure of a strike by the junior technicians and ministerial employees of RSEB when I was its Chairman. During the period of strike, the power supply improved with more effective technical management. We had taken the public into confidence by resorting to newspaper advertisement in a big way pointing out how the strike was unjustified. One of the reasons for the collapse of the strike was that it did not have public support.

At a personal level, the success was more in that there was no personal rancour left behind. The strikers shouting Hai Hai! would invite me for family functions like marriage and would extend all courtesy and hospitality to me. I made it a point to attend such functions.

When I was in the Home Department, a Judge of the Jaipur Bench of the Rajasthan High Court had ordered that I should be personally present in a contempt matter pending before him. It related to some orders which I had passed years ago when I was Registrar, Cooperative Societies. Before I went to the court I perused the relevant files to acquaint myself with the details of the case. The Additional Advocate General, who was to take care of the government interest, gave clear evidence of the fact that he had not made adequate preparation. I sought the court's permission to address it, which the Judge graciously granted. I remember I spoke for more than 45 minutes, a spectacle watched by a number of lawyers who had assembled in the court out of curiosity when they heard that the Home Commissioner was pleading his own case. In the event, the presiding judge had some caustic remarks to make against the Additional Advocate General. He also dictated his judgment in the open court 'purging' me of all the charges and awarding me a princely sum of Rs 100 as compensation.

There was a case of a Deputy HoD who had cast himself in the role of Leader of Opposition to his HoD whom he considered to be an undeserving Leader of the House! The matter related to some purchases where the allegations made against the HoD was that the purchases were not according to specifications. Schedule of specifications was copiously referred to, which gave an aura of authenticity to the allegations. The office had recommended in the file further action. I asked for the schedule of specifications. Nobody had thought of it. When the schedule came, I found that the allegations were based on, a superseded schedule, and the purchases were in accordance with the extant schedule!

Lesson: See for yourself the rules and regulations.

There was a recruitment scandal involving a senior officer and his henchmen. The officer was well connected and well heeled and enjoyed the protection of his department. The matter was referred to me while I was in Home Department. The most revealing and, at the same time, daring aspect of the recruitment modus operandi related to a fake caste certificate. The enquiry revealed that on the basis of a certificate issued by a so-called Tehsildar of a non-existent tehsil in Banswara an employment was given to a favoured person. It was unfortunate for those involved in the racket that I happened to be Collector, Banswara and knew the district well.

Lesson: Nothing is to be accepted at face value, without proper verification.

By the time I became Home Secretary, I had held a number of posts of HoD, the last being that of RSEB Chairman. I had firm ideas about the role of Secretary to Government vis-à-vis HoD. With this background, I had no difficulty in striking a rapport with the DGP. After my retirement, a warm farewell was organized for me by DGP Raghunath Singh in the Police Academy.

Lesson: Home Secretary and DGP complement each other. An IAS officer cannot become DGP but an IPS officer can be Home Secretary. Only that in the latter event, the Home Secretary and DGP will be in a state of permanent confrontation!

The last day of my service, 31 October 1984 was a traumatic day. The day broke with the shocking news about the assassination of Smt. Indira Gandhi. Quick consultations with the DGP followed and we had agreed upon a series of pre-emptive/precautionary measures to be taken and put in place. Later I talked to the CM who was also Home Minister about the steps that had been taken. He along with his Council of Ministers were huddled in the drawing room at his residence, all in a state of gloom. I also asked the CM what were his instructions for me, he said that I should get in touch with the CS.

CS, Anand Mohal Lal was in his office in the grip of an emotional upheaval. He said that he had lost his 'guru behen' as both of them were followers of Ma Anandmayi. Anand Mohanlal said that I could relinquish my charge. When I reminded him that that may not be the right thing to do in view of the administrative imponderables, he corrected himself and said that I could hand over my charge to him, which I did. I could claim that my successor was the CS!

Late in the evening that day, I left office quietly to return home and into retirement.

Outsider but with Insider's Knowledge and Experience

31 October 1984 was the end of another phase. It also heralded the beginning of yet another phase. This phase lasting over 16 years, with occasional breaks, saw me intimately involved at different times in a number of tasks. I was

- Chairman of a High Power Committee constituted by NABARD to examine the cooperative land banking structure in the country and suggest improvements.
- A consultant to the National Wasteland Development Board with headquarters at Jaipur.
- A consultant to the JDA.
- Chairman of a study group on Cooperative Development of Sikar district.
- Vice Chancellor, University of Rajasthan.
- I had also carried out enquiries:
  - into allegations against the then VC, University of Rajasthan,
  - relating to irregularities in financial dealing by RIICO with an entrepreneur,
  - against Chief Electoral Officer Harish Pandey,
  - against Chief Electoral Officer Sudhir Verma regarding photo identity cards, and
  - against Gajendra Haldea, Commissioner, CAD, Bikaner.

The last assignment in government related to certain pending demands of government employees. A committee headed by me was required to make recommendations.

At one level I was busy keeping myself occupied and, at another level, it was a voyage of discovery.

Consultancy with JDA in 1992–93 led me into a study of the Lal Kothi scheme. The Lal Kothi story begins with an LAO giving his award of monetary compensation in respect of some land acquired and also adding a recommendation of allotment of plots of different sizes to those whose land was acquired. The latter recommendation was clearly beyond his legal jurisdiction, but it gave rise to the claim of 'awardees' for plots. Later, a category of sub-awardees also cropped up. These were those in whose favour the so-called 'awardees' had alienated their plots. I had held that these categories had 'no legal legs' to stand on and the JDA was not obliged to provide them with 'Jaipur foot'. I understand that the legal position has since been sustained even by the Supreme Court. But, the problem is still festering.

In a quarter of a century of its existence, the JDA apparently has had as many as 25 Commissioners. Whatever might have been the objectives with which JDA was established, it has failed to inspire. My report which I had titled 'Beyond the Existing' is apparently gathering dust in the office of the JDA.

Same is the fate of the Report on Cooperative Land Development Banking System submitted to NABARD on the last date of 1985. The Chairman of NABARD changed and his successor was none too keen to pursue the matter.

The enquiries I had conducted against the three IAS colleagues were interesting. My recommendation in respect of each one of them was that the allegations were not substantiated and they deserved to be exonerated. The recommendations were accepted.

One of the allegations against Harish was that he alone as CEO raised before the CEC a number of questions in a meeting, when all the rest were silent. The validity of the points raised by him was not commented upon. *How could a Pande question a Seshan?* My conclusion were that he was merely sinned against the sinning. Though vindicated, Harish did not live long to enjoy a peaceful retired life.

One of the allegations against Sudhir was that he inaugurated a showroom belonging to his distant relation and later obtained computers from the same source. The purchases had been made by following all prescribed procedures and could not be faulted. In passing I had emphasized the advantage of government servants functioning under anonymity.

Gajendra Haldea is a good officer but he had to contend with a Minister who would like to function also as Commissioner, CAD. Cronies crowded around the Minister, and for obvious reasons, the Minister felt that action was warranted against Gajendra. Enquiry revealed that none of the allegations against him was sustainable.

The enquiry into RIICO's dealings with an entrepreneur revealed how documents could be fudged. RIICO officials depended on photostat copies produced by the entrepreneur whether of contracts entered into or bills paid. A systematic comparison with the originals revealed the faking/forging of documents. Consequent on the findings of the enquiry, one of the senior officials resigned. When one of senior officials was asked whether there was a system of verifying utilization of earlier instalments released before the release of subsequent instalment, he responded by saying that in that event he would have no time for any other official work. I remember to have asked him what other work, for which he had no reply!

Lesson: Reliance only on photostat copy is risky.

One afternoon in May 1997, I received a phone call requesting that I should take over as Vice Chancellor (VC), University of Rajasthan. I sought a day's time to think over. I had to consult not only with my family members, but also my cardiac physician, as I had undergone a bypass surgery a few months earlier. The next day I conveyed my consent. I told myself that here was something coming unsought and hence merited acceptance, however taxing the job might be. Since I had earlier conducted an enquiry against a VC, I had no illusion about what the acceptance would entail. At the same time, for one who had started as a lecturer after graduation, VC-ship could be a fulfilling achievement.

I thought I would be on the job for three months, as the incumbent VC had proceeded on three months leave. In fact, when I took over, a press correspondent asked me for how long I would be in that post? I told him, "Not a moment longer than necessary, but even if it were to be for one minute, I would sit firmly on the seat". During the Independence Day get-together at the Raj Bhawan, political leaders of all hues whom I ran into offered me their good wishes and assured me of their full cooperation. In the event, I was VC for 17 months.

These months were action-packed. One had to contend with those who were used to being back-seat drivers, who would like to have free and all-time access to the VC, whether at home or in the office, who could be vociferous and cantankerous, who would misbehave in a manner insulting to the institution and person of the VC. It took some months to make all such persons to get used to a different type of acceptable behaviour code. Though there were exasperating moments, one could instil a greater sense of discipline both amongst the teaching and student communities. By and large, the Science Departments were on proper rails with a comparatively higher degree of commitment amongst faculty members as well as students.

Rajasthan is a border state and the state institutions are vulnerable to externally sponsored activities against the interest of the nation. What would you say if a foreigner claiming to be a student is sponsored for doing a doctoral thesis on:

(a) The Working of the Interior Ministry in His Majesty's Hashemite Kingdom of Jordan.

or

(b) The Harem Life of N-Jagirdars in the 19th Century.

or

(c) The Flora and Fauna in the Thar Desert.

In the first case I remember to have said, "Let the candidate go to Jordan". In the second, "The subject was neither relevant to the University nor to Rajasthan history nor, for that matter, to the history of the country to which the candidate belonged!" In the third, I had said how a student of Music could suddenly develop an interest in flora and fauna!

There was another instance where four Germans, one working in a bakery, two others as plumbers and the fourth as a nurse apprentice were sought to be sponsored for post-graduation course in Environment. I said that if with similar qualifications an Indian could get admission for such a course I would have no objection.

Instances could be multiplied but, suffice it to say that accessing education facilities for foreign scholars, all sorts of candidates with questionable antecedents sought entry into the University. Foreign students belonged to two categories: one, those sponsored by Indian Council of Cultural Relations (ICCR) and second, the so-called self-financing candidates. I had in general taken the line that all such cases/matters would need to be scrutinized by the intelligence machinery of the government. On one occasion when the issue was taken up with the ICCR, the Deputy. Director General rushed to Jaipur to personally intercede against a particular candidate sponsored by the Council being entertained.

There was a doctoral thesis submitted by an African candidate. The guide was taking the thesis from table to table to get it cleared without delay. The external examiner had made copious adverse comments about the thesis, but the last sentence in the appraisal report was that "However, I recommend the candidate for being awarded the degree of Ph.D!"

I had said I agreed with the appraisal of the external examiner except for the last sentence. I wanted the thesis to be revised and rewritten.

In good time the VC's attitude towards candidates being recommended for Ph.D. or doctoral thesis being cleared became all too well known. As could be expected there were people both for and against the VC's strictness.

There are teachers who are visiting Professors in one college or the other abroad. I had taken the line that on the reopening day of the University, all staff—both academic and non-academic—should be present in the University colleges. A horrified teacher came and pleaded with me that if he was not in a Japanese University on its reopening date he would lose his visiting Professorship. What could you say to a Professor not showing a similar commitment to his alma mater?

A teacher-scholar wanted to go at University's cost to present a paper at a forum organized by a Food Manufacturing Company somewhere in France on the Nutritional Value of the Rations supplied to Napoleon's foot soldiers. What should one do—frown or smile. Another wanted to present a paper at a seminar funded by an American University—a South Korean Varsity being the venue—on a subject which had military connotations. Would you consider that it was only incidental that her husband was in the army?

There was the case of another teacher assisting an American scientist in some scientific endeavours. He was getting monetary consideration there and according to the University rules, there were regulations regarding his salary in the University. The American wrote a letter to the University pleading on behalf of his Indian collaborator in a language that was unacceptable. I got immediately a letter faxed to the University teacher asking him to return. Then came a letter of apology from the American scientist. If someone were to sell his soul for a mess of pottage, what can be done?

My intervention in such matters, contrary to making me unpopular, was respected if not appreciated. As time passed, there was a realization that the VC was not prompted by any self-interest and his unbiased approach was in the interest of the University. More people amongst those who came to 'scoff remained to pray'.

I was made a target of a sustained campaign by some self-appointed champions of the University that I was inaccessible to the students and staff. This was untrue as would be evidenced by the engagement diary. By prior appointment, anyone could visit the VC in his office. What was not allowed was the VC's office being treated as a 'Dhaba' where anyone could walk in or walk out any time without let or hindrance. Those who wanted to berate the VC were in need for a handle and this was one.

Conduct of examinations is one of the main responsibilities of the University. The tasks involved for a University of the size of University of Rajasthan (UoR)—with both constituent and affiliated colleges—are stupendous. The examination season is one where the pressure groups—both amongst the academic and non-academic staff—would like the University to become amenable to all sorts of demands—some reasonable and many unreasonable.

There is a Controller of Examinations who coordinates the conduct of examinations from their commencement to declaration of results. Over the years, the UoR has developed appropriate expertise so that all the operations are conducted smoothly. Some innovation introduced related to substitution of computerized tabulation of marks for manual effort. Declaration of results in 1998 got delayed for a variety of reasons, which also included non-cooperation from examiners who were insisting on prior payment of the past arrears, breakdown of a vehicle here or there, failure of computer, etc.

The Controller of Examinations had decided that the results of the final year examinations would be declared first, with the results of the first and second years to follow. In the meanwhile, the first or second year students would move up to the next higher class. The suggestion, under the circumstances, was acceptable and accordingly implemented.

But for those in the student community in search of a cause and a heroic role, also abetted by others, the delay in the declaration of results provided adequate reason to agitate. The non-academic staff was agitating separately with their demands. The leaders of Teachers Association also were spearheading an agitation with their set of demands, which remains unresolved even today.

All these separate agitations converged in point of time on a day when the Syndicate meeting was being held. Successful disruption of a Syndicate meeting was used always to boost up the morale of the agitators.

The Syndicate meeting was on, and as was told to me later, on the JLN Marg a student—who was later identified as belonging to an affiliated college, whose results had already been declared and who had also obtained his marksheet—sprinkled petrol on himself and much to the instigation of the crowd that had followed him, lit his petrol-soaked clothes. The plan must have been that his instigators would make an effort and succeed in bringing the fire under control. But that was not to be and to the horror of the bystanders including the police, the boy sustained burns and was hurried to the SMS Hospital, later to AIIMS, Delhi where he succumbed to his burn injuries.

The Syndicate meeting had concluded. The JLN Marg was also empty and when I was told about what had happened I was overwhelmed by a feeling of emptiness.

Late that evening, after quick consultations with my wife, friends and well-wishers, I put in my resignation as VC.

Another Day, Another Dawn

The following morning, Governor Tibrewalla called me up to tell me that it was a painful decision for him to accept my resignation. He was earlier the Chief Justice of Rajasthan. His judicial conscience must have prompted him to phone me up. It was gracious of him. My conscience was clear. I lost a throne but my crown was intact.

A number of persons from the University met me or phoned me up to say that I need not have resigned, as I could not be faulted for what had happened. My answer to all of them was: "Thank you. My resignation should help in the situation not going out of 'administrative control'."

I felt sad that a youngster for no reason had to end his life in the manner he did. He did not become a martyr; he ended up a scapegoat. Another chapter in my life came to an end.

Mid-summer 1999. The old order had changed and a new order has come into being. Surendra Kumar, CEO, called me up one fine morning to say that the government wanted me to inquire into a matter that had created a furore in the Legislative Assembly. It related to photo identity cards for voters. He said that the Minister had discussed the matter with the Speaker, the Chief Minister, the Leader of Opposition and all were of the view that I should conduct the enquiry.

I had accepted the assignment. When I was later perusing the authenticated version of the Assembly proceedings, I found that the Minister had given an assurance on the floor of the House that the inquiry would be conducted by a *'saksham'* and *'nishpaksh adhikari'*.

The findings of the enquiry were to the effect that there were no irregularities committed and in fact, Rajasthan should be proud that it had done a commendable job compared to most of the states. The government accepted my report and copies of the same were made available to all the legislators. I think there ended the matter.

It was on December 31, 2001, I submitted my last report to the government and it related to various demands of government servants. I presume action must have followed.

It is touching to find someone who has worked with me seeking some favour or intervention from me. He would refuse to believe that I am not in circulation! If through my intercession, he benefits and there is a smile on his face, it is a great reward.

There is a smile of recognition from someone who, like you, is picking up vegetables from an outlet. He may be a former Home Minister or a former Chief Secretary. There is a hail-fellow—well-met feeling and the talk meanders along to the good old days.

We were ten in our batch allotted to Rajasthan. G-10 has now become G-7. I miss Robin Mukherjee, Vishambar Nath and Kishen Joshi. They were good officers and sensitive souls. Amongst the rest of us, though we do not meet over long periods, there is an invisible bond that binds us. I will be stepping into my 80th year in a couple of months; the others are older to me. Individually and collectively, we have tried to give our best to Rajasthan and the country. *Speaking for myself, I should acknowledge that Rajasthan has given me more than what the best in me has been able to render to the state.*

Epilogue

The fears I had expressed at the beginning that any memoirs would lend to become self-centric has turned out to be true. That is the feeling I get reading what the moving finger has written. Well, if that is so, let it be so. I can always depend on the readers' indulgence.

Tail-Piece

Your wife has an effective role in administration. She is your most effective ego-buster!

3 ARUN KUMAR

Some Recollections

Writing about oneself is no simple task, particularly when the same is to be placed before young officers who have yet to go a long way in their career. It is difficult to resist the temptation of glorifying one's deeds and to put them in an objective manner. It is equally difficult to select a few instances from a long career spanning forty-two years. Even so, I have tried to recollect some incidents which I think may be of interest to readers. Some of the incidents chosen by me relate to my interaction with policy makers at the level of State Government, indicative of the cordial and mutually appreciative relationship that existed in the state between the political leadership and civil servants. Some of the events recounted describe how situations developed and how they were dealt with. Readers may draw their own inference.

On completion of my district training at Udaipur, I was posted as Sub-Divisional Officer at Mt. Abu in 1965. I would like to narrate two incidents which I cannot ever forget.

Mount Abu was a beautiful hill station and in those days several state level conferences used to be held there. One such conference of Chairmen and Executive Officers of Municipalities from all over the state was under way and late Shri Barkatullah Khan, the then Minister for Local Self Government, was presiding over it. Shri Khan was a very senior minister and later became the Chief Minister of the State. As SDO, I had nothing to do with the deliberations in the conference. When I came to my residence for lunch during one of the days of conference, I was handed over a visiting card. I was told that a gentleman driving a Fiat car stopped at the gate and came in. On finding that I had gone to office he left his card for me. I was greatly surprised to find that it was the visiting card of Shri Barkatullah Khan. I kept on wondering why had the minister come to my residence instead of calling me to the Circuit House, till I called on him in the evening. He told me that the previous evening a dinner was hosted by him in connection with the conference to which the SDO was not invited by his office. In a sub-division, SDO represented the State Government and he should have been invited to the dinner. I was amazed to hear the minister telling me that he had gone to my residence for apologizing to me for this lapse of his office. One can imagine my mixed feelings of embarrassment and importance at this edifying gesture of a very senior minister towards a very junior officer.

The other incident relates to the then Chief Minister, Shri Mohan Lal Sukhadia's visit to the district. Shri Sukhadia came by train to Abu Road and Collector and I were there to receive him. Of course, there was a huge crowd of local leaders, MLAs and workers to greet him. He spent a few hours in the Dak Bungalow and met a large number of people. From Abu Road the CM was to travel by road to various places in the district. His motorcade was ready for departure. As he was entering his car, the local leaders tried to sit with him in his car. He told them to follow him in other cars and looked for the Collector who was standing behind the crowd for following the CM in his own car. The CM invited the Collector to sit with him and drove away with the Collector. The message was loud and clear that in a district, it was the Collector who was number one.

One of my earliest postings in the Secretariat was that of Deputy Secretary in the Finance Department. This was 1968. Apart from other subjects, I was dealing with loss of government revenue. In those days the state used to be visited by very severe famines. Sizeable population with livestock used to migrate to greener areas. Still, large population and cattle stayed back in villages for whom food and fodder had to be arranged. In large areas of the state, fodder procured from other areas had to be transported by means of road or rail. One such consignment of fodder meant for Banswara district was moved by rail. As there was no railway in Banswara district, wagon loads of fodder were dispatched to Ratlam station in Madhya Pradesh, which was the nearest railhead for Banswara. By the time fodder reached Ratlam and was unloaded for being transported by road to places in Banswara district where it was required, it rained and the Collector felt that the fodder was no longer needed. The Collector talked to the owner of a straw-board manufacturing industry at Ratlam to buy the hay and the latter agreed to purchase it at a certain price. The Collector moved the State Government for approving the sale of fodder lying in the railway premises at Ratlam to the straw-board manufacturing unit at the price offered by its owner. As the amount involved was heavy, the Famine Relief Department sought approval of the Finance Department. In the

Finance Department the matter was examined in my office and it was pointed out that under the rules government goods could be disposed of only by open auction and an individual offer was unacceptable. The matter went back to the Famine Relief Department which in turn informed the Collector to dispose of the fodder by open auction.

In the meantime there was more rain and the hay lying in open on railway ground got damaged. Nevertheless, following government's instruction the Collector put it to open auction which obviously took some time. The maximum bid received in the auction was considerably less than the amount that the straw-board manufacturing unit had offered initially. The Collector again referred the matter to the government in the Famine Relief Department which sent the case again to the Finance Department. The Finance Department was in a fix what to do now. We advised the Famine Relief Department to sell it to the straw-board manufacturing unit at the price quoted by it earlier. The Famine Relief Department directed the Collector to do so.

The Collector dutifully contacted the owner of the unit. Regular rain had, in the meantime, set in and the quality of hay which was lying in open got further deteriorated. It had become practically unfit for use in straw-board manufacturing industry. The owner however, in deference to the Collector's request, agreed to take it for a paltry sum which was much lower than the bid received in auction. In addition, charges had to be paid to the railways for storing fodder on its land for several months.

In fact, we failed to realize that the hay which was no longer required as fodder was a perishable commodity and with onset of monsoon it would rot in no time, once it got wet. It was a raw material for the straw-board industry which was even prepared to pay a reasonable amount for it. When the Collector suggested its sale to the industry, the State Government should have accepted it in relaxation of rules for which the Finance Department was fully competent. But adherence to rules and procedures meant for safeguarding government interest, in this case, led to virtually a total loss of income.

I was working as Additional Commissioner, Commercial Taxes Department when the Finance Minister called me in the month of February 1973, just before the annual budget. He informed me that he wanted to levy a new tax on market value of lands and buildings in urban areas in the state and asked me to draft a new law for this purpose. No such tax was levied anywhere in the country and there was no precedent for such a law. The Finance Minster had selected me to draft the Bill in view of my experience in taxation and got me posted as Director, Lands and

Building Tax. Fortunately for me, the Deputy Secretary (Finance), who was dealing with taxation, was appointed to IAS through special selection from the judicial services and few could match his legal acumen and his skill in drafting. With his help, I prepared a Bill which was enacted in the budget session itself as the Lands and Building Tax Act.

The charging section of the Act sought to levy a tax on market value of lands and buildings in urban areas of the state. The amount of first rupees one lakh of the market value of the land or building was exempt from tax. If a person owned more than one land or building in an urban area, the market values of all the lands and buildings were to be clubbed and tax was to be levied on such aggregate value.

As was expected, the Act was challenged in the High Court by way of a writ petition. The matter was taken up for hearing and a very senior counsel from Delhi was engaged to represent the State Government. Both the Deputy Secretary and I went to Jodhpur (there was no Bench at Jaipur then) for the hearing of the case. During arguments a point was raised by the petitioner that the Act was ultra vires of the Constitution of India as it sought to levy tax, in case of more than one property, by clubbing all the properties together. It was argued that by clubbing the properties they assumed the nature of 'wealth'. It was only in the purview of Central Government under the Constitution to tax 'wealth' and the State Government's attempt to tax it in this manner was unconstitutional. From the observations of the judges during arguments, it appeared that this stand of the petitioner was likely to find favour with the Bench. We also thought that the petitioner's argument had considerable force and on account of this clause alone the entire Act might be struck down.

The Deputy Secretary and I worked out a strategy to deal with the emerging situation. It was a Friday and we suggested to our counsel not to complete his arguments so that the hearing could continue till Monday, Saturday and Sunday being holidays for the court. We also rang up the Finance Secretary from Jodhpur and requested him, in turn, to request the Chief Minister and the Finance Minister to remain in Jaipur on Saturday and Sunday as an ordinance might have to be issued. While driving back from Jodhpur on Friday evening we drafted an amendment to the Act deleting the clause by which tax was sought to be levied by clubbing all lands and buildings in an urban area. On reaching Jaipur we discussed our plan to omit the disputed clause with the Finance Secretary and the Finance Minister who supported it. The Chief Minister, who was to go out, had stayed back in Jaipur on our request. He approved the line of action that we had thought out to save the Act. The proposed amendment was processed on Saturday itself and an ordinance was issued deleting the clause which was the target of attack by the petitioner.

We went back to Jodhpur on Sunday and produced the amendment before the High Court on Monday when the hearing was resumed. In view of the changed provision of law the writ petition had become infructuous and a revised petition was filed in due course. Once the doubtful provision in the Act was removed, the other provisions of the Act were found to be in order and the validity of the Act was upheld.

Where on the basis of a small provision the entire Act could have been struck down, by omitting it, the Act itself was saved. We, still very junior officers, felt gratified that our proposal was readily accepted by the government. CM changed his programme on our request so that the ordinance could be issued the same day.

While working as Special Secretary (Planning), one morning the Chief Secretary (CS) called me as soon as I reached office. He handed over to me a one-page hand-written note and told me to process it without loss of time so that the lady mentioned in the note was able to fly to Tokyo by the first available flight. This lady, wife of an officer of the State Economic Service, had met the CS at his residence that morning. Her husband was undergoing training in Tokyo where he had suffered a heart attack. The Japanese authorities had sent a message to his wife asking her to immediately come to Tokyo where her husband's condition was critical. The CS, after the lady had met him, wrote the note directing the Finance Secretary to sanction an amount sufficient to cover the air fare to Tokyo and back besides incidental expenses. I personally took the note to Finance Secretary, got the money sanctioned and the amount was paid to the lady who was able to fly to Tokyo the next day. Later we learnt that the officer recovered fully and returned home safely with his wife. I was greatly impressed by the human touch displayed by CS in handling such a sensitive issue.

A short time later, the Finance Secretary (FS) asked me, being the Administrative Secretary, to recover the money given to the officer's wife for flying to Tokyo. I requested the FS to treat the amount as a grant to the lady. The money had enabled her to be with her husband at a crucial time and save his life. It was a heavy amount for a government officer and would cause great hardship to the officer if it was recovered from him. The FS would not agree with me and went to the extent of suggesting that if it could not be repaid by the officer, the foreign agency which had sponsored his training should be required to pay the amount. I told the FS that the well-being of our officer and his family was our responsibility and not that of the foreign agency. Even making such a request to the foreign agency would look ridiculous. I started comparing the magnanimity of the CS and the narrow attitude of the FS. For the State Government it was a petty amount but for the officer it was a huge sum. I was convinced that it would be unfair to recover the amount from the officer. When the FS insisted on recovering the amount, I sent the matter to CS knowing fully well his attitude in such matters. And surely he agreed with me, overruled the FS and the amount was treated as a grant not to be recovered.

Annual Plan discussions between the Chief Minister (CM) and the Deputy Chairman of the Planning Commission were to be held in Delhi and were usually attended by the Finance Minister, Planning Minister, Chief Secretary, Finance Secretary, Secretary to the Chief Minister, Special Secretary (Planning) and some key personnel of the Planning Department. Being the Special Secretary (Planning), other officers and I reached Delhi the previous day. The CM used to hold a preparatory meeting of the ministers and officers before the meeting in the Planning Commission. As the CM had not arrived from Jaipur, time for such a meeting was not fixed. I was staying with my in-laws who were about 15 minutes drive from Jodhpur House where the CM stayed. I told my Deputy Secretary to inform me as soon as CM arrived from Jaipur and the time for meeting was fixed so that I could join the meeting.

I waited in the evening for any intimation regarding the meeting from my Deputy Secretary but there was no call. Early in the morning next day, several hours before the scheduled meeting in the Planning Commission, I reached Jodhpur House presuming that the in-house meeting might be held a little before we left for the Planning Commission. On reaching Jodhpur House I was told that the Chief Minister was in his drawing room with the Chief Secretary and the Secretary to Chief Minister. I did not know that the meeting had already taken place the previous night. The moment I entered the room, the Chief Secretary fired me saying that I went away for staying with my in-laws and was not available for discussions with Chief Minister the previous evening. I tried to explain that my Deputy Secretary did not inform me of the meeting and as I was only 15 minutes away, I would have joined in no time. The Chief Secretary did not accept my explanation and continued with his barrage. I could not defend myself realizing that I was, indeed, not present in the meeting taken by Chief Minister the previous evening even if it was not because of my fault. All the reprimand in presence of the Chief Minister was taken by me silently. I was so demoralized that I kept quiet the rest of the day.

Of course, on coming out of the Chief Minister's room I scolded my Deputy Secretary for not informing me about the meeting and letting me down before the Chief Minister and Chief Secretary. The Deputy Secretary had mischievously done it just to show that he could substitute for the Special Secretary. Well, I learnt my lesson the hard way of staying together whenever in a team. I must add that later, the Chief Secretary became very fond of me as demonstrated by his proclivity to entrust important and difficult assignments to me during the rest of my career. The same CM appointed me later as Home Secretary and Chief Secretary.

I was posted as Special Secretary (Personnel) and a very close friend of mine was posted as Special Secretary (Planning). As Special Secretary (Planning) he was also the Administrative Secretary for the State Economic Service. He sought advice of the Personnel Department on certain matter but he did not agree with Personnel Department's views. The matter went on between me and my friend quite a few times without being sorted out. We then referred the case to Chief Secretary who was the Secretary for both the Planning and the Personnel Departments. He sent the file back with the remark that he agreed with Special Secretary (P). My friend claimed that the CS had agreed with Planning Department's views and I claimed that he had agreed with Personnel Department, both claiming 'P' for their own departments. After arguing for some time we resolved the matter ourselves and realized that we could have done that much earlier without referring it to CS. And that was perhaps what the CS intended us to do!

I was Managing Director of the Rajasthan Finance Corporation (RFC), a public sector organization meant for promoting industries in the state and in particular, for providing term loan to prospective entrepreneurs. The Administrative Department for the organization in the government was the Industries Department. The Chief Minster was holding the portfolio of Industries also. I had been in the Corporation for some time and the CM had never talked to me about anything to be done in any particular manner. I was therefore surprised to receive a telephone call from the CM one day. The CM personally spoke to me and told me that a certain gentleman would be meeting me in connection with some work.

This gentleman was known to be very close to the CM. On meeting me he mentioned the name of a person whose application for grant of loan was pending in the Corporation and requested for expediting it. I was unaware about it and told him that I would look into it. After he left, I called for the file and found that there were complaints about the applicant to the effect that he was not a genuine entrepreneur and had earlier taken loan from the Maharashtra Finance Corporation but had never set up any industry. My office was verifying the facts from our counterpart in Maharashtra. I told my office to pursue the matter and take a view quickly. Some more complaints came about the party and some more time elapsed in enquiring into the allegations.

After some time the CM again spoke to me on phone and enquired about the case. I told him that I would personally come over and explain the matter to him. He asked me to come over straightaway. I drove down to his residence and entered his drawing room where he was sitting with other visitors. He looked at me and asked me what the matter was. I looked at the people sitting around him and said that I would explain to him when he was free from his guests. He understood the hint and took me to the adjoining room where there was no one else. I explained to him the entire case and told him that loan could not be sanctioned to the party in view of complaints against him particularly one in which the party was alleged to have paid money to the CM also for the purpose. On hearing this, the CM just smiled at me and said *'theek hai, jaiye'*.

While driving back to my office I started wondering whether I should have mentioned to CM about the complaint against CM himself. I must say, thereafter CM never spoke to me about that case and I completed my tenure in the RFC which was one of the longest of my career.

One night in July 1990 while deep in sleep at about 3 a.m., I was woken up by the ringing of the call bell. I wondered who it could be to call at that unearthly hour. I was working as Health Secretary and an emergency was unlikely to crop up at that hour. When the bell kept on ringing, very reluctantly I went to the main door and peeped out to see a man standing in the verandah with some papers in his hand. I asked him who he was and why had he come at such an odd time. He told me that he was a cycle-sawar of the Vidhan Sabha and had brought *dak* for me. I told him to deliver it in the office next morning as I could do nothing with the *dak* in the night and went back to sleep.

The Legislative Assembly was in session. The next day, the Speaker of the Legislative Assembly spoke to me on phone about the night's incident. I told him what exactly had happened. I also told him that there was no office at the residence of officers and action on all communications could be initiated only in the morning when offices open. He seemed to be satisfied and I thought the matter was over.

After a lapse of five months in December 1990, I was surprised to receive a letter from the Secretary of the Legislative Assembly. My refusal to accept Assembly's letter in the dead of night was treated as breach of privilege and I was asked to submit a factual statement for perusal of the Honourable Speaker. I sent a reply mentioning the facts which I had already told the Speaker when he had spoken to me on phone. I also sent a note to the Chief Secretary mentioning these facts and requesting him to set up a centralized receipt in the Secretariat to receive *dak* of the Legislative Assembly meant to be delivered at residence after office hours and in night when the Assembly was in session. The *dak* could be distributed to the concerned Secretary the next morning for appropriate action. In pursuance of my suggestion an order was issued requesting Vidhan Sabha Secretariat for delivering all such *dak* meant to be delivered at the residence of Secretaries at a centralized place in the Secretariat to be passed on to the concerned Secretaries next morning. But this was not the end of the matter.

In September 1991, I was informed by the Secretariat of the Legislative Assembly that the Honourable Speaker had referred the matter to the Privileges Committee of the House. A copy of an undated letter, which the cycle-sawar had submitted to the Secretary of the Legislative Assembly, was enclosed. In this letter I was accused of misbehaviour with the cycle-sawar. I was also alleged to have threatened him never to come to my residence. I was asked to submit my written statement within fifteen days. I gave my reply mentioning the real facts and denying the allegation of misbehaviour and threatening the cycle-sawar, being totally false.

After two months I received another letter from the Secretariat of the Legislative Assembly informing me that the Privileges Committee was not satisfied with my reply and wanted to examine me in person on a given date. I wrote back to the Assembly Secretariat to clarify which conduct of mine constituted breach of privilege and what was the specific charge against me and what was its basis to enable me to present my case. I also asked for inspection of the original letter given by the cycle-sawar and other evidence in its support. I also requested that before my examination the cycle-sawar should be examined and I should be allowed to cross-examine him. No reply to my letter was received but I was examined by the Privileges Committee on the day fixed for the purpose.

In my statement before the Privileges Committee of the House, I narrated the correct facts as they were. I also pointed out that in the first communication received from the Assembly Secretariat only refusal on my part to receive letter was mentioned. The allegations of misbehaviour and threatening the cycle-sawar were made only in subsequent communication. It was therefore necessary to see at what stage the allegations were introduced to make the insignificant incident look like a serious matter of breach of privilege. I do not know what view the Privileges Committee ultimately took as I am still awaiting its final decision.

In 1996, I was working as Additional Chief Secretary in the Home Department. A note was received from the Additional Director General of Police (Intelligence) (ADGP) in which Bajrang Dal and VHP were reported to be circulating a video cassette and some printed matter which could adversely affect communal harmony in the state. Lok Sabha elections were shortly to be held and the possibility of fanning communal feelings to swing the votes in favour of BJP by screening these cassettes was expressed. I requested the Law Department to advise what action could be taken on the basis of the facts mentioned in the note against the people who were circulating the literature and video cassettes. The Law Department took the advice of the Advocate General (AG). The AG examined the matter and opined that no action under the provisions of IPC or CrPC was called for. However, while parting with the matter, he observed that the ADGP should not have delved in politics by stating that an attempt was likely to be made to swing votes in favour of BJP by provoking communal feelings. He should not have also recommended action under IPC or CrPC. The matter went up to the Home Minister and the Chief Minister. The CM sent it to Deputy Chief Minister for perusal. The Deputy Chief Minister agreed with the AG and added that action should be taken against the officer who had given political views and made allegations against certain organizations. The CM agreed with Deputy Chief Minister implying that action should be initiated against the ADGP. The file came back to me through the Home Minister.

I was shocked to see that action against the ADGP, who was only performing his functions sincerely, was approved by the CM. According to Secretariat Manual, no junior person could write a note after a senior person has recorded his note. I therefore wrote a 'routine note' which was separate from the main notes and did not form part of the main file.

While resubmitting the matter, I clarified that the ADGP had not suggested or recommended any action but had only brought certain facts to the notice of the government. It was I who had asked Law Department to examine what action could be taken in the matter. Secondly, the ADGP had only expressed his concern about the possibility of communal harmony being endangered just before general elections to the Lok Sabha. Such expression of views could not be termed as delving in politics. All officers had the freedom to express their views even if they involved the ruling party and the views expressed were unpalatable to it. It was the function of the Intelligence wing of Police to gather information from the field, analyze it and bring it to the notice of the Government. If the Government started taking action against officers, as was being proposed, they would hesitate in reporting the true situation in the field. This would deprive the State Government of correct information about the field and consequently decision-making at the government level would be affected. In view of all this, no action against the ADGP was called for.

On receiving the file the Home Minister called me and expressed his reservations in sending the file to CM when certain action already stood approved by him. I told him that it was not right to initiate action against any officer in the present case and the matter needed reconsideration. After some deliberation he sent the file to CM with a request to call him and me for discussion.

The CM called us for discussion and went again through the papers. After discussion he agreed that the ADGP (Intelligence) had only expressed his views on the likely effect the cassette and the literature being circulated could have on the communal situation in the state and on its likely impact on the Lok Sabha elections. He had not recommended any action. CM observed that Intelligence Branch of the State Police was an important agency for keeping the government informed of the happenings in the state enabling the government to take correct decisions. Any attempt to stifle flow of factual ground information might have dangerous consequences. Instead of putting up correct picture, the officers might then express only such views as would find favour with the government. He even recalled what happened during the Emergency when the officers fed the government only with such information as the government wanted to hear and emphasized that such a situation should not be allowed to develop. He finally ruled that officers should be entirely free to bring to the notice of the government such facts as they observe and their implications on law and order situation. He agreed with me that no action was called for against the Additional DG (Intelligence). The file came back to me through the Home Minister. I was happy that the most cherished right of an officer to express his views freely and frankly was upheld.

There is a small town called Kumher near Bharatpur, predominantly inhabited by Jatavs, which is a Scheduled Caste. On 1st June 1992, three persons of Jatav community went to see a movie in the local cinema hall. They did not have tickets and told the gatekeeper that tickets were with their fourth friend who was to join them shortly. A scuffle followed between them and two gatekeepers who happened to belong to the Jat community. A report was lodged by the Jatavs and police was dispatched to the cinema hall. The cinema hall manager also filed a report stating that after the scuffle 200–300 people stoned the cinema hall causing enormous damage to it. The next day passed off peacefully. On 3rd June, some Jatav labourers were returning to Kumher in the evening when they were attacked by the same two Jat employees of the cinema hall. Another FIR was filed with the police of this incident.

When the battered Jatav labourers reached Kumher, people became agitated. A mob of about 200 Jatavs gathered and went to the bus stand and the bazaar damaging public and private vehicles, shops, besides beating innocent people. A petrol pump belonging to a Jat was damaged and the owner also beaten up. Jeep of an Assistant Registrar, Cooperatives was also attacked and its driver injured. Three FIRs were filed with police relating to these incidents. During this violent agitation a rumour was also spread that a woman Jat passenger was stripped at the bus stand which caused tension in the Jat community.

As a protest against the riot, a bandh was observed on 4th June by the local Vyapar Mandal basically for demanding arrest of the culprits responsible for the incidents of 3rd June. The district administration made extensive arrangements for dealing with the bandh.

A place close to Kumher had a pumping station from where water was supplied to Kumher town. A Jat mob forcibly occupied the pumping station on 4th June, tampered with some pipelines and disrupted water supply to Kumher town demanding arrest of persons guilty of the incidents of the 3rd June. After intervention of the district administration, water supply was restored and the mob promised to behave. The SP also convinced them that no woman was stripped as alleged and the culprits of the violence would be apprehended soon. The mob dispersed with a promise to wait and watch till the 6th of June.

The promise was, however, not kept. A crowd of 200–300 strong men occupied the pump house and water supply to Kumher was again stopped on 5th June. The Superintendent of Police rushed to the place and talked to the crowd. Though the crowd restored water supply and dispersed, it informed the SP that a Jat Mahapanchayat would congregate at the same place at about 2 p.m. on 6th June to consider action taken by police against the culprits of the incidents of 3rd June. If the police had not taken effective action till then, the Jats would take action themselves.

When I received this information as Home Secretary, the DG, Police happened to be sitting with me in my office in connection with some other matter. The two of us conferred and came to the conclusion that things were not moving as they should be and the situation seemed to be escalating. Both the Collector and the SP were very competent officers, yet seemed to be unable to tackle the situation effectively. We decided to send a senior officer to Kumher who could guide the district administration. The DG, Police briefed IG, Crime, an experienced officer, and dispatched him to Kumher. The IG reached Kumher in the evening of 5th June and discussed the developments with the Collector and SP who assured him that the situation was well under control. The Collector and SP informed him that they had planned a raid in the early morning of 6th to apprehend Jatavs responsible for violence on the 3rd June, which was the main demand of the Jats.

In the night between 5th and 6th June, Jatav colonies in two villages close to Kumher were attacked by some persons. There was widespread arson and 35 hutments of Jatavs were set on fire. Two FIRs were registered with the police regarding this incident.

As planned by the district administration, a predawn raid was carried out in Kumher on 6th June. The Jatavs put up strong resistance but 46 persons were arrested. Some explosives were also recovered. Three cases were also registered regarding these recoveries.

As announced by the Jats, they started gathering at the place of Mahapanchayat on 6th June much before the time declared by them. For keeping surveillance over the Mahapanchayat, some revenue and police staff was deployed. The crowd was carrying *lathis, pharsas, gandasas* and even fire arms. The Mahapanchayat resolved to take law into its own hands and to eliminate Jatavs of Kumher. This information was carried to the SP around 1 p.m. by the police persons stationed there. He immediately redeployed his force so as to prevent entry of the crowd in Kumher town. The crowd entered Kumher from by-lanes setting fire to sundry things. The mob became violent, setting fire to houses and killing persons. Police had to resort to firing. Violence also spread to some nearby villages. In view of large-scale arson and violence the Army had to be called out and it took a few days to restore normalcy. In all, 14 persons died and many more were injured. Some cattle also died and a lot of property was damaged. A Commission of Enquiry was appointed to look into the whole episode.

I have narrated the incidents prior to the main incident of 6th June in some detail just to show how seemingly small events may develop into major law and order situation. But what is more important is that both the Collector and the SP, able officers as they were, being close to area of operation, could not see the series of incidents in their proper perspective. Their view was restricted to the immediately preceding event and they worked for the next immediate step to deal with the situation. They could only see the dots and not the whole picture. In contrast, the DG, Police and I, sitting in Jaipur, could see the wider canvas and the overall picture emerging out of the individual incidents which did have a nexus with each other. Though no one could predict precisely what was going to happen but serious trouble was brewing could be sensed in Jaipur. That is what caused us to dispatch a senior and experienced officer from Jaipur. He also seemed to have been swayed by the confidence shown by the Collector and SP to handle the situation. Being at a distance sometimes provides better appreciation of what is happening in the field and provides a better perspective to guide the field officers.

I was working as Chief Secretary when in the month of June 1998 the Director of Meteorology, Jaipur informed me that a cyclone gathering in the Arabian Sea was likely to strike Saurashtra coast in a few days. It would also enter Rajasthan and might pose a threat to life and property. I called a meeting of Secretaries of the concerned departments and DG, Police and invited the local Director of Meteorology to brief the officers about the cyclone and its likely impact in Rajasthan. All the officers were asked to take preparatory action. The Chief Minister was also apprised of the situation. I also spoke to the Chief Secretary, Gujarat, who happened to be my batchmate. He was unaware of the approaching cyclone. I suggested to him to contact the officer of Meteorology Department in his state and take necessary action.

On the 6th of June, the Cabinet Secretary had called a meeting at Delhi of the Chief Secretaries of Gujarat and Rajasthan to resolve a pending issue between the two states. I went to Delhi on the 5th and before leaving Jaipur, I spoke to the concerned Secretaries to be prepared to meet the cyclone. While in Delhi, I received a message in the night from Jaipur that the cyclone was likely to reach Rajasthan any time in the evening of the 6th. I spoke to the Chief Secretary, Gujarat, who was also in Delhi, to get the meeting adjourned as I was going back to Jaipur in view of the impending cyclone. I also spoke to the Cabinet Secretary and requested him to postpone the meeting as I was rushing back to Jaipur to oversee the arrangements for dealing with the after-effects of cyclone.

On reaching Jaipur, I contacted the local Director of Meteorology who briefed me about the progress of the cyclone. Though its intensity had diminished, it was expected to be very severe while striking Gujarat coast and was to enter Rajasthan with high velocity winds and rain. I spoke to the Collectors of Sirohi, Jalore, Barmer and Pali districts where the cyclone was to reach first and reviewed the arrangements with them and the concerned Secretaries and Heads of Departments. According to the

Meteorology Department's forecast, the cyclone was to hit Rajasthan at about 11 p.m. The CM was also kept informed of the development.

I was in my office in the evening, monitoring the progress of the cyclone. It had already struck Gujarat with great fury. I was constantly in touch with the Collectors. I was pleasantly surprised to see the Chief Minister enter my room at about 10.30 p.m.

The information given by the Meteorology Department turned out to be very precise. The cyclone entered Jalore district around 11 p.m. with heavy rains and high velocity winds as predicted. The worst was over by about 2 a.m. Only then the Chief Minister left my room after having cheered up Collector, Jalore where the effect was severest.

As the population in the districts likely to be affected was forewarned, no human life was lost though some cattle, sheep and goat did die. Damage to property was also minimal. As all the departments were fully geared up for the eventuality, no time was lost in providing medical help, restoring power and water supply wherever it was disrupted. Roads were repaired and life returned to normal in a couple of days. The Collector, Jalore who was a lady, as well as field officers of other departments, did excellent work, both before and after the calamity. Our preparedness, to a great extent, minimized the impact of cyclone.

In the end, I must express my boundless faith in all young civil servants joining as engineers, doctors, experts in other fields or administrators. They are all professionally highly qualified and greatly motivated to serve the society, the state and the country. This motivation to give one's best has to continue till the end of one's career. A lot is talked about incentives and disincentives for promoting higher levels of performance in government. But, at the level at which we function, it is not for the sake of reward or fear of punishment that we do our work. It is not even recognition of good work which draws the best out of a devoted worker. It is essentially the inner satisfaction that one gets on doing a job well that spurs one to put in his or her best at all times. Maintaining highest degree of integrity, one should, therefore, continue to work conscientiously to the best of one's ability without caring for rewards or recognition. The greatest reward is one's own satisfaction that one derives on doing a job well and the feeling of having contributed something for the good of the people. This will keep up the morale and motivation throughout one's career.

4

K.K. SAXENA

Memories Recollected

I have chosen to narrate the experiences of the period, when I was young in the service and did not have the accumulated knowledge of previous postings. With more experience behind, one is always in a better position to handle various situations.

I have narrated about my training and my first regular posting, to give an idea of the circumstances then prevailing, while the other narrations, mostly relate to situations and the handling thereof.

The effort to improve matters, must invariably be made. The extent of success in this, depends on several factors. Some of them are in our control, while some are not.

Probation

We had learnt about our state allotments at the Mussoorie Academy, well before the close of the session there. The training districts were also communicated to us. I was allotted the Udaipur district. We were to proceed to our districts, after a brief stay at Jaipur. We were required to call on the senior officers stationed there.

We had our scheduled meetings with the Chief Secretary, the I.G. Police and several other senior officers. Under directions from the Chief Secretary Shri Bhagwat Singh Mehta, we had to call on the senior officers, of a few other departments, which we did.

When we went to see Shri Mehta at his residence, he asked his usual 'Good Boy', 'Bad Boy' question, implying, which amongst us, consumed alcohol and which did not. He told us, to carefully see, all the dak papers, that came to us. This was a good bit of advice, as it acquaints the officers, with the current matters and correspondence, at the dak stage itself. He further cautioned us, not to blindly affix our signatures. Through his advice to call on senior officers of the other departments, he wanted to stress the multifaceted character of administration and the need for cooperation between various departments. He had placed us quite at ease, even in the first meeting with him. Our meeting with the 'hukka' smoking I.G. Police Shri Goverdhan Sharma was both educative and interesting. In those days there were no DGs. In fact, all the senior officers received us, with a great deal of informality and warmth. Interactions with these officers, were lessons by themselves.

Thereafter, we left for our assigned districts. I reached Udaipur in the evening and was housed in the dak bunglow. Later, in the Collectorate, I learnt that we were entitled for stay, in the Circuit House. I took the concerned staff to task and shifted to the Circuit House straight away. This took care of my food requirement. While the circuit house served food, the dak bunglow did not. Within a month or so, I moved into the house allotted to me. The orderly given to me, would cook for me and also have his meals, at my house. Simple home made food, was welcome indeed.

My training schedule had been properly charted out and I religiously adhered to it. If a probationer has to learn anything, he has to take the initiative himself. I did the same. I tried to familiarize myself with the functioning of the various sections of the Collectorate and also carried out my court work.

During the training period, even IPC cases were tried by us. If I had any problem, I did not hesitate, to walk over to the chamber of the District and Sessions Judge, to seek his advice. As for interactions with the Collector, they were not many, because he would invariably be busy, with something or the other. Besides, I had three Collectors, within my training duration. Interaction with the last Collector, Late Shri K.K. Joshi was more, he being comparatively young. He told me to prepare details of different acts, that specified functions of the Collector/DM. For this I had the services of a typist, otherwise unavailable to trainees. My notes, are reported to be still tucked somewhere, in the Udaipur Collectorate.

We reassembled for about a month, at the state training school (OTS), housed in the then Peeramal Hotel at Jaipur. We were required to study the state laws and appear at the departmental examination.

The 1965 conflict with Pakistan took place, during this time. This gave us an opportunity, to understand and study, some wartime measures and exercises in civil defense. Trenches had been dug up in our training cum residential campus, for shelter against possible air raids.

All through the training period, the guiding principle was, that while all officers were helpful and cooperative, the initiative to approach them for any problem, would invariably be, with the probationer.

Incidentally, I got married during my probation period. That probation still continues.

First Independent Charge

After completing my district training at Udaipur, I got my first regular posting as Vikas Adhikari, in the Rohet Panchayat Samiti of Pali District.

When I reached the Panchayat Samiti House in the evening, I learnt that the place had no electricity. A staff member from the Panchayat Samiti, mercifully produced a kerosene lamp. I realized that I had to buy some of my own, the very next day.

Being tired, I fell asleep, fast enough. When I got up in the morning and looked for a toilet, I found that my house had none. One was expected to use the nearby fields, for the purpose. I did not find this amusing and shortly thereafter, left for a scheduled meeting at Jaipur, with instructions to my staff to get the toilet done up, before my return.

On getting back, I realized that there were a few other problems. There was no supply of any newspaper and the dispensary in the area, had only a compounder as its head. To cap it all, there was no drinking water of the type, we are used to. We had to take it, from a close by *tanka*, which stored the accumulated rainwater. Gradually, I got used to it.

The office was shabby. I had to get it whitewashed and done up. This Panchayat Samiti did not have a regular Vikas Adhikari for sometime. One of the extension officers had been officiating as a Vikas Adhikari. One day the petrol pump dealer, supplying petrol for the Samiti Jeep turned up, with a pile of bills for payment. There was no proper record, through which, they could be verified. I called for a meeting of the concerned staff and instructed them, in the system of speaking office files, which would contain all the notes and action taken. I had all the bills verified, by the officers using the jeep and then co-related it, with the jeep log book entries. After full verification, payment was released to the petrol dealer, who was pestering for it, all the time. In the process, a proper system of file maintenance got developed, for the future.

My experience in the Panchayat Samiti showed, that while there was plenty of paper work, precious little was happening at the ground level. Running the Panchayat Samiti Schools and disbursing the salary of the teachers, it seems, was the main activity. The salary, of course, was very regularly disbursed, on the first of every month.

As for my social life there, I bought a table tennis set and played with the staff, after office. Occasionally, I joined the school boys in their volley-ball or simply went cycling, around the village. Luckily, I had a good Pradhan from the Rohet Thikana, who would occasionally ask me, to come over for a meal.

While I was posted at Rohet, the General Elections were announced and I was put on duty, as a Zonal Magistrate. I requested the Collector to be associated with him, to be able to get an overall view. He agreed. So the election became a period of training for me. We used to tour all over the district. The Pali Dak Bunglow, where I stayed had no mess. Luckily, for me, the district SP asked me to join him, for lunches and dinners, at his residence, next door.

On getting back to Rohet, one day my orderly told me, that a dog had fallen and died in the *tanka,* which used to provide drinking water to us. I had the matter reported to the medical staff. The dog was removed. The water was treated with extra doses of chlorine and declared fit for consumption.

While my experience at the Panchayat Samiti was useful, not many activities could be carried out, due to paucity of funds. Some of them were even left incomplete, which was a pity. Nevertheless, this posting gave me an opportunity, to live and work, at the very grass roots.

Sub-Divisional Charge

When young, one is at times rash. If power is conferred on him or her, there is a tendency to display it. Things were no different with me. My posting as Sub-Divisional Officer, Ajmer was a welcome change, after the roughing out as Vikas Adhikari Rohet, which had no electricity, no doctor, no regular drinking water and a somewhat medieval existence.

Having settled down on my new job, I commenced my touring, as was required. The Pushkar Municipal area, was in my jurisdiction. It has always been an important religious place. Foreigners had taken a liking to it and hordes of them, could be seen, roaming in its narrow lanes.

Pushkar was a small municipality with an elected chairman. With so many tourists, there was a mushroom growth of wayside restaurants. The owners merrily used the streets, as an extension of their premises and parked their stools and *modhas* there. Driving on the streets was difficult. More so, when vehicles confronted each other, from opposite directions. Unmindful of inconvenience to the tourists and passersby, restaurant owners continued to occupy the street space, with the municipality and its elected office bearers, turning a blind eye. Some of these entrepreneurs were also stated to be closely related, to the elected personnel of the municipality. Everyone knew everyone else. It was only the traffic, that had to put up with all the congestion.

When I noticed all this during my initial visits, I asked my driver and the accompanying staff, to tell the encroachers to remove the obstructions from the public way. These instructions were resisted and then grudgingly complied with temporarily, only to reoccupy the place, the moment my visit was over. The street side dhaba owners felt, as if some of their sacred rights were being interfered with. After several visits, I realized, that there was no intention to keep the road clean. Instructions to do so, were treated as a hostile act and complaints against them, were made to the chairman of the local municipality, who most likely passed them on, to the minister from that area.

It was in this background, that the Pushkar fair was held. The SDO Ajmer is supposed to be the officer in charge, for organizing this fair, within the overall control of the Collector, of course. The Collector, however, would hardly interfere.

The Pushkar fair goes on for a few days. I had tried to look into all the arrangements, in detail. As the fair is an annual feature, things ever otherwise, are well organized. While the fair was on, the local minister visited it a few times and gave an uncalled for, unilateral verdict, that the arrangements were not satisfactory, without elaborating any further.

I was dismayed, as all care had been taken and the fair was going on smoothly. I soon learnt that the disgruntled dhaba owners had used this opportunity, to poison the ears of the minister, through the elected representatives of the municipality. How was I do deal with an unsubstantiated verdict? I would certainly not suffer it, without a rebuttal. In the presence of the chairman of the municipality and his associates, I enquired from a very large number of villagers, tourists and visitors to the fair, if they had any problems of any kind. The answer was uniformly negative. People against me, could see, what I was trying to convey. They got the message alright and the rest of the fair passed smoothly, without any adverse comments. I had however learnt an important lesson. The local politician would always side with his people, even if they decided to level incorrect allegations against an officer.

The matter did not end. With continued occupation of the street space, I spoke to the SP and also wrote to him demi-officially. The offending furniture strewn or the streets was confiscated and regular legal action was initiated. This may appear to be a very small matter in retrospect. It is for the common citizen to respond, whether the narrow streets of a prominent religious/tourist centre like Pushkar, could be encroached for commercial activity and personal gain. My complainants tried to mend their fences, during my subsequent posting as Collector, Ajmer.

Another situation that I handled as SDO Ajmer, is fresh in my memory. I received an urgent message, that there was a serious law and order situation in the Makhupura village near Ajmer, on the Nasirabad road. I was told about an altercation, between the staff of the public health and engineering department and the local villagers, while the PHED staff was laying down the pipeline, for bringing water from Banas to Ajmer. It was communicated that the villagers were obstructing this work. Ajmer always suffered from drinking water deficiency. This pipeline was being laid, to increase the water supply to Ajmer. Naturally it was important, that the work be speedily completed. The problem arose, because the huge pipes that were being laid, obstructed the passage of the villagers to their fields. They could not go to their fields, nor could they take their animals across. The MLA of the area was a young person. He had collected the villagers and objected to the laying of pipes, without ensuring proper passage for the villagers. The PHED was in a hurry to complete the work, perhaps under some deadline pressure.

On hearing about the situation and in view of the law and order implications, I visited the site, alongwith the additional SP. It was clear, that the demand of the villagers was quite justified. They lived on one side of the road, while their fields were on the other side, where the pipeline was being laid, near the road. The PHED staff had not taken care to ensure proper passage for the villagers, who were agitated and had brought the pipe laying work, to a standstill.

On assessing the situation and the genuine demand of the villagers, I told the concerned Assistant Engineer (AEn) of the PHED to put up a few pathways *(Pulias)*, so that the villagers could reach their fields, along with their animals. When the AEn dilly dallied, I told him in no uncertain terms, that my instructions were meant to be carried out. I assured the villagers that necessary action would be taken, to cool their tempers and to defuse the situation. The AEn was perhaps too junior an officer, to make a commitment himself. I told him firmly, that unless the pathways construction material was placed on the site, within a day, I was going to use my judicial powers and stay the pipe laying work. I knew, I was overstepping my powers about the stay order, for a case, which had not even been filed. How could I convey a decision, without a proper legal hearing, to the concerned parties. Even though, all this was in my mind, I repeated my threat, knowing full well, how urgent was the pipe laying work, for the residents of Ajmer. I told the AEn, that I would visit the site again, the next day, and physically see, whether my instructions about the needed material on the site, were carried out or not. After defusing the crisis at the site, we returned back.

The AEn concerned would have communicated my instruction to his higher ups, because I was approached by some of them, to convey the urgency of their work. I knew that court procedures are time consuming and even if a stay order was issued, it would be criticized on the simple ground, that the SDO was trying to obstruct, such an important government work. Besides, there were courts above me, that would vacate my orders. Despite this, I did not relent in my position, on the stand taken by me, for I wanted no further confrontation between the villagers and the PHED staff. Thereafter, I did not bother to find out what the PHED officers were doing, although I briefed the Collector, about the situation and my instructions.

Next day, late in the afternoon, I went to visit the site, in my jeep. In those days, the SDOs had no jeeps allotted to them. Jeeps had to be requisitioned from the district pool. The site visit showed, that my threat had worked, for there was building material in place, for the construction of pathways. This satisfied the villagers, who well understood, that the construction work, would take its own time. I never cared to find out, how the PHED complied with my instructions, in so short a time.

Anyone proceeding by road from Ajmer to Nasirabad can see these pathways, over the pipelines, even now. As for me, I was able to resolve a crisis fast enough, even though I had to adopt, an angry posture.

Long after that, I worked as Principal Secretary in PHED. This time it was my duty, to ensure laying out a bigger pipeline on the same route, for ensuring water supply to Ajmer. There were no loopholes of the earlier kind, denying passage to the villagers, to their fields.

I debated with myself, whether to narrate or not, the experience that now comes to mind. Ultimately I felt, that even personal problems suffered in the course of official duties, are worthy of narration. Having been posted as SDO, Ajmer, I wrote a letter to Collector Ajmer, about my accommodation and was sent an allotment order. It was only on landing at Ajmer, that I discovered that the house usually meant for the SDO, had been given to the City Magistrate and the one meant for him, had been allotted to me.

I further discovered that the SDO's house had a better location and accommodation. On discussing the matter with the Collector, I was told that the City Magistrate had a bigger family, so he needed a bigger house. Plainly speaking, I was not happy about this and gave vent to my feelings. I also did not shift into the house allotted to me, for sometime and looked for private accommodation. That I found, was neither good nor within my affordable limits. Another problem, that I faced with the allotted house, was that it was located right on the Ajmer Pushkar Road and had no garage. My personal car had to be parked, on the main road and was always exposed to being hit, by any passing vehicle. My entreaties fell on deaf ears, till the Collector got transferred and a new Collector joined. On hearing my problem, he allotted a big Mir Shah Ali house to me, which was meant for supertime scale officers. I happily shifted into it, on a monthly rent of fifty four rupees, which was all that was due from me. Somehow, my happiness was short-lived, as another supertime scale officer got posted in Ajmer and rightly claimed the house, to which he was entitled. I repeated my request to the Collector, that I should be allotted the original house of the SDO. Late Shri B. Hooja was considerate enough to agree to this. I got my due and the city Magistrate shifted, into the house meant for him.

I realized, that, not all senior officers are unreasonable. I lived in the SDO's house, till my next posting. Incidentally, this arrangement has continued for nearly four decades now. One has to keep pressing for one's rightful claims, for a happy ending.

First District Charge

My first district charge was Jaisalmer, which I got, after five years of service. I was asked by the Chief Secretary to take over soon, as my predecessor wanted to be relieved.

After taking over charge and on enquiring about the problems, I was told that continuous famine was the only problem. In the district, there was not much scope for famine works, because of the sandy nature of its terrain. The per square kilometre population ratio was also quite low. I recollect that, in the newly opened college, I managed to get roads built up through famine funds, using the labour of the famine area, by twisting the rules, for a right cause.

Water transportation was the main activity, for tackling the acute famine conditions. Only the Dabla area and the Chandan-Lathi belt had underground water. From there it had to be sent to the remote corners of the district, through tankers. We had a fleet of them, needing regular maintenance, necessitated by continuous usage.

When I visited the Bahla area of the district, I noticed, something like a graveyard on a flat piece of open land. On getting nearer, I realized that I had mistook the small tankies to be graves. In fact, whenever there was the smallest rainfall, the villagers stored the rainwater in their family tankies, which were covered by a lid and securely locked. Like bank money, this was then used by these residents in times of need.

This area was so inaccessible that our tankers could hardly ply there. We had therefore made arrangements for water transportation to this area through military tankers. On learning from the villagers that the driver of the military tanker had evaded his duties, the matter was taken up with the military authorities. The guilty driver was suitably punished. Site visits have their own advantages indeed!

On one hot summer day, I was once standing on the terrace of my house, in the early morning hours. I noticed that one truck was carrying water, but the lid of the water container was missing and most of the water was getting spilled. It was pretty early and my jeep driver had not turned up. I picked up the jeep keys and gave a chase to the water truck. I caught up with him at some distance. It was supposed to carry water to the Sam area under contractual arrangement. The driver was brought to book and made to do extra rounds for his lapse. The local papers got hold of this news and made much, of the chase, given by the Collector.

In view of the severe famine conditions, the Chief Minister, Finance minister and the Relief Minister jointly visited the district and gave orders for immediate cash dole distribution. As oral orders are not enough, for such an action, I talked to the Relief Secretary and obtained regular orders, through wireless, along with the financial clearance. The wireless was a fast and reliable mode of communication in those days, as phones were often out of order, in the sandy area. Having obtained the sanction, it was only a question of quick and fair distribution of doles. Along with the dole distribution parties, I told the few senior officers available, to make surprise checks, for the fair distribution of doles. I would myself undertake some of these surprise checks. This ensured that there were no complaints. For the left over cases, a second round was organized.

I had meanwhile, visited the famous Tanot Temple near Longewala and prayed for rains, in the district. The Tanot temple had withstood all the bomb attacks, in the 1965 war with Pakistan. It was believed, that all prayers were granted there and thus my prayer for rains. To the utter surprise of everyone, the rains came on time. There were intermittent spells, going well into September. This brought much cheer to the people and also a problem. There was not enough animal or manpower, to till the lands, in the wake of a very good rainfall. The district just did not know how to cope with so much rain. Some of the border roads got breached, as no culverts had been provided.

In view of the good rainfall, I talked to the Development Commissioner on phone and requested, that some tractors of the Agro Industries Corporation, be placed in Jaisalmer, for the sowing of crops, in the large area. The Development Commissioner thought, that this was an unusual request and did not pay much heed to it. Luckily for me, some of the National Dailies, splashed the heavy Jaisalmer rainfall news, prominently on the front page. In their interview with me, I had repeated my request for a few tractors. Thereafter, the Development Department, got in touch with me, to work out the modalities. A few tractors, finally reached Jaisalmer, even though we were midway, into the sowing season. They had to be hired on fixed, hourly rent basis. The farmers had poor resources and the banks were not organized to advance loan, for such purposes. Despite all this, a rather extensive area came under cultivation that year. The Jaisalmer Darbar was kind enough to repay my visit, bringing with him a present of fresh *Bajra Suttas.*

The Jaisalmer I knew, was all desert. Some parts of the district have now been completely transformed, with the coming in, of the Rajasthan Canal network.

Jaisalmer has a rich historical heritage. Apart from the *Sonar Quilla* (The Golden Fort) the *Havelis* are a great specimen of sculptural genius. I had initiated steps for the protection and preservation of this heritage, some of which, was in the danger of being sold. It is now an important tourist destination, with hordes of foreign tourists, visiting the Patwa Havelis everyday.

In those days, Jaisalmer was very popular with the film World. Sunil Dutt's 'Reshma Aur Shera' and K. Asif's 'Love and God' were shot, while, I was posted there. It was good entertainment for us. Otherwise, we had to be satisfied with the solitary, open air movie hall, at the district headquarters. Sanjeev Kumar the hero of 'Love and God' applied for a gun license. I refused it, on the ground, that he was expected to apply for it, at the place, of his permanent residence.

Jaisalmer was and is famous for the great Indian Bustard. My next door neighbour, the District S.P. Shantanoo Kumar was a great bird watcher. He had tamed a falcon and used to carry it on tours, so that he came to be known as *"Baaz wala S.P. Sahab"*. Once we encountered, a big group of the great Indian Bustards, while on our way, to receive the Chief Minister, at the district boundary. We got so engrossed with the majestic presence of these birds, that we barely managed to reach our destination in time.

Jaisalmer is a very good training district. It toughens one up. Lost in the vastness of the desert, one realizes how small one is, in the seemingly endless expanse of nature.

Chittor District

Among the district charges held by me, I remember Chittor most, as I had a rather long spell there. These days when short tenures are the rule, a period of about three years, could be called long enough. Chittor was an interesting district. While the city itself was small, the district had five sub-divisions and geographically, it was well spread out, with Pratapgarh at one end and Rawatbhata at the other. We had to cross the Neemuch and Mandsor area of Madhya Pradesh, to reach the Pratapgarh Sub-Division, till a new road within the district got built up. For reaching Rawatbhata, one could either go through Madhya Pradesh area or the Bundi, Kota districts. There was a third route also, if one decided to reach Rawatbhata by a boat in the Chambal, from the Bhensrorgarh side. The present Chambal bridge came up later. Rawatbhata being the centre of nuclear power generation, we were in constant touch with their authorities and also witnessed some of their installation related activities.

The Chief Minister being from adjacent Banswara, local politicians had easy access to him. They would flaunt their connections and one had to be careful, on that count. The Pradhan of one of the Panchayat Samitis was a specialist in this job. He would try to bully, the Sub-Divisional Officers, with the talks of his influence. During one of the visits of the CM in this area, a tricky situation once got created, when some political workers obstructed the CM's entourage, by prostrating themselves on the road. They were removed. CM was however unhappy and conveyed his displeasure. The Pradhan concerned lost no time in criticizing the district administration in general and the Collector, SP in particular. Luckily, the evening public meeting of CM went of very well, thanks to some very strict arrangements by us. The Pradhan might have felt disappointed, when the CM asked us to join him, for dinner that night.

It was in this background, that a land allotment case came to me, in the discharge of my revenue court duties. In the districts, only the officers keep changing. The staff and the politicians remain the same. They are more aware, about the background of cases and their implications. My staff promptly passed on the information, that the case, concerned the Pradhan in question. For me, this was irrelevant, as I would invariably look into the merits of the case, rather than who were the parties involved. As for the Pradhan, he never ever directly approached me. As the CM used to visit the area frequently, he must have spoken to CM about it, who in turn asked me to have a look. The Pradhan may have been happy, by putting me into some kind of a pressure.

Back in the office, I had a look at the entire case and the related laws, I came to the conclusion, that it was a hopeless case. I waited for a while and informed the CM of the factual position, during his subsequent visit. He told me to do, what I liked. Obviously, he had no time or interest, for such petty matters. This was good for me. The case proceeded as per procedures and the allotment rejected, having been found, against the law. The Pradhan, I was told, pursued the matter, till the Board of Revenue, but found no relief.

In our younger days, with not enough experience behind, tricky situations confront us. With more experience, one learns to cope with them better. One cannot blindly follow orders from above and get away. Nor can any administration worth its name, side with this or that group, in cases of communal conflicts. Miscreants on either side, need to be promptly booked. Ethics in administration, is an ongoing process. One has to deal with situations and keep sight of what is lawful and just. While it is easy to dispense law, it is not easy to dispense justice.

Being part of an administrative set-up, one is not only responsible to the Government, but also to himself and to the society. When the interests of the employers come in conflict, with the interests of the people and society, we need to opt for the latter. Terry L. Cooper has dealt with this subject beautifully in his book. "The Responsible Administrator". He has rightly observed, that if the public interest is your fundamental controlling principle, you must weigh the probable public impact for each alternative.

Apart from being responsible to their organization superiors and the elected officials, public administrators are responsible to the citizenry too. Administrators have to be able to explain their conduct to the citizenry, as consistent with either the wish of the citizenry or the larger public interest. Citing the case of Eichmann, Cooper brings in the Nuremberg principle and its articles, which mention that individuals are ultimately responsible for their deeds and must be held accountable, before the bar of justice.

Public service is a duty. Self seekers have no room here, though they often creep in and occupy cushy positions. Power, in fact is a trust, to be used for public welfare and not for personal ends.

My posting in the Chittor district gave me an opportunity to deal with a variety of situations. The Birla Cement works based there, was a source of constant problems. There were rival groups of workers. They would fight all the time and often rush to the district officers, at all odd times. There were several arrests and cases galore, yet things did not improve.

This being an internal matter of an industrial unit, the role of district administration was limited and mainly related to law and order maintenance. The factory management ultimately engaged a retired Chief Secretary of our State, to head that unit. This itself showed the seriousness of the situation, within the factory. While showing all due courtesy to our retired Chief Secretary, I never gave him the impression, that he could influence our decision, in any way.

It was in these circumstances that one day he met me and informed that some kind of a union election was fixed by the workers in the factory, on the next day and that this meant trouble, because the groups would invariably clash physically, to establish their supremacy. Thereafter I sent my own officer, for an on the spot assessment of the situation. He confirmed the apprehension of the retired Chief Secretary, who was now heading the Birla Cement Works Chittor.

There was little time and much to organize. Of the two rival groups in the cement factory, one had its support base in Udaipur and was backed by a powerful politician. The other group had its support base in Bhilwara and was backed by another powerful politician. It was expected that loads of workers/miscreants from both these places would come, outwardly to support their groups in Chittor, but ready to come to clash on the smallest pretext.

In such a situation, one has to muster adequate force. I sat down with the SP and organized that part. Another aspect, was the legal handling of the matter. The SDM incharge of the city came to me for guidance and I gave him a well drafted legal order, banning any activity against prescribed law. We got these orders pasted in different parts of the factory.

The location of the Birla Cement Works in Chittor is such, that there is Udaipur road on one end and the Bhilwara road on the other end. In between them, was a vacant guest house.

As the day broke, we stationed the forces, duly armed, at all vantage points, so that their presence was quite visible. I parked myself with the SP at the guest house, with a small force and kept track of all the developments. The area between the entry point from Udaipur and Bhilwara was placed under curfew. When the groups of rival supporters, tried to enter Chittor, from the Udaipur and Bhilwara sides, they were not allowed to proceed, in view of the curfew orders. Within the factory, the prohibitory orders, took the wind out of the sails of rival groups. We had ensured that there were not only the prohibiting orders, but enough force and will to enforce them, if the need arose. The supporters of the rival groups, waited at the outskirts of the district, till evening. Some of rival workers of the factory wanted an interpretation of the prohibitory orders, within the factory premises. They were curtly told, that the orders were clear and needed no interpretation.

By evening, the workers and their supporters from the two nearby districts were clear, that no nonsense would be tolerated and anyone violating the orders, would be strictly dealt with. The support groups from Udaipur and Bhilwara, returned back to their districts. No peace was disturbed, either in the Birla Cement Works or in the Chittor city. We knew that our strong action had averted a crisis and also planted the fear of law, in the minds of the workers.

While the problems of the Birla Cement Works continued, the strong hand of law was there for everyone to see. By the night of the day in question, the officers and forces on duty, could relax in the security of their homes.

Law and order has become far more tricky and difficult now. There are all kinds of situations, often created by the mischief mongers. Terrorist activities, often take the administration by surprise, because our intelligence falls short of expectations. With no advance intelligence, one cannot plan preventive action. Red alerts are announced, when the damage has been done.

The security of the citizens, is the responsibility of the administration. The intelligence agencies have to be good enough, to nip the danger in the bud, or give enough time to effectively deal with it. An innocent group of citizens, with no prior warning, can always be a soft target. When any checks and restrictions are required on a regular basis, there is simply no escape from them. The administration cannot be a spectator, to the ghastly killing of innocent citizens, by the terrorists, so often witnessed recently.

A Final Word

The service objectives have always got to be the beacon light for the public servants. Amidst several demotivating factors, one's own will, plays a great part.

Unlike the politicians, who have a limited tenure, the public servants have security of service. They have no reason to ignore their basic job, of working for the people. The only punishment likely to come to them, is in the form of transfers here and there. This in anycase, is a part of the job profile. Minus the fear of transfer, the public servants are bound to be, a more confident lot. If a large number of public servants acquire this trait, the politician would not be in a position, to play one against the other. Unfortunately, the lure of cushy postings weakens their spines, turning them into yesmen. There is no need to be an obstinate 'No' man, but there is certainly a need, in being a part of an objective system of administration, where public interest reigns supreme.

Pariksha, the famous story of Premchand, one of our greatest modern story writers, always comes to mind, while talking of the expected attributes of a civil servant. For selecting the Deewan of the State, the choice fell on a young sportsman. Although himself injured, he pulled out the loaded cart of a poor farmer, that had got stuck. The story symbolizes, what is expected from a public servant. Unless we have such men entering the services, they would just be another wage earning mechanism. Standing up for the underdog, is what public service is all about.

5

P.N. BHANDARI

Experiments in Administrative Innovations

I have served in various official capacities during the last three-and-a-half decades of government service. From the very beginning, I was deeply interested in finding new solutions to old problems. In spite of the complexities of the administration, I have had an abiding faith and confidence in the innovative measures. Away from the beaten track, I have tried in public interest to introduce measures, leading to simplification of procedures and practices. My experience every time gave me a new insight in the philosophy of the administration.

Proactivism in Administration

Our society is basically status quoist and public administration is also a reflection of that culture. Red-tapism is, in a way, synonymous with status quoism. I have always felt that the context and relevance of rules and procedures, which were introduced in a particular background, changes from time to time. Hence, the rules and procedures also need a fresh look against the new background. Unfortunately, our bureaucracy often gets circumscribed in *Babooraj* and even the senior-most officers find themselves as much shackled by rules as the lowest level officials. If the senior officers act and react in the same manner as do the lowest functionaries, then what is the need of having an army of senior officers? I have always tried to interpret the rules and regulations in the new context and I have been greatly inspired by judicial activism. The courts have, time and again, risen to the occasion and given new context to the legal provisions. The founding fathers of our Constitution perhaps never imagined that under the writ jurisdiction, even a postcard could be treated as a writ, but over the years the courts have taken remarkable strides on the front of social justice, through the mechanism of public interest litigation. In many important policy issues, the courts have launched new experiments and have tried to mould the laws in the new environment. In my view, on the pattern of judicial activism, the administration can also adopt proactive posture.

Loan Melas: A New Concept

In wider public interest I have never hesitated in stretching the meaning and interpretation of outdated and irrelevant rules and procedures and this has ultimately received wide acceptance. As District Collector I organized loan *melas* for the farmers and perhaps for the first time persuaded the banks to disburse loans outside the bank premises. Disbursement of cash outside the bank premises at that time was considered unthinkable. When I was Collector, Udaipur, a complaint was made to the Reserve Bank of India (RBI) for flouting of the established banking rules in the loan *melas*. The Deputy Governor of the RBI personally came to look into the so-called flouting of the standard banking practices. However, he was very much impressed with the methodology of our loan *melas* and this led to change of thinking of the RBI, and some of the issues connected with such loan melas. The Deputy Governor realized that the *melas* had eliminated the middleman as well as the red-tape. Later, Shri B. Sivraman, the then Deputy Chairman of Planning Commission and former Cabinet Secretary also visited one of our loan *melas* and he was simply thrilled at the promptness and the simplification of procedure. At his instance, the Agriculture Secretary, Government of India wrote to all the Chief Secretaries to organize similar *melas* in their states and a documentary film was got prepared by the Agriculture Ministry, Government of India for propagating this campaign technique for irrigation wells etc.

One is reminded of the unconventional approach of the former Chief Election Commissioner, Shri T.N. Seshan. Without any significant amendment in the law, he gave a new dimension to the various provisions and brought about revolutionary changes in the election practices. The liberal and unabated use of blackmoney in the elections was substantially curbed. The higher judiciary has also given new direction to the dispensation of justice. Formerly, their role was confined to the letter of law, but now there is more and more stress on equity. The courts are transforming from courts of law to courts of justice. The whole country has generally welcomed the judicial activism. No country or society can move forward with static rules and procedures.

In Udaipur, as Collector, I discovered that while the entire district was lagging behind in most developmental activities but it was leading in well deepening programme. That amazed me. On further probe, I found that in large number of cases, no deepening took place. Loan and subsidy were just distributed with heavy cuts being taken by the lending officials. I stopped all cash payment to the farmers. For deepening, the blasting units of State Ground Water Department (GWD) were deployed and payment was to be made by lending institutions directly to them. Overnight this rampant malpractice stopped, apart from generating all-time high work for the GWD.

I recall another event in Udaipur. I happened to meet Mr Zumro, who was the Chief of CARE in India, looking after Food for Work programme. He was on his way to Bikaner, for reviewing this programme in the Rajasthan Canal Project. I apprized him with our campaign of constructing ten thousand wells. He was greatly impressed with the campaign and instantly allotted 50,000 metric tons of wheat for this project. We were to take delivery of wheat from Food Corporation of India (FCI) godown in Udaipur. We had no funds for transporting such a huge quantity from Udaipur godown to hundreds of villages, where the farmers were constructing wells under our campaign. I thought of seeking help from FCI itself. The FCI was also collecting wheat under the levy programme from villages. Suddenly it struck to me to take delivery of wheat in villages instead of Udaipur godown of FCI. My officers discouraged me on the ground that FCI had an all-India policy for levy collection and they were unlikely to modify that policy for Udaipur district alone. But I persisted and met Shri Yatindra Singh, a very senior officer of our cadre, who was then chief of FCI in Rajasthan. I suggested to him that if delivery of wheat is allowed to us in villages, FCI would save the transportation cost from each village to Udaipur. We too would save transportation cost for carrying CARE wheat from Udaipur godown to each village. Unlike typical bureaucrats who are 'busy' most of the time, in making queries, hunting precedents, 'actively' considering the matters and seeking horizontal opinion of sister departments, besides seeking guidance and approval from above, here was an officer, who to my pleasant surprise, instantly agreed to my proposal. The nation saved transportation cost of one lakh MT wheat in this exercise.

Leisurely Schemes on Fast Track

During my Collectorship in some of the districts, schemes under the Small Farmers Development Agency (SFDA) used to be sanctioned.

These schemes were supposed to be completed in 4–5 years. Among other activities, loan and subsidy used to be given for digging of wells, installation of pumpsets, etc. I felt that the schemes could be compressed in a very short time and the farmers can get faster benefits. We planned to complete the schemes in six months instead of five years. Instead of the individual farmers approaching the banks and other functionaries, we organized camps in each Panchayat Samiti, where officials of all agencies would be present right from Collector down to Patwari, from Block Development Officer to Gram Sewak, the Central Cooperative Bank (CCB), the Primary Land Development Bank (PLDB), the Lead Bank and a host of other connected organizations. All certification, documentation and loans used to be provided in a single-day camp. In the normal course, the poor farmers had to go from pillar to post to get their loans sanctioned but through these camps, where I used to be invariably present till late in the night, we were able to cut the red-tape totally. Farmers could concentrate on real developmental activities, without being required to chase officials and other functionaries at every level. SFDA officials from GoI visited our camps and were simply amazed at the speed and quality of implementation through campaign strategy. Nowhere in the country, the SFDA schemes had been implemented in so short a period and with so much of convenience to the farmers.

In all my assignments, I had launched a series of campaigns and without a single exception, they were a roaring success. Instead of merely issuing instructions, I used to have constantly live interaction with all the players and stakeholders from top to bottom. The organization would be constantly humming with some campaign or the other.

Shake Up in Cooperative Loaning

As Collector, Bharatpur, in 1973, I launched a campaign to push up the various developmental programmes through cooperative loaning. Initially, there was lot of resistance at the level of the CCB and the PLDB. Applications would be entertained only if it politically suited the Chairman of CCB/PLDB. I initiated a series of steps to simplify cooperative loaning. I was able to convince the Registrar of Cooperatives that many of the procedures were outdated and irrelevant. In view of my initiatives, the government specially conferred the powers of Registrar, Cooperative Societies upon me, by name. When I was transferred as Collector, Udaipur, again, these powers were conferred upon me by name. Later of course all the Collectors were conferred with these powers.

The cooperative loans used to take months before they could be sanctioned. The loans, it appeared, was a test of borrowers' endurance. Through the campaign technique and constant simplification of procedures in Bharatpur, not to speak of the remarkably superior quality of loaning, in sheer statistical terms, we achieved 300 per cent of the targets for the schemes, which envisaged digging of pipe bore wells, surface wells, pumpsets and dairy activities. As against a target 3,700 applications, we advanced loans to 12,318 farmers. In financial terms, as against a target of Rs 151 lakh, we achieved a loaning of Rs 469 lakh. Under the SFDA scheme in Bharatpur, during the previous three years, 1,800 farmers were sanctioned loan, while during the 3-week campaign, 3,000 applicants were sanctioned loan. An amount of Rs 75 lakh was sanctioned during the previous three years while during the 3-week campaign, loans worth Rs 150 lakh were sanctioned.

I raised several issues before the higher authorities regarding the cooperative loaning which were leading to delay, harassment and very often corruption. Large number of these practices were dropped or modified at my instance. Previously, the PLDB alone would receive applications. And, if they were not favourably inclined, they would avoid even the receipt of applications. But we authorized the BDOs also to receive applications in the camps. The loans were sanctioned previously only by PLDB Board. During our campaign, a sub-committee of the PLDB was authorized to hold the meeting and sanction the applications in the camp itself.

Individual land valuation procedure was very cumbersome and prone to manipulation. Frequently, they would inflate the land price and show low expenditure to clear the application, while in other cases, low cost of the land and high family expenditure would be shown to reject the application. On my initiative, District Level Committees were appointed for tehsil-wise land valuation, instead of individual costing. This saved a lot of time and also avoided manipulations. Furnishing of family tree, dating back to several previous generations, was also considered to be unnecessary. Similarly, the practice of sending every file for legal advice too was avoidable, apart from adding to the expenses. It was agreed that the cases would be sent to the Legal Advisor only where the Secretary, PLDB was in doubt about the title, etc.

We discontinued the previous practice of attaching quotations of pumpsets of a particular dealer with every application. Previously applications would move fast or slow, based on which firm's quotation was attached. We discontinued this practice and rather attached a general quotation, without indicating any firm or make. This ensured farmer's freedom to purchase any pumpset of approved make. This freedom to choose meant a saving of almost Rs 800 per pumpset, which was quite a substantial amount for farmers in 1974. Besides, the Cooperative Inspector would hold public enquiry, before grant of loan, inviting objections if there were other claimants on that land. This public enquiry was a futile exercise and led to lot of delay. We convinced the Cooperative Department that revenue record was sufficient and was acceptable even by the highest court of the land. Once the title was certified by revenue functionaries, there was no need for further enquiry about the title.

In the past, entire subsidy used to be given by SFDA to the PLDB at one time. I started giving proportionate subsidy in camps along with each instalment given by the PLDB. Earlier, after paying the first instalment, the PLDB did not bother for months together to release the subsequent instalments to the farmers but under the new policy introduced by me, they were forced to release the subsequent instalments also in time, in order to earn subsidy. The controversy regarding our SFDA not paying the subsidy in lumpsum reached the State Government and the Agriculture Ministry, GoI. Ultimately, at the level of the GoI, our decision was endorsed and it was clarified that the SFDA was well within its right to release proportionate subsidy instead of depositing the entire subsidy in advance.

To protect the farmers from a variety of delays and harassments, we ensured that loans were disbursed, not in the hush-hush environment of bank counters but in the widely attended camps. The key note of the entire campaign was that the applicant was not required to visit any office or functionary for anything connected with the preparation and processing of loan applications. Consequently, all connected functionaries of revenue, development, cooperatives and banks were available in the camps with full records. What used to involve months of agonizing delay, was accomplished in just one-day camps.

Embarking Upon Technical Solutions

In Kota, as Collector, I noted that the irrigation authorities used to traditionally construct canals on the higher ridge. Farmers on the lower side used to get the canal water due to gravity while on the other side of the canal, they were invariably left out. In a Cabinet meeting held in Kota, I mooted a scheme for providing outlets on the other side of canal also from where the farmers could lift water since flow due to gravity was not possible on that side of canal. The Chief Minister instantly gave in principle clearance, although the irrigation officials scoffed at the idea. I however pursued the scheme and for the first time a large number of farmers who were never supposed to get the benefit of canal water, could get the irrigation water. Later, as Irrigation Secretary, I directed similar approach in Mahi Canal also, which benefited hundreds of tribal farmers.

Metamorphosis of a University

In 1981, I was inducted as Vice-Chancellor of Udaipur University at a very turbulent time. There was all-round chaos. The law and order situation in the University had crumbled. A student was brutally murdered in a clash between two groups of students in the hostel. My predecessor was suspended.

The students were pressing for early elections of the Students Union. I was firmly convinced that one of the major causes of student trouble in the university was elections. Just to display their aggressive leadership, the student leaders create hue and cry. I told them that till there was complete normalcy to the satisfaction of the district administration, no elections were possible. And, the district administration would not accept normalcy, till I gave them the green signal! Gradually, I noticed that the student front was becoming orderly. Many of the problems were being created by the students as pre-election stunt, but once the elections were deferred, they slowly gave up their aggressive style. Our Chancellor, Air Chief Marshal O.P. Mehra was surprised at the unusual calm on the student front in the university. I told him that the compulsory membership of the union and subsequent elections were the major causes of all the trouble. The Chancellor accordingly asked the other Vice-Chancellors in the state to emulate our example and they all fell in line, though with lot of mental reservations and doubts. The postponement of elections paid rich dividends in restoring the academic environment of the university.

I remained Vice-Chancellor of Udaipur University for about four years. This field was totally new for me but many a time, I felt that the scope for innovation significantly increased in an unfamiliar area. All over the country, in Agriculture Universities, internal grading system of examinations was prevailing. I felt that in an average university, with so much of student unrest, pressures and tensions, the teachers cannot freely function in internal grading system. The students succeeded in getting higher grades while subjecting the teachers to threats and assault. When I took over as VC, I found the university atmosphere very vitiated and even the teachers were manhandled and assaulted on many occasions. I took the initiative in switching over to external examination system and this dramatically improved the environment. The students started devoting more time to studies and the strategy of threatening the teachers was no more relevant—rather with the fear of external exam, the students started depending more and more on the teachers for preparation. There was a sea-change in the university environment and one could not believe that in this very university, many Vice-Chancellors had been manhandled in the past.

Bringing Examinations Back on Rails

Our law faculty examinations were running behind schedule by almost six months. Unfortunately, the law students were most lawless and they took admission more in order to continue on the rolls of university rather than for academic pursuit. While all other examinations were put back on the normal schedule but the session for the law faculty was deliberately kept by me a few months after the regular session. This helped us in several ways. First, since the admission to the law faculty would not be over till a few months after the start of the regular academic session, I could take the technical view that since all the admissions in the university had not been completed, therefore, the elections cannot be held. Second, the initial pressure of problems which we faced throughout the university due to simultaneous admissions could be phased out since the admission to law faculty got postponed. Similarly, since the examinations of the law faculty got delinked from other examinations, the pressure and the tension which the university used to face earlier during the examinations also got phased out. Gradually we reduced the gap between the admissions of law faculty and rest of the university.

Curb on Walk-outs

On an average there were 57 walk-outs every year, before I took over as Vice-Chancellor. After each walk-out, a truck load of students would march towards the office/residence of the VC and force him to declare the date for re-examinations. However powerful the VC may be, he had no option, under the severe student pressure, but to yield and declare dates for fresh examinations. The examinations schedule and the university session used to be totally upset as a result of frequent walk-outs. The academic session was running behind by almost two years, and obtaining university degree in time was almost a dream. The students used to very much lag behind in competitive examinations etc., because of such dislocations. The general students and their parents were greatly upset by such walk-outs but they had no option but to watch as mute spectators. I approached the

Chancellor and persuaded him that the authority to conduct fresh examinations in case of walk-outs should be with him, rather than with the VC. Before the commencement of the examinations, we gave wide publicity to this new arrangement. We advised the students to approach the Raj Bhawan in case of walk-outs. Earlier, while the VCs were helpless, under the revised dispensation, the students became helpless and they could not even think of pressurising the Governor (Chancellor) for declaring fresh dates for examinations. The students suddenly realized that pressure would not work in this area and walk-out would mean loss of one year. After this, walk-outs just became a thing of the past.

Examination Reforms

An important reason for walk-outs by students was that occasionally the questions in examination papers were out of syllabus. Sometimes, the problem was exaggerated but on other occasions, it was genuine. Paper-setting was done by university examiners spread all over the country and inspite of all the precautions, such mistakes were not uncommon. The walk-outs had become a common feature of the university system. We set up high-level committees for each subject and got question-banks prepared. The question-bank was quite comprehensive and included all possible questions. This totally changed the scenario and the fear of the unknown in the examinations totally vanished. The students could think of other reasons for walk-outs but not on account of the questions being too tough or out of syllabus. The other effect was that students started preparation from the very beginning and frequently sought the guidance of teachers.

Formerly, out of 12 questions in a paper, students could answer any five and very often they depended upon selective study. However, alongwith the question-bank, we also introduced a system of three or four sections in each paper and the students had to attempt at least one question from each section. This ensured a comprehensive study by students. I noticed that the usual tension which pervades the university community during the examination season had substantially disappeared because there could be nothing new in the question paper which was not there in the question-bank. Incidently, this solved another problem. The paper-setters were spread all over the country and sometimes we could not receive the papers well in time. With the question-bank in our hand, there was no more tension on this account. Even at the eleventh hour, any teacher could be asked to tick-mark out of the question-bank and set the paper.

I used to visit various campuses of the University, sometimes announced and on other times, unannounced. In one of such visits during the examinations, I found that there were hardly any students in one college and I asked the Centre Superintendent about this. He informed me that students were taking the Sanskrit paper and therefore the number of students was rather limited. I asked why more papers of other subjects could not be taken up in a single day. The Superintendent was amazed at my question and told me that students could have any combination of subjects. Therefore, if more than one paper was scheduled on the same day, it would be impossible for a student to appear in both the papers on the same day and same time. He also elaborated that this practice was in operation for decades without any problem but somehow I was not satisfied with the situation. I pondered over the matter and finally raised this problem before the Academic Council and at my instance, it was decided to club the various subjects and the students could choose only one subject out of two or three subjects. For example, we clubbed English Literature and Sanskrit. A student could take either English Literature or Sanskrit. Generally, we had clubbing of three subjects. This ensured that on every examination day, there used to be three papers instead of one as in the past. This ensured that the long drawn examination schedule of about three months could be completed in one month.

Copying was another headache in the examinations. Members of the Flying Squad had been frequently manhandled and they generally hesitated to discharge their duties enthusiastically. I introduced one Police Sub-Inspector as an additional member of the Flying Squad. This very much emboldened the teachers. They could handle copying cases with greater firmness. After a few days I was told that the Sub-Inspector did not promptly come to join the flying squad duties. This defeated the very purpose of surprise checking. We decided that the Sub-Inspector would also get the same remuneration as other members of the Flying Squad. With this decision, the problem was over. Now, the Sub-Inspector started taking initiative and would frequently enquire on telephone from the Examination Superintendent if his services were required. This simple step of induction of Police Sub-Inspector in the Flying Squad and paying him even a token honorarium made a remarkable difference in the general discipline during the examination days.

Going Deep into Mining Issues

I joined Rajasthan State Mines & Minerals Ltd. (RSMM) under a severe handicap. My predecessor was a very distinguished officer, who during his long spell in RSMM had earned a name and was also picked up as a UN consultant. Any departure from the policies laid down by him was almost considered heretical. I, however, felt that in the highly unionized environment, productivity was not sufficiently high and there was need for privatization. I informally sounded the Board members. Without going into the details, they were simply not inclined to change the earlier policy. But I persisted. I somehow floated an all-India tender and the response was very good from very competent parties. The rates too were substantially lower than what we were spending. In the face of the low tender rates, the Board had to finally endorse my stand. I am glad that the decision to switch over to private contractor for overburden removal proved a great success and the profits of RSMM shot up. The trade union's nuisance value could also be curbed, after the induction of contractor's labour with much higher productivity.

In RSMM, I noticed that some of the customers were being supplied richer ore, compared to the average customers. However, the rates being charged from both categories of customers were same. I felt that there was no justification for supplying richer ore to a select few customers. I, therefore, started blending this richer ore, so that the quantity increased and the quality of ore was uniform for all the customers. This blending added to our revenue by several crores. This unnerved many quarters, because questions were likely to be raised as to why this additional revenue was missed by supplying richer ore to certain customers, without charging any extra amount. After I was shifted from the organization, I received a letter from the Mines Secretary, asking me to either prove the supposed losses under the old policy or it would be presumed that there were no losses under the old policy. I was amazed at the audacity. I should have been complemented for saving several crores by switching over from the old scheme to the new scheme but surprisingly an attempt was being made to dump the issue as inconsequential. I shot back a letter, saying that the extent of losses could be determined in due course but if it was strongly felt that the new policy was wrong, they should at once revert to the old scheme. The bluster did not work. The matter ended at that. Obviously, nobody could dare revert to the old policy, in view of the substantial revenue increase under the new policy.

Liquor Licences: Defaulters Preferred!

When I joined as Excise Commissioner, as per the policy, licences for IMFL were being given to non-defaulters on a fee of barely Rs 100. The market value of the licence was perhaps one thousand times higher and therefore I was rather uncomfortable in granting licence for barely Rs 100, when it could fetch even more than Rs 1 lakh. I, therefore, modified the policy and informally publicized that licences would be given to defaulters. In the past, the department was chasing the defaulters for heavy dues but they were not traceable but now every one started proudly proclaiming to be a defaulter and claiming the IMFL licence. In the subsequent informal meetings, I conveyed that in view of the unusual rush of defaulters, I cannot accommodate all the defaulters. Hence, my criterion was that higher the default, higher would be the priority. We negotiated with the big defaulters to clear their old dues and obtain the licence. Through this campaign, most of the dues which had become irrecoverable could be recovered. Incidentally, most of the higher dues were against fictitious names, but with this scheme, the defaulters had no hesitation in owning their *benami* dues.

Paradigm Shift in Revenue Administration

As Principal Secretary, Revenue, I felt that the performance of the Revenue Board was on the decline. A posting in the Revenue Board was treated as symbolic of government displeasure and such posting meant a fall in the social status. The output of such officers posted on government displeasure was also significantly low. Many of them felt that they had nothing to worry any more as the government cannot send them to a worser place. While I am saying this, I am conscious of many honourable exceptions such as Shri T.V. Ramanan, Shri M.L. Mehta, Shri Arun Kumar, etc., who displayed the same dedication to work as on other posts. In spite of these handful of exceptions, I was quite convinced that unless the system was changed radically, the future of thousands of litigants in the rural areas was bleak. We, therefore, introduced a scheme by which we would invite applications from willing officers of selection scale of IAS for being promoted as members of the Revenue Board in the super time scale of the IAS. The selection committee was headed by the Chief Justice. The selection process ensured that the Revenue Board members would not lobby for getting back to the secretariat postings. We also provided for extension up to two years for officers showing good performance. This scheme was a great success. The environment of the Revenue Board suddenly transformed and average disposal of cases significantly improved. The time and energy which the hon'ble members were earlier deploying for getting back to the secretariat, was suddenly diverted for higher disposal of cases.

I also noticed in the Revenue Department that the Settlement Officers were underworked, although they had jeeps at their disposal. On the other hand, the Revenue Appellate Authorities were overworked and had to go to far off places for holding Camp Courts in buses. We conferred powers of Revenue Appellate Authority on all Settlement Officers. By this arrangement, without any financial burden, the number of Revenue Appellate Authorities increased by 100 per cent.

The distribution of work was done in such a manner that the Revenue Appellate Authorities were given district headquarters, involving no journey. The Revenue Appellate Authority-cum-Settlement Officers were given outside districts so that they could go to hold the camp courts with their files loaded in their jeeps.

Whenever a new system is introduced, it faces resistance and the same was the fate of this scheme. The advocates of divisional headquarters protested because under the new decentralized system, every district was given the facility of camp courts. The advocates of neighbouring districts however welcomed this arrangement as they started getting cases, which were formerly concentrated at divisional headquarters. The litigants also welcomed this as each district was provided with the facility of camp court and they were not required to go to the divisional headquarters.

In the Revenue Department, I felt that the Settlement Department was no more relevant. It had ceased to be a major source of revenue to the State Government as in the past. Settlement operations very often left everything unsettled and triggered lot of litigation. I initiated a series of measures for a phased winding up of the Settlement Department. Not only the Settlement Officers were made ex-officio Revenue Appellate Authority but a large number of lower officials were also shifted from Settlement Department to the Collectorates.

After my exit from the Revenue Department, the process slowed down but I am happy that the issue has again been picked up and the Settlement Department is perhaps going to be wound up. Government departments and agencies are created to serve the cause of the public but over a period of time, the public cause recedes in the background and vested interests often develop in each department for its perpetuation, whether its activities are relevant in the changed context or not. The vast British Navy continued long after Great Britain had ceased to be an empire. The Jagir Department continued long after the *jagirs* were abolished. And I would not be surprised if the Settlement Department in one form or the other, manages to survive even after its abolition. I often wonder if the urban areas can manage without settlement operations, what is the need of such operations in the rural areas.

Cutting Delays: An Unorthodox Approach

Another problem was the long delay of cases in the lower Revenue Courts. The witnesses would frequently turn up for tendering evidence. But cases were frequently adjourned on flimsy grounds and the poor witnesses had to go back, time and again. We introduced a system where evidence would be recorded by some advocate or retired officer in the presence of the counsels for both the parties. This ensured that the entire evidence would be recorded outside the court and the Presiding Officer of the Revenue Court would be only hearing the arguments and decide the cases. This substantially saved the time of the Presiding Officers of the Revenue Courts and also saved the witnesses from the infructuous trips for tendering their evidence. This could also generate substantial work for younger advocates, who were otherwise having light case work. This system was introduced at the fag end of my tenure as Principal Secretary, Revenue but somehow it was not followed up vigorously and it could not sufficiently pick up. Lately, there is some thinking to revive the system. If the system is revived in practice, the activity of recording of evidence could be shifted from the revenue officials so that they get more time for the disposal of the cases.

Thousands of cases are pending in the Revenue Courts. Every year, the institution is much higher than the disposal. As the old cases become older, the disposal of such cases tends to be slower and as the court files become bulkier and bulkier, the Presiding Officers tend to concentrate on the disposal of the new cases. In more than 80 per cent cases, the government has no stakes and the litigation is between the private parties. We decided that retired officers of proven competence and integrity should be appointed for disposal of such cases and payment to be made on per case basis. Justice delayed is said to be justice denied but under this set-up, much of the delay could be eliminated.

In RSEB and RSRTC we already have this model, where retired officers of the administrative/judicial services deal with the enquiries. The lower revenue officials feared that it would lead to reduction of the posts and promotion avenues. Some Tehsildars filed a writ in the High Court and protested against the dispensation of justice on contract basis. However, the Chief Justice, while presiding over the Bench, very much appreciated the scheme and observed that inherently there is nothing wrong in the scheme if it could lead to faster disposal of cases. This was one of the two measures which were taken at the fag end of my tenure in the Revenue Department. For lack of follow up, the schemes could not take off. Lately, in the light of downsizing of the civil services and the emphasis on faster disposal of cases, there is some rethinking on this issue and I am hopeful that at long last the scheme may be revived and operationalized.

Initiatives in Commercial Taxes Administration

As Commissioner, Commercial Taxes, I realized that stay orders were playing havoc with our revenues. Awards resulting into crores were blocked because of stay orders. We got the Act amended so that the Tax Tribunal could grant stay at a time for three months only. In the past, once the stay was granted, the tax practitioners could obtain adjournment from time to time, at the level of the Court Reader. Under the amended provisions, however, no stay order could continue beyond three months and every time it was required to be extended by the Presiding Officer of the Tribunal after appropriate hearing. It was further provided that no stay could operate beyond one year from the date of first stay order. This mechanism put a big check on the tendency to obtain stay orders and prolong them on frivolous grounds. The disposal of old cases was very prompt and put a check on frivolous stay matters. I happened to talk to some of the High Court Judges on this issue. They felt that if a similar provision was introduced for judicial courts, 75 per cent of the litigation would reduce, because presently the cases are prolonged only because of stay orders.

In Commercial Taxes Department, for the issue of 'C' form, a paltry amount of Rs 12 was required to be deposited in the bank and based on the deposit receipt, the 'C' forms were issued by our Commercial Taxes Officers (CTOs). It was a very trivial issue but I felt that so much of time was being wasted by the tax payers at bank counters for such a minor work. I, therefore, directed that this amount may be got deposited in the offices of the CTOs rather than in the bank. It gave a big relief to the assessees because they were not required to stand in the long queues at the bank counter. I was pleasantly surprised to receive telephone calls from several bank managers thanking me for the step. The queue at the bank counters became shorter with the shifting of depositors of 'C' forms to the offices of CTO. The bank branches could concentrate on the transactions of bigger amounts rather than frittering away of time and energy on paltry amounts.

I also discovered that a large number of assessees were registered with us who were not paying any tax. In fact, they were not required to pay any tax as they were all tax paid dealers. I am not aware of any private gains to the officials or the counsels but the department gained nothing by assessing them. We removed these 50,000 dealers from our jurisdiction, which was widely welcomed.

Ends and Means

As Commissioner, Commercial Taxes, I found that more and more CTOs and ACTOs were showing interest in being posted at Makrana. My curiosity in Makrana increased and I paid a visit to that area and organized a *sammelan* of our assessees. I observed that the semi-educated marble dealers were being exploited in a variety of ways. I introduced the system of spot-payment of the sales tax when the truck was passing through our check-post. Earlier, the system of payment was based on monthly basis and it required maintenance of elaborate accounts. These accounts were often being questioned. From time to time surprise checking was done by the Inspectors and this led to lot of complaints about harassment and corruption. I suggested that the rate at which the marble was being valued for sales tax purposes was much less than the market rate. Therefore, they should voluntarily revise it upwards and on my part I offered them to exempt them from all checkings. They readily agreed. One of the participants in the *sammelan* said that what they were unofficially paying to the lower staff, will now be paid officially to the department. I transferred all the Inspectors from that area and kept these posts indefinitely vacant so that no checking could take place as promised. The result was remarkable and the income increased by leaps and bounds. A delegation of Inspectors met me and pleaded that such exemption from checking was not permissible under the rules. My counter-question was that what was the purpose of checking? It was to check evasion and ensure higher revenue. If the department did not get enough revenue in the last so many decades inspite of checkings and after the total shifting of the Inspectors, the revenue had shot up, how can the checkings be justified. The Inspectors had no answer. The scheme proved a great success. Later, it was extended to certain other areas also.

Something similar happened in the cinema checkings. I called a meeting of the cinema owners and told them that a large number of persons are being found, time and again, without tickets which meant loss of revenue to the department. They readily accepted the charge and explained that in most of the cases, they were helpless. They had to deal with so many departments and if officers and lower staff of those departments insisted on seeing the cinema shows without buying tickets, they found themselves in a tight corner. I offered a composition scheme to them under which if every year, they paid 15 per cent higher revenue, we would exempt them from all checkings. They readily agreed. This resulted in higher revenue to the department and elimination of harassment and corruption on this front. The staff meant for checkings was diverted for other fruitful activities.

Opening Communication Channels

In Commercial Taxes Department I used to organize frequent meetings with the trade and commerce and others concerned. Based on the suggestions in such meetings, simplifications measures were introduced from time to time. Out of the total number of notifications, which had been issued in the department since its inception, 50 per cent were issued during my tenure. The publishers of literature on commercial taxes felt greatly harassed because by the time they would come out with any publication, it would become outdated due to issue of many more notifications, after that.

In retrospect I often wonder how so much could be achieved by me in the Commercial Taxes Department. One of the reasons was overcoming of the hierarchy problem. The Commissioners of Commercial Taxes Department have been generally super-time scale IAS officers but the administrative heads (Special Secretary, Finance) have been traditionally in the selection scale of IAS. In a situation when the Head of Department (HoD) is very senior and the Administrative Secretary is very junior, there is very often an ego clash and the HoD would not like to pursue matters with his junior officer, even if he happens to be the Administrative Secretary. In the past, the Special Secretaries, Finance also tended to cold shoulder the proposals of the Commissioner because they were not appropriately pursued by the HoD and meetings between the Commissioner and the Special Secretary, Finance were rare. I overcame this problem. I did not have any hangover of seniority and, therefore, I interacted very frequently not only with the Special Secretary, Finance but also with his Deputy Secretary, who was 13 years junior to me. The Deputy Secretary was very bright, intelligent and hard working. I used to spend virtually half the office time with the Deputy Secretary, pursuing my proposals and responding to various queries through direct discussions instead of lengthy correspondence. This significantly reduced the gulf between the Commissioner's office and the administrative department. The direct informal discussions created a very healthy atmosphere. We have had many competent Commissioners in the Commercial Taxes

Department in the past but I guess many of their schemes could not be translated into the action because of the communication gap or lack of live contact between the field department and the administrative department.

Urban Development without Tears

As Commissioner, Jaipur Development Authority (JDA), I had to deal with an auction of a plot involving Rs 12 crore. The amount was stuck up in litigation. With my special efforts, the entire amount was recovered. I had only granted instalments. The rate of interest fixed by me was also 3 per cent higher than prescribed in the JDA regulations. Ignoring the positive resolution of the long-drawn stalemate, in the biggest auction deal, I was asked about the provisions under which the instalments were granted. According to me, the right to recover includes the right to recover in parts, i.e., in instalments. Incidentally, I was personally called in the High Court and the Hon'ble Judges had orally directed us for settling the matter out of court. The opening sentence of the agreement indicated that the agreement was being finalized in the light of the directions of the High Court. It is reflective of our *Babooraj* mentality that if the entire amount had remained stuck up in litigation for years together, no questions would have been asked but since departing from the general practice, it became a serious question of propriety. Incidentally, property of Dr Hellig's bungalow and Hind Hotel, worth crores, remained stuck up in litigation for more than a decade, because of this rule-bound approach.

In JDA, an overbridge had been planned but the scheme was languishing for several years because of acquisition problems. I personally visited the area and had long discussions with the concerned persons and offered them reasonable compensation package. I also provided them our bus to see the alternative sites. We also helped them with our transport in shifting them. The human touch melted their resistence. The long-pending stalemate was broken in a remarkably short time. One party whose land came just below the proposed bridge was evading any settlement. After inspecting the site I suggested to the party that if it cooperated with us in the construction of the bridge, we can exempt it from land acquisition. How could the bridge be constructed on that site, without his land being acquired which fell just below the proposed bridge. The party could not believe but still it readily agreed for any scheme saving his private land. We offered that only a supporting pillar would be constructed in his land and if that was allowed the party could retain the land below the bridge under its own ownership. The party jumped at the offer and the work was started. Today, this overridge in 22-Godam area is handling very heavy traffic. If we were not pragmatic in our approach, perhaps the project could not have materialized for years.

We also succeeded in widening of roads which were stuck-up in litigation. In Lal Kothi area, from a narrow passage of only 8 feet, we were able to have a wide road of 60 feet by demolishing certain old structures, which were under stay. Hardly any compensation was required to be paid in this case. We convinced the party that by merely widening of the road, the market value of his property would shoot up. In the long litigation, nobody had highlighted this issue. The party readily agreed and it felt very grateful to us in spite of our demolishing his structures.

Mobile Committee

In JDA we used to frequently go for site inspections and at the end of the visit, very often I found that the officers had different perceptions on some of the issues because during inspections they were all moving in different cars. Many a time what would strike one officer may not be noticed by another officer. I, therefore, immediately ordered for a mini-bus and for all site inspections we started moving jointly by mini-bus and we would hold our meetings in this mini-bus while being mobile. Through this mobile committee in the mini-bus, the decisions were much faster. Increasingly, the emphasis shifted from office work to field work, thanks to the frequent trips in the mini-bus.

After inspections we used to give spot decisions for constructions etc. On a few occasions I found that the stock reply of the engineers was that Notice Inviting Tenders (NIT) had been issued or that the tenders are under process. I was not very comfortable with this system. I decided that instead of inviting tender from time to time for different areas we will have a one-time tender which would continue for the entire year or may be even beyond that. Formerly, the tenders used to be invited at the level of Executive Engineer for each separate work but under the new system the general tender was finalized in the high level committee consisting of the Chief Engineer and the Chief Accounts Officer etc. While calling for tenders, we merely specified certain major activities like construction of roads/drains/walls etc., which were commonly required in the entire JDA area. This system significantly speeded up our functioning. We had a substantial saving on our advertisement cost due to one-time tender advertisement. The usual complaints, which used to be received earlier against the lower officials, were eliminated once the tenders were finalized at the top level management. The time lost in frequent processing of tenders was also saved as, instead of approving a particular party for a particular job, we had fixed certain rates, at which the works could be awarded from time to time. Previously, if a contractor failed, the work could be awarded to another contractor at his risk and cost but this took several months and it often involved litigation. However, under the new arrangement, if a contractor failed, on the very next day, another contractor could be inducted on the same rates without requirement of fresh tender. This system was widely acclaimed.

Land Acquisition without Tears

As Secretary, Urban Development, I came across a few cases where complaints were received about determination of the land acquisition rates. We pondered over the matter and decided to follow a new scheme. We decided to give 12.5 per cent developed plots in the same agriculture land, surrendered by the farmer. This was totally equitable. Whether the land is good or bad, in every case, the farmer would get the same equitable share in that very land. This was totally transparent and no favouratism or discrimination was possible in this. Besides, in such acquisitions, no funds were required. This method being voluntary was much faster and avoided all litigation.

'Sweeping' Reforms in Municipalities

As Secretary, Local-Self Government, I was constantly worried about the poor level of cleanliness in the municipal areas. The regular sweeping staff was highly inefficient and indifferent. I hit upon an idea. Under this scheme, all the vacancies were filled up by shifting the sweeping staff from certain wards so that a few municipal wards became totally vacant. We authorized the ward members to make sweeping arrangements through contractors engaged by them in such wards. The municipality would give them a lumpsum amount for sweeping operations, which was somewhat less than what the municipality was actually spending earlier in that ward. The ward member could hire or fire this private staff unlike the municipal staff which could not be touched. This experiment was very successful. I am sure, if this is vigorously pursued on a larger scale and further regular recruitment in municipalities is stopped, the level of cleanliness would remarkably improve and the expenditure too would come down.

Arbitrary Arbitrations

As Secretary, in PHED and earlier in the Irrigation Department, I came across many cases of fake disputes and questionable arbitration awards. Under the standard contract agreement in all engineering departments, in case of dispute, the matter would be referred to arbitration. A panel of three names is proposed by the department and the contractor picks up one person for arbitration. My experience was that the contractors used to concoct the disputes and make exaggerated claims. They had nothing to loose if they failed in the arbitration, because the option of choosing the arbitrators was with the contractors. The arbitrators very often used to charge on per day basis. Hence, more the hearings, more the fee for arbitrators.

We dispensed with arbitration provisions. If any contractors was genuinely aggrieved, he could file civil suit. Highly exaggerated claims cannot be made in civil suits since court fee is required to be paid on the claimed amount. In contracts already finalized, we fixed arbitration fee on percentage basis. With this amendment, the tendency to unduly prolong the proceedings came to an end.

The Fall of 'Price Fall Clause'

Another standard clause in purchase orders of engineering department was the 'price fall clause'. If the supplier had supplied the material to someone else at a later stage, on lower rates, then the department would claim the same lower rate from him for existing supplies also, even though the earlier contract with the supplier was for higher rate. This clause created lot of heart burning and led to lot of avoidable litigation. To my mind the clause was rather unjust and unfair. If the market rates go down, the department would take benefit but if the market rates go up, the department would ignore that. My feeling was that in whatever way we saddled the suppliers with extra financial burden, the suppliers would indirectly inflate the cost of supplies. Removal of this clause was widely welcomed. Lot of bad blood and litigation was avoided by this decision.

Topsy Turvey Tenders

As Secretary, PHED, we had floated tenders for Jodhpur Water Supply Scheme. After the sealed tenders were opened, I received a letter from a new party saying that the rates had been manipulated by a cartel and he was willing to supply the pumps at Rs 4.5 crore less than the lowest quoted rates. I decided to invite fresh tenders. Accounts wizards may question the propriety of this decision but I did it, against the advice of many senior officers. Their first argument was that the tender had already been opened. Second, they said that the party giving the offer was totally sub-standard for supplying the biggest size pumps in the country. I however persisted. In the second tender, the party which had quoted the lowest rates in the earlier tender, was hell bent on not allowing any other party to take that work. It drastically reduced the rates by Rs 12 crore in the revised tender and we finally placed order with that party. In retrospect, I knew that the new party was sub-standard but outwardly I strongly supported that party's request for floating fresh tender. My objective of breaking the cartel was achieved with the inclusion of a sub-standard party and we could save Rs 12 crore of state exchequer by somewhat departing from standard practice.

Radical Reforms in Power Sector

As Chairman of Rajasthan State Electricity Board (RSEB), I used to have an average waiting list of 2.5 lakh farmers for energization of agriculture wells. Every year, 25,000 connections used to be given and 35,000 new applications were received. On an average, it took 12 to 13 years before an applicant could hope to get connection. It was difficult for the farmers to wait for such a long time. Hence, more and more farmers were resorting to theft. While we stepped up checking against theft but I felt that a large number of these farmers would avoid committing theft, if they could get early connection. We started an out-turn scheme, called 'Nursery Scheme'. On an average, the initial cost was ten times higher in this category and the tariff was also 100 per cent higher; connections were being given in about 12 weeks instead of 12 years. There was lot of debate on this issue and at one time, facing vehement opposition from the opposition party in the State Assembly, the then Chief Minister was forced to withdraw this scheme. But, by that time the scheme had taken firm roots. More than 40,000 farmers had taken connections under this scheme. As the news spread about the withdrawal of the scheme, the farmers built up pressure on the MLAs of the ruling as well as the opposition party. It was recognized that in spite of being costly, the Nursery Scheme was cheaper than irrigation through diesel sets. It was also recognized that the scheme was totally voluntary. If some farmers can afford it, others should not object. It was also publicized that the higher amount charged from the better-off farmers was used in supporting the connections of the poorer farmers. The success of the scheme had amazed everybody. The Planning Commission and the World Bank applauded the scheme. I was invited to address several national level workshops about the scheme. In an international seminar on Power Sector Reform organized by the World Bank in Tokyo, I was the only Chairman of the State Electricity Board (SEB) to have been invited. At the end of my presentation, Shri Montek Singh Ahluwalia, the then Finance Secretary warmly congratulated me and told that he should have learnt about the scheme in India rather than in Tokyo.

The scheme had exploded many myths. All over the country, it was strongly believed that the agriculture sector is a holy cow. Even, a marginal increase in tariff would provoke violent agitations. But, the success of the scheme proved to the hilt that tariff was a peripheral issue. The farmers were more concerned with quality of power. In a way, the semi-educated farmers had taken a more progressive view, while the public representatives did not dare to even marginally raise the tariff. This thought is now gradually spreading to other states. This concept can significantly improve the financial position of SEBs which are on the verge of bankruptcy. Today, with financially weak SEBs, the farmers are worst hit by the energy crisis. Tomorrow, with financially stronger SEBs, the farmers would greatly benefit.

Marathon Brainstorming Sessions

In RSEB I used to have meetings in each district at different levels. There were four sessions: one with the public representatives, second with trade and commerce, third with the officers and fourth with the workers. Each of these marathon meetings would very often continue beyond six hours. This was a unique experience in the RSEB. In the past, an overwhelming majority of workers did not have even the glimpse of the Chairman. Here again, the rigid hierarchy was relaxed. I was in live contact with such a large number of persons, officers, workers, and the people at large, instead of confining my meetings to senior officers only. In the meetings, I would speak less and listen more. Many of our senior officers have "hearing problem", in the sense that they do not have patience to listen to others. At the end of such a meeting with the workers, one Chief Engineer told me that he had discovered many new things which he did not know earlier, even though he had been in RSEB for more than 30 years. I told him the secret. If your antenna is sharp and you are receptive, you would remarkably add to your knowledge every day, otherwise you will be adding to your ignorance with every passing day. No officer can survive on his past laurels alone.

In RSEB I used to organize periodical meetings with suppliers where they could raise their grievances. This forum was somewhat new for them. Initially, they were scared to raise their grievances lest the officers below got annoyed but in due course they mustered enough courage to raise their issues. Based on our feedback, we could introduce large-scale improvements in our system. From time to time, due to certain lapses, many parties had been black-listed. In a few years, in certain categories, the number of normal parties was less than the number of black-listed ones.

Consequently, competition between the competent parties got reduced. We reviewed cases of all black-listed parties and offered them to consider fresh orders to them, if they were willing to rectify their past lapses. Through this mechanism, we were able to get large number of past lapses satisfactorily settled and with the removal of their names from the black-list, the number of competing parties also substantially increased which resulted in lower rates to the RSEB.

Agenda-less Meetings

In RSEB, every Monday, I used to hold an agenda-less meeting. All senior officers attended the meetings. Any officer could raise any issue whether it pertained to his wing or not. This broke the watertight compartment between the various wings of RSEB. Proposals were elaborately debated and collective decisions were taken. The atmosphere in these agenda-less meetings used to be very informal and based on the rich experience of the officers, we used to get very useful suggestions. Above all, so much of paper work could be avoided and faster decisions could be taken.

In RSEB, I found a large number of workers, who had become disabled, while discharging their duties. They were virtually getting salary without doing any work. I devised a scheme under which those who sought voluntary retirement, one of their relatives, if found suitable, was to be given employment. This scheme was widely welcomed by the workers and we were able to substitute hundreds of unfit workers by fit workers, higher paid salary workers by lower paid workers, and old workers by young workers. In the normal course, for removing surplus workers, huge funds are spent on VRS schemes but in our scheme, without paying even a single rupee, we were able to dispense with the services of hundred of unfit workers.

Settlement Committees: A Rational Approach

In my short tenure as Principal Secretary, Industries, Settlement Committees were constituted in RIICO and RFC. I had initially constituted such committees in the RSEB and the experiment was a great success. In a single year about 5,000 cases were decided by the Settlement Committees in RSEB. The courts specially encouraged these Settlement Committees. Large number of writs were pending in the Rajasthan High Court. In case after case, the High Court ordered that the petitioner must first approach the Settlement Committee and then the High Court, if the issue remains unresolved in the Settlement Committee. I also approached the Chairman of State Commission for Consumer Affairs and persuaded him that the heavy backlog of appeals can be significantly reduced, if the parties are directed to first approach the Settlement Committee. Although this was totally unprecedented, large number of such appeals were sent by the State Commission to our Settlement Committees. About 85 per cent of the cases were amicably settled and were finally decided. The State Commission had to hear and decide the remaining 15 per cent contested cases only which could not be resolved in the Settlement Committee. The constitution and working of these committees was very much appreciated by High Court and the State Commission. In one of the judgments, the Commission directed Rajasthan Housing Board also to constitute similar Settlement Committees. Prior to the formation of these committees, large number of writs used to be filed against the RSEB but after these committees were formed, the number of such writs drastically came down.

Fighting Famine: An Unconventional Strategy

My tenure in Sikar district was less than nine months but I still fondly remember those days. In 1972, we were in the grip of the worst famine. In a desert district like Sikar, the scope of *pucca* works was rather limited, mainly the desilting of ponds used to be taken under the famine programme. I was totally against such unproductive works. Even during good rainfall, the ponds do not get filled up. I saw no logic in desilting and deepening of the ponds. We had received instructions for engaging 50,000 workers on famine works and we were also told to take up the work on ponds. I discussed with our MLAs and other public representatives and suggested that instead of such unproductive works, we could take up the construction of private irrigation wells.

As is very often the fate of any new proposal, the proposal was scoffed at. The public representatives felt that private works had never been taken up under the famine programme. I, however, pleaded with them to canvass for the scheme at the state level. Their initial attempts were not successful. I kept on pursuing them. After appropriate spadework with the public representatives, I personally took the proposal before the Famine Commissioner for construction of 4,000 irrigation wells. The Famine Commissioner was quite elderly—of my father's age. He was very sceptical about the success of the scheme but the way in which I presented the scheme, he did not wish to discourage a young and enthusiastic officer like me. Hence, he accepted the scheme in principle and indicated to me that in the first phase, he would like to give sanction for 1,000 wells. I pleaded with him that whatever may be the reduction at later stages, but at least at his level, the full scheme of 4,000 wells should be cleared. At long last he cleared the scheme in toto. The same day, I took the file personally for approval of the Famine Minister. In the meanwhile I had informed our MLAs that I was proceeding to the Vidhan Sabha with the scheme to take the approval of the Famine Minister. I also requested the Minister-in-Charge of our district to specially recommend the scheme to the Famine Minister. The Finance Minister was surprised that in a maze of red-tape, how could the file move all the way in a single day. He too was reluctant to take up such a big scheme but in the presence of many of our MLAs, he did not wish to give the impression that he had reduced the number or the size of the programme. Hence, after a pause, he too gave his approval on the file.

Under this scheme, an amount roughly Rs 5,000 was to be spent on the wells, out of which Rs 2,500 was to be spent for labour under the famine and the remaining Rs 2,500 to be given as government loan for each well. In the famine operations, traditionally, the workforce was most unproductive. Allegations of fake labour and fictitious muster rolls were rampant. Under this scheme, the labour was to be selected, not by government officials but by the well owners themselves, not more than two labourers from any family. The result was dramatic. Instead of unfit and unproductive workers, the best workforce was selected and the output went up many times. Another significant change was that the supervision of the workforce was to be done by the well owners rather than government officials. Normally, for a workforce of 50,000 labourers, an army of supervisory officers would have been engaged but in this scheme, in view of the dispersal of labour and personal supervision of the well owner, very limited officers were required for supervision. We also realized that digging of wells was not sufficient. Ultimately, because of very low water table, the wells will have to be energized. The farmers would require bank loans. Hence, we approached the Lead Bank officials of our district. Initially, they did not evince much interest in the scheme. Then, we approached another bank and this was given wide publicity in the press. This alerted the Lead Bank officials and they suddenly realized that if another bank advances loans for pumpsets on such an extensive scale, they will have only a marginal role in the banking operations of the district. Hence, the Lead Bank agreed to advance a loan of Rs 2,500 per well. This news appeared in the newspapers. I was surprised that on the basis of that news item, the government cancelled their part of loans for the wells. Rarely, we find such a promptness in government working. Anyway, we were not adversely affected, since the Lead Bank had agreed to step in. In a nutshell, for the first time, we were able to take up private works instead of public works under famine operations. We also succeeded in switching over from the traditional *kuccha* works to *pucca* works under the famine operations. The heavy expenditure on supervisory staff was drastically reduced. We often talk of one window service, but translating it into action is not always easy. In this scheme, we insisted and ensured that the farmer will not be required to leave his village for anything. The bank officials were required to disburse the loan on the well site. If the land was to be mortgaged with the bank for loan, the tehsil officials were required to do registration in the village itself rather than requiring the farmers to go to tehsil headquarters. The entire scheme was operationalized with the full cooperation and active support of public representatives. In the bank loan sanction committee, even the local MLAs and Pradhans of Panchayat Samitis were included. The bank officials were very reluctant to include public representatives in such committees but we were able to persuade them, on the condition that the Bank Manager will have the veto power. Applications for the wells were screened and sanctioned in public under the full gaze of villagers and rarely there was any difference of opinion.

Processing of 20,000 applications in barely two weeks was a herculean task. Our sanctioning committees moved from village to village—it resembled a typical election scenario. Normally, the people have to go from pillar to post for everything but in this campaign we insisted upon the government officials to visit the well site, for everything.

Exploring Administrative Law

In 1998, after being promoted in the Chief Secretary's scale, I was posted as Chairman of the Civil Services Appellate Tribunal. It was supposed to be a very dull and dreary assignment. The postings in the Tribunal, as in the Revenue Board, are very often indicative of the displeasure of the government and as a reaction to that, the concerned officers also very often tend to become indifferent in their work. In this context, when I joined the Tribunal, the Registrar asked me if I would like to sit on the bench for a day or two every week. I was surprised, why for a day or two, I told him, I will be on the bench every day.

Keeping with the leisurely pace of work in the Tribunal, the court work used to start quite late. I wanted to have early sittings but the advocates were not used to that and they resisted on the ground that they have to be in the High Court during the early hours for admissions etc. Without getting into clash with the advocates, I started the court work in the early hours and suggested that such of advocates who are busy in the High Court, may come later in the day. By this flexibility, we increased the working hours of the Tribunal. Many advocates preferred to come early and finish their work. Earlier, the cases used to be taken up as per the serial order of the cause list. I often found the advocates rushing, when their case was called for hearing, while others had to wait for long because their cases were lower in the cause list. I changed the system and made it totally informal. Whether the case was high or low in the list, we would take up the case, if counsels for both the parties were present. Thus, nobody was in hurry. Instead of going by the serial number of the cause list, we used to take up these cases first, where the advocates would turn up first. Earlier, if the advocates were not present when the case was taken up, many a time, the cases would be dismissed in default. We discontinued such dismissals in default. This created a very informal and tension-free atmosphere in the Tribunal.

On a Faster Track

When I joined the Tribunal, there was a large backlog of old cases. Many cases were as old as of 1988. We launched a campaign for disposal of the old cases. Again, there was resistance from the advocates. They used to take adjournments for one reason or the other. Here again, I wanted to firmly proceed with this campaign without getting into conflict with the Bar. We would agree for adjournments but instead of the earlier adjournments for three to four months, we would adjourn for three to four days. Noting our firm determination, the advocates started cooperating in the disposal of old cases.

The new work culture in the Tribunal was infectious. Our two members of the Tribunal also started taking active interest in the fast disposal of cases. The advocates also realized that dragging on the old cases was counter-productive. During my tenure of 13 months in the Tribunal, we were able to virtually clear all the cases from 1988 to 1997. Most of the cases of 1998 had also been finalized.

The Hon'ble Judges of the Rajasthan High Court were also very impressed by our disposal, which had gone up by more than four times of the average disposal. Most of our decisions were affirmed by the High Court. In the High Court, the pendency of old service matters was quite high and even writs of 1988 were pending. I called on the Hon'ble Chief Justice and suggested that on the ground of alternative remedy, the pending writs could be transferred to the Tribunal as appeals. This would ease the pressure of work on the High Court. This system also had the advantage of all the cases initially getting filtered at the Tribunal level. The

High Court informally decided not to entertain service matters directly. This reduced the institution of service matters in the High Court.

Our initial disposal of cases was rather slow and the advocates used to argue for long. After a month, I felt that it would be very useful, if we could study the files in advance. With this advance preparation, we could curtail the long arguments of the counsels and the disposal was very fast. In 98 per cent cases, we would dictate the order in the court in the presence of the advocates. We also resorted to many time saving measures. We used to admit all the appeals, without arguments. We were told that in the High Court, perhaps more than half the time is taken on hearing arguments for admissions alone. In the High Court, such 'admitted' cases came up for final arguments years later. We, in the Tribunal, were able to save this time by not having any arguments at admission stage unless any stay was involved. We also started giving top priority to disposal of 'stay' cases. The attraction for obtaining stay and allowing the matters to linger on for months, if not years, was gone because we started disposal of stay cases on top priority.

RIICO Turned Entrepreneur-Friendly

My last assignment in government service was as CMD, RIICO. I had barely five months to retire. Many thought that my tempo of work would finally slow down, but no, I was brimming with activity till the last day, rather the last hour. I was as enthusiastic about my work on the last day of my service, as I was on the first day of my service. While handing over, I told my successor that no file or decision had been left pending by me. In the normal course, an officer would take several months before he gets a hang of the department, but through the weekly agenda-less meetings, I was able to take stock of the problems of the organization in great depth and in a quick manner. The agenda-less meetings used to last for several hours. Officers, whether senior or junior, were encouraged to freely express their views. The traditional one-way channel in which the senior officers give directions and the junior officers merely follow, totally changed. It became a two-way traffic. We adopted a collective decision-making approach in which all officers, whether senior or junior, were actively participating in the decision-making process. The rich experience of the field officers in the normal course would have never come up so prominently but for these meetings in which hierarchy became irrelevant. Everyone in the meeting had a common objective of identifying the burning problems and finding their ready solutions. Very soon, the message went round the organization that the top management attached high importance to any useful suggestion, irrespective of the fact whether it was given by a senior officer or a junior officer. In fact, we involved members of trade and commerce also in such exercises by holding separate meetings with them, in which they were encouraged to be brutally frank and instead of defending the status quo, we were very prompt and positive in our reaction.

I am glad to say that as a result of series of policy decisions, emerging from these marathon meetings, our sale of land was seven times higher than the average annual disposal and the revenue too was highest ever. But, in my view, even more important was the series of radical policy decisions, simplifying the procedure and removing irritants of our allottees. Sometimes, even if certain improvements are introduced, they are confined to official circulars and the concerned people have only a faint idea about such improvements. We, however, not only put all such notifications on our website but also widely published such simplification measures through the media.

About sixty major policy decisions were taken during my five-month tenure in RIICO. Because of the constraint of space all such decisions cannot be narrated here. From RIICO's point of view many of them may be minor issues but for the entrepreneurs they were major irritants. I mention a few decisions. RIICO would insist for project report before allotting a plot in the industrial area. I questioned the relevance of such project reports. Our main task was to provide land for industries and not to sit in judgement over the feasibility of such projects. We decided to dispense with project reports. This saved lot of time and expenses of the entrepreneurs and speeded our land allotment.

Due to some unavoidable reasons, if the entrepreneur wanted to change the product, it would require RIICO's approval. We also dispensed with this condition. RIICO, I felt, as seller of land, had nothing to do whether he was making one product or the other. In my view, market forces should decide what product needs to be produced from time to time. Allotment of bigger plots used to be done earlier at the level of CMD. We decentralized and authorized the Regional Managers to allot any size of plots. Land allotment was made almost like purchase of platform ticket. If there was any change in the partnership (partners may be located in different cities), all the partners were required to come to RIICO office for executing the revised partnership deed. I felt that once having allotted the land, such meddling by RIICO was uncalled for. RIICO had nothing to do whether one partner was replaced by another. We had allotted the land for setting up of some industry and so long as the industry was running, in my view, we were unconcerned with the composition of partnership. Plots used to be auctioned by RIICO for commercial purposes but if the entrepreneurs wanted to change the use within commercial category, it would again require RIICO's permission. Thus, if a commercial plot taken in auction for cinema was required instead to be used for a hotel, RIICO would not normally allow change of land use. In my view, it was unfair to perpetually bind any one to stick to a particular project. Having purchased the land for commercial purposes, which is the costliest category, we allowed any such change of use automatically in the same category (industrial to industrial-commercial to commercial), instead of adopting a case to case approach as in the past. I often feel that at some level or the other, the case to case approach often degenerates into a cash to cash approach!

Land allottees were supposed to provide proof of commencing commercial production. Various formalities were involved in this. We removed all these rituals. A mere information through registered letter was sufficient. Earlier, original lease deed was kept in RIICO's office. The entrepreneurs faced problems in obtaining loans etc., without lease deed. We directed our offices to return the lease deeds if there were no dues against them. In the past every map for construction of factories required RIICO's approval but we authorized the entrepreneurs for self-certification up to a particular size and beyond that, a certificate from registered architect was enough. Permission from RIICO was no more required. Earlier, permission was not being given for construction above the shops located in the RIICO industrial area. With the pressure of population, all over the country, vertical expansion of buildings is inevitable. Hence, we allowed such constructions by charging industrial rate for every storey. If for any reason the entrepreneur was not able to commence production, he was not permitted to transfer his land. There must be strong reasons for not being able to start production. I felt that it is futile to force such persons to commence production. It was equally futile not to allow such plots to others who were willing to take up production. Land was our key resource and idle plots reflected badly upon our working, while others were waiting for plot allotment. Hence, we allowed such transfers. There was no incentive for payments made before time. We started giving 5 per cent rebate to those who paid at least 75 per cent charges, before time. In the past, permission was not being given for mortgaging the plot for obtaining loan etc., from financial institutions. This restriction was removed. Besides, sub-division of plots was not permitted, before commencement of production. To my mind, there was no logical link between the two and so we removed this restriction too. Service charges, I discovered, were being levied even from closed units. I felt it was unjust and harsh to such units which were closed. We exempted the closed units from service charges. The earlier restriction of giving land on rent was also removed. Our motto was the productive use of the plots allotted by us. Hence, if the entrepreneur is not able to fully utilize the land, let the tenants productively utilize our key resource, i.e., land. Earlier, RIICO's NOC was required before an entrepreneur could obtain power connection. This caused undue delay. Once RIICO had allotted the land, further micro-managing was uncalled for, hence we removed this requirement.

A Faith Fortified

In a nutshell, time and again, my faith has been fortified that administration can be made more responsive, the tendency to function thoughtlessly and indifferently can be curbed, in the new context, rules and procedures can be given a fresh look, precedence can be given to logic and reasoning instead of outdated rules, that administration should focus on major issues rather than getting bogged down in trivialities, with the active help of the public and public representatives, a new and a forward push can be given to the various development schemes, and the stigma of red-tape can be removed with simplification of rules and procedures.

6 INDERJIT KHANNA

Some Reflections of a Senior Civil Servant

Broadly, this paper is divided into three parts. The first deals with the public perception of the civil service and the public servant, the second with my professional experiences which may be relevant for officers undergoing training and the third part would dwell on the way ahead.

Public Perception of the Civil Service and the Public Servant

The four words—civil, service, public, and servant—are crucial in terms of understanding the role of the bureaucracy. As individual, and as a group of persons, we must always be *civil* in our behaviour, we are appointed to *serve* the society, our actions are constantly under *public* gaze and we are meant to be *servants* of the people. This, then, is the image that the civil service and the public servant is expected to live up to.

In real life today the public perception of the civil service and the public servant is, unfortunately, quite negative and contrary to what the image should be. As a common citizen, if one exchanges experiences of visits to any government office, e.g., tehsil, police station, municipality, urban authority, electricity office, water works, transport office, passport office, a bank, etc., with friends, one only hears words of criticism and rarely words of appreciation. This is because of the long wait, no satisfactory response, absence of officials, non-availability of files, etc. The citizen is, therefore, generally exasperated by his experience and would be only too happy if somehow his visit to a government office becomes unnecessary.

The general public also seems to hold the view that work in government can only be got done if one either pays a bribe or has contacts which can be used for the same. Most government servants do not personally encounter difficulty in getting odd jobs done in government because they adopt the latter course. It would not be out of place to share the views expressed in an e-mail which I had received around May 2007. It was from the Director of an Institute of Management in Rajasthan. He is a graduate from IIT, Delhi and IIM, Ahmedabad. He had set up this institute some years ago. The problem he was now facing related to land. His mail clearly stated that he had been told by friends that the work would only be done either by paying a huge bribe or giving good publicity to important personalities. This perception only seems to strengthen the common belief mentioned above.

Today, the public perception of the civil service is also reflected as a reaction to the authority displayed by members of the civil service. Their government vehicles display red or blue lights, the senior civil servants are invariably accompanied by liveried support staff, gunmen, etc. It is also not uncommon to see gunmen following civil servants when they are out shopping or on their morning walk. The recent spat between an MP and an Airline pilot has been highlighted by Soli J. Sorabjee in his comments under the caption 'soli–loquies' published in the *Indian Express* of 13th April, 2008. He also refers to the late arrival of a VVIP for which no regret was expressed nor any explanation offered. This is the mindset; the *lal batti* culture which, he says, needs to be obliterated. In all this there is no humility, only an aura of authority which brings about an attitude of contempt in the minds of the people vis-à-vis public servants.

Three important quotations of very responsible persons recently highlighted in the 7th April 2008 edition of the *India Today* magazine are worth referring to. The frustrations of former Prime Minister Rajiv Gandhi with the system are quoted: "We have government servants who do not serve but oppress the poor and the helpless, police who do not uphold the law but shield the guilty, tax collectors who do not collect taxes but connive with those who cheat the state and whole legions whose only concern is their own welfare at the cost of society". Secondly, a very respected member of the Indian Civil Service, L.K. Jha, is said to have defined the bureaucrat as "a strange creature who sits on files, sleeps over reminders, eats his own words, turns a deaf ear to complaints and binds his hands and feet with red tape".

Thirdly, the Finance Minister P. Chidambaram, while describing the quality of governance in the country at the *India Today* Conclave on 15th March, 2008 had said: "We distribute vast quantities of foodgrain through our public distribution system. The finding is 36 per cent of the foodgrain does not reach the poor. We have laid out the largest guaranteed wage employment programme as a safety net for the poor. The finding is that there are pockets in India where this programme is not giving the guaranteed wage to the very poor. We have the largest school lunch programme in the world; 130 million children eat a school lunch. The finding is that the quality and the quantity of the food at many places leaves much to be desired. We have a very large road building programme. But many of the roads that are laid are of such poor quality that they have to be re-laid every five years, they vanish after three or four years".

The Prime Minister in an address on 21st April 2008 on the occasion of the Civil Services Day observed: "We must introspect and recognize that there is a great deal of public dissatisfaction with the functioning of government, at all levels of government. This challenge the civil service must endeavour to address as a collective entity". He added that the government also needed to improve its 'human face' as it moved away from running industries and controlling economic activity to managing public services delivery. The latter observation is very important from the point of view of the bureaucracy understanding the changing role of the government. That is necessary because if the country is to move forward at a faster pace than it is presently moving, the mindset of members of the civil service at all levels—from the village level to the level of the Cabinet Secretary—has to change to be perceived as a 'human face'.

The above observations are a telling account of the quality of our delivery systems, and the implementation of developmental programmes all of which reflect the poor quality of output as delivered by the civil service. Obviously, this public perception is a cause for dismay and certainly requires that our younger officers—individually and collectively—rise to the challenge of providing an efficient and honest civil service.

The Training Period

Generally, we all join the government and the civil service with an objective to serve and, with a fair amount of idealism. When we joined the civil service, we were young, at an average age of 23 years, and largely fresh out of college/university. At Mussoorie we had our first formal encounter with the system. The Director at the Academy, a very senior member of the Indian Civil Service, was a strict disciplinarian and a man who led from the front, by his own example. On the very first day of our training the class room doors were closed at 9 a.m. Those who came late by even a few seconds remained out of the class and were given half a day's casual leave. The next time a probationer was late it was a day's leave without pay. Quite obviously, though a few may have fretted and fumed, we were all soon attending classes, PT, riding classes and all other functions on time. The Director himself was never late. Quite often he would be present at the early morning PT sessions, the morning or afternoon riding classes and at the other functions in the evenings in the Academy. His personal example ensured that the other faculty members and staff followed suit.

The Director was also concerned about the well-being of the probationers. We were required to submit a daily report in case of any difficulty being faced by us in our hostels and residential rooms. To ensure that these were promptly attended to, he went through these himself, as was evident by the fact that he would sometimes come to our rooms to look at the problem and have it attended to. This also ensured that we did not make frivolous complaints.

At the social level too, he saw to it that there was interaction between him, the faculty, their families and the probationers by inviting us over in groups in the evenings for tea to their residences.

Apart from acquiring knowledge from the classes we attended, particularly on subjects which we had not studied at college/university, our training at the Mussoorie Academy did add to our spirit of idealism and our desire to serve. It has also built friendships which have lasted over more than forty years.

The next stage of our training brought us to the district and face-to-face with reality. Our role model here was the Collector. At Kota, where I was posted for my training, the Collector was a sober and practical person, in touch with the people and yet one who kept his distance from those with whom such distance was necessary. He upheld the principle we had been taught at the Academy to not only be honest and fair but also to appear to be honest and fair. The latter is very important because the public is closely watching us and our actions and their perception of the government is formed as a sum total of the actions of all members of the government whom they see or interact with frequently. I also vividly recall even today the advice given to me by the Collector on completion of my training, as I was leaving to take up my first independent assignment as a Sub-Divisional Officer. He said, "whenever you take up a new assignment, do not criticize your predecessor and in your enthusiasm and zeal do not rush to make changes in the system till you get a good grasp of your work". The very fact that I remember this advice nearly forty years after it was given to me is evidence of the fact that it had meaning, as also an impact, on me.

Governance

Let us first look at what possibly constitutes good governance. Governance is something above and beyond government. It must be participatory, and its foundation must be built on true decentralization. Accountability, predictability, transparency, free flow of information and a strong civil society are also factors which contribute towards good governance. Another set of factors are in the realm of law. Quite obviously, the government has to be legitimate, its legitimacy flowing from the will of the people. It has to be based on constitutionality such that all actions have to be within the boundaries established by the Constitution, and it has to ensure the rule of law.

On the economic side are issues relating to economic policies being market-oriented and the concern for socio-economic equity and poverty. Some may wish to question the former, but generally it is accepted that good governance must encourage economic policies which promote initiative and enterprise. At the same time, governance must reflect its concern for equity, justice, happiness of the people, reduction of poverty and a better quality of life for everyone. Indeed, the benefits of economic development must reach the poorest of the poor.

One very important aspect of an administrator's work is the extent of his responsiveness. The common complaint we hear is that administrators do not respond to telephone calls. This reflects on their non-responsive nature and creates a poor impression on the calling party. I have heard some administrators trying to justify such non-responsiveness by saying that they receive so many phone calls everyday that it is difficult for them to respond in all cases. This is, in my view, an idle excuse. We must manage our time properly and ensure that we respond to people who are seeking to speak to us. A similar situation holds in terms of meeting visitors, rather than avoiding persons, and in terms of responding to letters in a reasonable time. All three aspects, on which civil servants are severely faulted today, can easily be remedied by their responsiveness in such cases.

Some Experiences in the Context of Good Governance

No doubt, the quality of governance is of paramount importance. At the core of all efforts and actions of good governance has to be the common man, the '*Aam Aadmi*'. It is my view that the well-known adage, "that government is best which governs the least", is undoubtedly the direction in which we must be continuously moving. This does not imply an elimination of government, but rather a serious effort to reduce the government-citizen interface to the bare minimum particularly in terms of mundane activities so that such interaction happens, if at all, infrequently and in a routine and effortless manner. This will reduce, if not eliminate, harassment and corruption. Let me give three examples. Years ago, road tax for vehicles was paid every year. Now, it is paid as one-time tax. Driving licences were given for five years, now they can be given up to 20 years. Likewise, at one time passports were given for five years, now they can be given for 10 and 20 years. In each case, the citizen has to go less frequently to government offices for his needs. What good governance, therefore, requires are systemic changes to reduce government-citizen interface so as to reduce opportunities for harassment and corruption.

Let us now take a few examples of good governance from a state neighbouring Rajasthan, i.e., Gujarat. The experiences go back about 25 years when I had the opportunity of working in that state for two years. Past experience had led me to the conclusion that the payment of an electricity bill and a water bill results in loss of one man-day of work per month if one were to pay the bills oneself. This includes the time taken from when one leaves home, reaches the concerned office, waiting time and then the time taken to return home. In Ahmedabad there were no water bills as water came for a short time, though with clock-work precision, in the morning and evening but the Municipal Corporation factored in this aspect while calculating the property tax. The citizen, therefore, did not have to bother on this score. In the case of the electricity bill, one had only to attach a cheque to the bill and post it back to the Ahmedabad Electricity Company (AEC). There was no need for searching out any office of the AEC or identifying oneself before making payment. Next month, the new bill would be accompanied by the receipt for the previous month. The system worked flawlessly for 24 months when I was there. Shortly thereafter, on return to Rajasthan, during a campaign of 'Prashasan Shahar ki Aur', I suggested to the Collector of one district to introduce and enforce the system of payment of electricity and water bills by cheques. He declined giving his own example where he had been sent an arrear bill by the RSEB, which he did not accept, of many many months earlier. Such a reflection of lack of confidence in the system, by those who are part of the system itself, clearly calls for a change of mindset when issues of governance are concerned. A third example is that of the Gujarat Fisheries Cooperative Federation, whose refrigerated van came to our Society every Thursday at the designated hour of 2 p.m. Finally, the fourth example is of the City Bus Service run by the Ahmedabad Municipal Corporation. At each 'Pan' stall the time table of the bus services, indicating starting time and time at terminating station, running on that route was available and with a fair amount of precision they would arrive at the right time. All these are relatively simple matters but certainly such as to make the life of a common citizen more easy and hassle-free. That, in my view, is what governance is all about.

Coming back to Rajasthan, let me take two more examples. The first relates to the question of abolition of octroi. Around 1992, the government had set up a committee headed by Shri Mathura Das Mathur, former Finance Minister to look into this issue. As Finance Secretary I was a member of this committee. The revenue from octroi at that time was around Rs 150 crore per annum. I had favoured the abolition of octroi on the ground that this would eliminate a lot of harassment, and corruption in the system. The Chief Minister, who was also the Finance Minister, was a little surprised when he was told of my views but did not question my views. The committee did recommend the abolition of octroi. However, it was only about six years later in 1998 that the Chief Minister and the government did abolish octroi though by then the liability had increased to more than Rs 400 crore. The moral of this story is that the objective of government is the welfare and well-being of the people, even if it means some loss of revenue to government which can be compensated by other revenue earning efforts, and in taking timely decisions.

The other example relates to levy of three taxes on one urban property owned by one citizen, each to be paid annually. Obviously this causes hardship to the citizen who has to run to three different offices every year: the Jaipur Municipal Corporation for payment of house tax, the JDA for payment of annual lease money and for payment of land and building tax to a separate department. In each case assessment had to be done, giving rise to discretion in the hands of lower level functionaries, leading to harassment and corruption. Common sense indicated that all three taxes on one property should be merged into one tax. As Chief Secretary of the government, around 2001–02, I saw the report from the Administrative Reforms Commission headed by Shri Shiv Charan Mathur, a former Chief Minister. One of the recommendations was to merge all these three into one tax and charge the property owner accordingly. The procedure recommended was also simplified with the rate prescribed at Re 1 per square yard for the land, plus Re.1 per square foot for the constructed area. It was to be on a self-assessment basis. Though a very simple and good recommendation, and despite my fully endorsing it, unfortunately, this recommendation was not initially accepted by the government due to an apprehension of curtailment of revenues, though later in 2003 the government did abolish the Land and Building Tax

Department. Two taxes on one urban property to be paid every year, however, still remain and are, in my view, a source of harassment to the common man.

My brief tenure of about 10 months as Commissioner, Tribal Area Development in 1983–84 was a rewarding and learning experience. In my view, the primary objective of work was to enable employment opportunities to be made available to the tribals residing in this area. Four activities which appeared to have potential were fishing, beedi-making, poultry and sericulture. As regards fishing, I found that the many water-spreads in the area were given to contractors who were exploiting the tribals. My suggestion of allotting the water-spreads to co-operatives of tribals initially met with resistance from the Finance Department on grounds of loss of revenue. After considerable persuasion, emphasizing that this activity could provide employment to over five thousand tribals, this was eventually agreed too. The important aspect of providing employment rather than some meagre revenue from contractors, who were also exploiting the tribals, was thus met.

As regards beedi-making, the area had 'Tendu' leaf and manpower but no tobacco leaf. I learnt that in Kerala where there was neither Tendu leaf nor tobacco yet by getting these two raw materials from other states they were able to employ about 20,000 persons in the activity of beedi-making in just one district, which they marketed as 'Kerala Dinesh Beedi'. While initially marketing the product, to compete with established brands from neighbouring states, the MD gave one match box free with each beedi packet. This incentive was evolved as a marketing strategy. Though they initially incurred some loss, in a few months, the impact of this marketing strategy was evident and they were able to capture the local market. This was a venture in the cooperative sector with around 20 societies in Cannanore district. Unfortunately, my tenure ended and I could not establish this activity in the area.

The third activity was in the field of sericulture. The growing of the mulberry plant was introduced and the Disease Free Layings (DFLs) were brought in from Bangalore. With help from the university, academic institutions and NGOs the activity was initiated. It was interesting to learn that one such activity had five different sets of employment opportunities—mulberry farming, DFL raising, basket making, reeling and weaving.

Poultry rearing activity provided me with a slightly different experience. The common perception was that this activity could not succeed in a tribal area as the tribals would eat away the birds. When I visited a rural tribal family to whom a unit of hundred chicks had been given three months ago I found that the mortality was only about 5 or 6 chicks. I categorically enquired from the lady rearing the chicks as to how many birds had been eaten by the family. Her reply was that she was rearing the chicks like children, then how could there be any thought of eating the birds. Obviously, common perceptions can be so very wrong!

In brief, good governance requires good leadership, a stable government and a concern for the common man or '*Aam Aadmi*'. There must be harmony and respect between the political wing of government and the civil service. Decisions have to be swift with no 'dilly-dallying'. Decisions must not be taken with short-term gains in mind but with a long-term view. Finally, there must also be a transfer of power to the people in real terms.

Decentralization and Delegation of Authority

Decentralization and delegation of authority is at the core of all aspects of governance. One must release power in favour of others, let them take decisions, help them to use that power justly and fairly and make them accountable for their decision-making.

The 73rd and 74th amendments to the Constitution, enacted by Parliament in 1993, have been path breaking efforts in terms of decentralization of power to local authorities in the rural and urban areas. They have sought to create a third tier of government at the district and lower levels. The Panchayati Raj Institutions (PRIs) and Urban Local Bodies (ULBs) are now expected to plan and execute development schemes within their respective jurisdictions. The amendments are intended to develop people to take their own decisions. These elected representatives, who number more than 3 million across the country, being nearest to the people are certainly going to be more accountable than others who are far removed from the grassroots level. While the objectives of these two constitutional amendments in terms of holding of regular elections, reservation of seats for weaker sections and for women and the non-dissolution of bodies have generally been met, other important objectives of transfer of power and decentralization in terms of the transfer of funds, functions and functionaries from the state level to the local bodies are yet to be achieved in adequate measure. One of the major reasons for this is that at the state level, both in the political field and within the bureaucracy, there is reluctance to part with power. On our part as individual civil servants, and collectively as a civil service, we must make every possible effort to ensure that this process of decentralization through the delegation of power and authority becomes a reality. Of course, in the process, we have to build in systems of accountability such that the decision-making authority realizes that its decisions cannot be arbitrary as they will be subject to scrutiny.

A very important feature of the two constitutional amendments is the provision of reservation of one-third seats and office of chairpersons for women. This is truly a revolutionary effort in terms of empowering women. As a consequence, more than one million women are elected every five years to hold office in local bodies throughout India. Their number is also increasing and some states, like Rajasthan recently, have increased this percentage of reservation for women in local bodies to 50 per cent. Experience over the past 15 years of this process of reservation for women in PRIs and ULBs has clearly established that their empowerment is a reality. An issue to be pursued is the introduction of reservation for women to seats in the State Legislatures and the Parliament.

With 3 million persons being elected to office every five years, one million of them being women, it becomes necessary to ensure that these elected representatives have the capacity and knowledge to enable them to take wise decisions. Experience over the past 15 years has shown that much still needs to be done in terms of capacity building of these elected representatives. Numbers need not be a reason for despair. In each state there is an institution for training of elected representatives and officials of PRIs and ULBs. Many such state-level institutions have regional/divisional centres. A three-pronged effort can be made to enable that these elected representatives are suitably trained and equipped to handle their responsibilities within a period of 3 to 6 months from the date of their election. The state-level institute could train the chairpersons of the district and block level bodies, as also the members of the district level bodies, while at the district-level, training could be organized for the members of the block-level bodies and the Sarpanchas and at the block level the members of the Gram Panchayat could be trained.

Generalist-Specialist Controversy

This is another long-standing criticism, particularly of the IAS. It is felt that members of this service keep changing jobs so frequently that they can never do justice to their work as they never acquire the specialized knowledge of any department. In common parlance, they are seen as "jack of all trades but master of none". To a limited extent there is validity in such a perception. To overcome this criticism, it is necessary for the government and the civil servant to work towards a process of specialization. It is my considered view that the first 10 years in the IAS is a period of learning for each member of the service. Apart from the formal period of two years training, the remaining period of about eight years should ideally cover two years as a Sub-Divisional Officer, two to three years as a Collector, two years as a Deputy Secretary and two to three years as a head of department. The next 10-year period is one where the officer should specialize in about two fields and the last 15 years is one where the officer is primarily involved in policy making in his field of specialization. This would require a strict adherence to the principles of tenure. In Government of India an officer has a stable tenure of five years and invariably remains in the same ministry. This develops in the officer a specialization in relation to the subject matter of his ministry. At the state level it has somehow to be ensured that an officer has a tenure of at least three years on one post. This requires considerable political will.

Another aspect in this regard is with respect to postings in the Government of India. In my view, such postings are necessary for every IAS officer. While the state-level experience provides the micro-understanding, the Government of India posting provides a national perspective, and in most cases, an international perspective also, both of which are very necessary for maturity in decision-making.

In terms of preference for postings and in the arena of specialization, officers normally tend to prefer the ministries/departments of economic affairs, commerce, industry, finance which are 'seen' as more glamorous. Peer-group perception is also a factor that makes this so. In fact, the ministries/departments of rural development, agriculture, health, education, social justice and empowerment, women and child development, etc., provide a much more rewarding experience and innumerable challenging opportunities. Let me here share the view of one of my senior colleagues in the service. Most of his career, both in the state and in the central government, was spent in the ministries/departments of finance, industry, commerce and a tenure abroad in the Indian Embassy as Minister, Economic. His last posting was as Health Secretary to the Government of India. A month before his retirement we both happened to be travelling from Delhi to Jaipur. During the course of conversation, he said, "I have found my tenure as Health Secretary to be my most rewarding experience". This was quite contrary to what one would have expected from him, but it was telling in terms of the fact that there is so much more in government than postings in finance, economic affairs, commerce and industry departments.

Corruption

Corruption has emerged as the most pernicious threat to governance in India. There is a perception of its encompassing all spheres of governance.

The bureaucracy is under constant glare and criticism on account of corruption within its ranks. The unfortunate part is that while corruption is a rampant malaise nothing seems to ever happen to those who are corrupt. Delays in investigation, delays in court cases and political interference result in most corrupt officials being let off the hook. There is corruption which the common man encounters in his day-to-day interaction with government functionaries and there is corruption at high levels. Much has been written on this topic but I would only refer the reader to two articles in the press. One is a special report in the *Sunday Times of India* of 28th April 2002 under the caption ' Common man's tryst with corrupt India'. The box item on this page also refers to Transparency International's Corruption Perception Index (CPI) 2001 and ranks countries on a clean scale of 10. The surveys reflect perceptions of business people, the general public and analysts. India's rank was 71 out of 91 countries and the Index was as low as 2.7. The second article is in the *India Today* magazine of 7th April 2008 which has the cover story article on bureaucracy under the caption 'A lot to hide'. It is a scathing attack and refers to cases against senior civil servants which have been going on for years, during which period many have been promoted, retired and got their pensions. Lack of action in corruption cases naturally results in more persons daring to be corrupt.

It is easy to slide down the slippery path of unethical behaviour simply because it seems advantageous. However, the measure of a person's character is what he would do if he knew he would never be found out.

The malaise of corruption can only be attacked by examples being set at the highest level and by firm and swift action against corrupt officials.

Cost and Time Overrun of Developmental Projects

A common criticism of developmental projects in the infrastructure sector in areas like power, roads, buildings, irrigation projects, etc., is that they are never completed on time. This not only delays the flow of benefits of the projects to the people, but also results in cost escalation. A news item published in the *Hindustan Times* of 4th May 2008 under the caption "Delayed projects could have fed half of India's poor for 4 months" refers to a report on the status of 897 infrastructure projects of the Central Government worth Rs 3,59,451 crore surveyed between July and September 2007. This report is by the Ministry of Statistics and

Programme Implementation. The news item states that 318 government projects running behind schedule had cost an additional Rs 24,670 crore to the exchequer and that this money could have fed half of India's below poverty line population for close to four months.

The cost and time overrun is primarily due to poor project planning, changes in design after the project has been initiated, and inadequate budgetary provisions from year to year. As Director of Primary and Secondary Education for three years in the mid-seventies, I came across hundreds of school buildings and class rooms lying incomplete. The investment in such infrastructure ran into hundreds of crores of rupees at that time. To give another set of examples, during the very early part of my tenure as Chief Secretary, in the cities of Ajmer, Jaipur and Delhi, I came across five government buildings where, against the revised project cost of Rs 155 crore, an expenditure of Rs 93 crore had been incurred over the past 5 to 6 years but each of these five buildings was incomplete and, therefore, their benefits could not be derived by the intended beneficiaries. Within a period of about 12 to 14 months, by providing Rs 25 crore for these buildings, they were completed or brought to a stage where they were put to use. The moral of the story, no doubt easier said than done, is to try and ensure that new projects are not taken up till the ongoing projects are completed.

In the context of infrastructure, two other examples of challenges being converted into opportunities are being shared. These are both from my experience during the tenure as Chief Secretary. In one case of two institutions, the Entrepreneurial Management Institute (EMI) and the Institute of Fashion Design, both of which were running out of rented premises, I found that the latter had land but no money to construct its building while the former had money but no land on which to construct its building. Getting both the institution heads together it was agreed that the Institute of Fashion Design would part with some of its land to the EMI and from the amount received from EMI would construct its building, while with the remaining money EMI would construct its own building on the land it bought from the Institute of Fashion Design. To the credit of the state PWD, which took up the construction of both these buildings, they were up within one year.

The other example in the field of infrastructure is that of a role of facilitator which one can and should play. National Highway Authority of India (NHAI) was responsible for the construction of the golden quadrilateral while Gas Authority of India Ltd. (GAIL) was responsible for laying a 1,100 km gas pipeline from Gujarat to North India. Both were central public sector undertakings which were responsible for these works in the early part of this decade. Sometimes, a view is taken that since such works are being executed by central undertakings the state administration has little role to play. To the contrary, I would say, that the state administration has a very important and proactive role to play as a facilitator since the direct and indirect benefits of such projects accrue to the people of the state. During their execution, the projects provide employment to the people of the state, while after completion their benefits, in one case, the use of roads and in the other in terms of gas availability, are available to the people of the state. The facilitator's role is possible in terms of helping in matters relating to land acquisition, clearing of encroachments and generally being there for the project authorities. The Delhi-Mumbai section of the golden quadrilateral with about 700 km of road length in Rajasthan was completed on time while the GAIL pipeline project, which was held up on account of litigation over a 40 km stretch in Sirohi district, was also successfully completed through the good offices of the Collector in resolving local disputes. Both central undertakings acknowledge the facilitating role of the state officials.

The flip side of the cost and time overrun issue is available in the example of the construction of units 1 to 5 of the Suratgarh Thermal Power Plant. At each stage of its construction, i.e., units 1 and 2, units 3 and 4 and finally unit 5, they were completed ahead of schedule resulting in cost saving and also earlier flow of benefits to the people in terms of power supply. Unit 2 (250 MW) of stage I of the project was completed six months ahead of schedule, resulting in a saving of Rs 80 crore. Units 3 and 4 (250 MW each) of stage II were completed 4 and 5 months ahead of schedule respectively, each resulting in a saving of Rs 80 crore per unit. In the case of unit 5 (250 MW), this was also commissioned four months ahead of the target date of commissioning resulting in a saving of Rs 100 crore in a project cost of Rs 754 crore.

In the case of this very project the process of decision-making in the context of sanction of unit 5 is also worth mention. Around October 2000 it was explained to the Chief Minister and the state government that if this unit was sanctioned quickly we could get BHEL to supply the equipment on an urgent basis provided an advance was paid to them by January 2001. Since much of the infrastructure was already available through the construction of units 1 to 4, the per megawatt cost of unit 5 was likely to be Rs 3.02 crore against Rs 4.60 crore in units 1 and 2. The idea appealed to the Chief Minister and the state government, sanctions were given, budget provided so that advance was paid to BHEL and unit 5 was also completed ahead of schedule. A clear case of quick decision-making with benefits accruing earlier than scheduled and with saving of about Rs 100 crore (over 13%) against a project cost estimate of Rs 754 crore.

Idle Infrastructure

I have observed that infrastructure built at the cost of the public exchequer quite often lies idle and unutilized. Most buildings in educational institutions lie idle in the afternoons and evenings. We should take up multiple use of such buildings to increase the return on investment. To give another example, in Jaipur city, there are residential colonies of government/government undertakings where houses/flats lie vacant for years on end. In just the four cases of the Income Tax Colony, the two RBI colonies, the PNB Colony and the IFCI Colony, a couple of hundred flats have been vacant for many years. What a colossal waste of government expenditure. Obviously, the expenditure was made unmindful of the occupancy factor.

Mindless Road Digging in Cities

The lack of coordination among departments and between private sector companies and urban bodies is quite evident in the mindless manner in which roads are dug up from time to time for laying pipes or cables in cities. The departments involved are JDA/UIT, JMC/municipalities, JVVN, PHED, telecom companies, etc. While there is meant to be a coordination body for this purpose, its effectiveness is totally absent. In five years the same road may be dug on five different occasions by different departments. Once dug, its restoration may take six months to one year causing innumerable hardship to the residents and tremendous inconvenience to traffic. Similarly, the same road is repaired time and again rather than money spent on laying new ones. The public response is that nobody seems to bother so why complain. This is a relatively simple matter if only some officials were to be conscientious and persevering.

Performance Appraisal

The Annual Confidential Reports (ACRs), now called the Annual Performance Appraisal Reports (APARs), have been in vogue probably since the civil services came into being. Their formats have been revised from time to time. Up to the Joint Secretary level there is a self-appraisal by the officer himself, followed by three levels of reporting, i.e., the Reporting Officer (RO), the Reviewing Officer and the Accepting Authority. Prior to the commencement of the financial year, which is the reporting year also, the officer and the RO are required to sit together and frame the targets for the next year. Unfortunately, this is rarely done. This is where the problem starts. At the end of the year the officer is sent the APAR form by the authority concerned, to fill his self-assessment. Ideally, the self-assessment should be a response to the targets fixed before the start of the year. Since prior target setting is seldom done, the objectivity of performance appraisal is questioned. The fault is not in the performance appraisal process but in its implementation.

The officer is given one month's time to submit the APAR with his self-assessment to the RO. If he does not do so within the period of one month, the instructions provide that the RO can give his remarks and assessment without the self-assessment and submit the same to the Reviewing Officer who, after recording his remarks, should submit the APAR to the Accepting Authority. It is my view that an RO should not take more than a week or 10 days to record his remarks. The Reviewing Officer and the Accepting Authority should not take more than three days each for putting their remarks on an APAR. If this discipline is followed, there is no reason why all APARs should not be completed by 30th June. The unfortunate part is that there is delay at every stage, by the authority which circulates the APAR form, by the officer concerned, by the RO, by the Reviewing Officer and by the Accepting Authority. The result is that sometimes APARs are not written and available for many years. This results in problems for the officer, and creates a lack of confidence in the process of recording APARs. Once again, the fault lies not in the system but the poor manner in which the system is managed.

Sometimes, officers try to cover up their delays by saying that with excessive workload they have no time for writing APARs. This is unacceptable. The problem only arises when officers do not record their remarks as soon as the APARs are received, but allow them to accumulate. Such officers can only be classified as inefficient or perverse and vindictive. The latter assertion is made since it is known that ROs, Reviewing Authorities and sometimes Accepting Authorities delay in writing their remarks to either keep subordinates under their thumb and pressure or to ensure that subordinates do not forget them even after they have moved on to other posts. At times the officer himself delays filling up his self-assessment since he does not want the RO/Reviewing Officer or Accepting Authority (Ministers, in some cases) to record their remarks in the hope that they would resign from office or retire. In the worst case scenario an officer may even connive with his Reviewing Officer to have the APAR misplaced when he finds that the RO has not given favourable remarks. I have also known of ROs writing APARs of the same officer for five years on one day, after the tenure of the RO is over. I have stated these details on the basis of unfortunate experiences which I have actually encountered. I can also state with authority that the Chief Secretary is probably the officer who receives the largest number of APARs, as RO/Reviewing Officer or as Accepting Authority. He has to set the example of adhering to the guidelines in letter and spirit, in regard to the recording of APARs. Only then will most others follow suit. I have particularly mentioned these points to highlight these situations which, though true, can easily be remedied if the movement of the APAR is closely monitored and the instructions for recording APARs are scrupulously followed.

Apart from the procedural aspects mentioned above, which do corrupt the system, and also give rise to criticism of the APAR system, the performance appraisal system itself is sometime criticized for being subjective. For a variety of reasons this is not a tenable argument. Firstly, if performance targets are made out initially, as required, the appraisal at the end of the year will necessarily be objective since the officer is being appraised against agreed targets set more than 12 months ago. Secondly, if perchance the RO has been either harsh or too kind in his appraisal, the Reviewing Officer or the Accepting Authority can certainly moderate the same. Finally, the APARs are merely a tool on the basis on which over a period of time, say 5 to 10 years, an officer is screened or judged for his promotion. With three persons assessing his performance every year and at least 10 APARs to be looked into, this itself implies that 30 assessments of the officer's performance are being looked into to decide whether he is fit for promotion or not. In view of these factors it would appear that today there is no better option to the APAR system if it is made to work in accordance with prescribed instructions.

In the context of performance appraisal and promotions I would like to refer to a telephonic interview given by Dr Dipak Jain to the *Hindustan Times* soon after his appointment as Dean to the Kellogg Graduate School of Management, US. This interview was published under the caption "From mediocracy to meritocracy" in the paper on 20th June 2001. In response to a question as to why Indian managers perform so well abroad but not at home, he said, "The answer is very simple. In India, we don't appreciate the difference between a horse and donkey. When I was a Professor at Guwahati, me and a colleague (who was extremely irregular at work) both got an increment of Rs 140 at the end of the year. Now, where is the incentive to work? Job security in India ensures that optimal efforts become zero. While in the US meritocracy alone counts, in India, mediocracy rules. And nepotism takes care that you are not dislodged from your position. This system is unfortunate because it does not allow talent to flourish. Though we, by our sanskaras, are hard working, sincere and gifted, there is no conducive environment for these traits to thrive". This is, unfortunately, very true and applicable to the Indian bureaucracy and the environment in which it functions.

Motivation

The motivation in any system or organization can be extrinsic or intrinsic. Both are necessary though the latter is probably more so in developmental organizations. Extrinsic motivation is generally in the form of an incentive while intrinsic motivation results in creativity and innovation. In the case of the former there is an apprehension that the motivation may disappear if the incentive is removed, whereas in the case of intrinsic motivation there is greater likelihood of members of the organization continuing their efforts since the creative and innovative work becomes an inspiration for further action.

In the civil service there is precious little we can do within the system to motivate employees. There can be no out-of-turn promotion and no monetary incentive to employees. Therefore, generally, there is little to motivate employees to perform better. However, certain things can still be done which may help employees to feel happy about their working environment and, therefore, to feel somewhat motivated. The first is to set an example by one's own work. Coupled with that, rather than always admonishing subordinates for their failures one should encourage them by proper guidance and giving time to explain matters. A little socializing can also help. In earlier days, particularly in the districts, the local officer's club provided opportunity for such interaction in the evening, and on holidays. Sports like tennis, badminton and table tennis were not only forms of exercise but also good recreation. To this were added a host of indoor games. I can particularly recollect the role of such activities in building friendships at the sub-division, district and head of department postings which are lasting till today.

Some other small incidents can also be cited which are not written in any book but which can result in providing necessary motivation to subordinates. For example, you tell your boss that you would like to visit a particular place on leave for some personal work and he responds by saying that there is some official work to be done there, which you should do. The boss is not only facilitating your visit but also getting some work done.

Obviously, he would do this only for someone with whose work he is more than satisfied.

Another small incident which I can recall occurred some 35 years ago when I was a Deputy Secretary. I happened to be slightly unwell and applied for two days' casual leave. The secretary of the department wrote back on the application, "I know that the Deputy Secretary would be working at home. No leave is required". I have always taken this to mean an appreciation of one's work.

Fifteen years ago, when I joined the UGC in November 1993, I had requested the Chairman that I needed to take two spells of leave, one for about a week in the last week of December, and about four weeks' leave in February-March 1994. The Chairman graciously agreed. Just two days before I was to proceed on leave in December he was unfortunately hospitalized but insisted that I proceed on leave as planned. He kept his promise on both occasions. The gesture did have its impact on me.

Incentive Works

The Kota Thermal Power Station was commissioned in the early 1980s. In 1990–91 its Plant Load Factor (PLF) was around 42.78 per cent. Prior to that, the PLF, with one exception, was between 41 and 57 per cent, whereas, it should have been well above 65. Obviously, the efficiency and productivity were well below the required levels. In that year the Governing Board of RSEB decided to introduce an incentive scheme for all staff, technical and non-technical, at the plant. To achieve the twin objectives of higher generation and cost reduction, the generation-linked incentive was based on the overall PLF. In the very next year, i.e., 1991–92 the PLF went up to 66.35 per cent and in the subsequent year it went up to 77.01 per cent, thereafter, it has always been between 73 and 90 per cent. Because of the efficient levels of production the plant management has been receiving awards at the national level. When the Suratgarh Thermal Power Station was commissioned from 1999–2000 and onwards the incentive scheme was made applicable there and the PLF here also has been maintained above 75 per cent. This example clearly reveals that if appropriate incentives are built into the salary structure of organizations, and this is what the private sector does, the productivity levels can be considerably enhanced.

Reward System

Any organization requires a system of rewards which is fair and transparent. It need not necessarily be monetary. The objective of a reward system must be to motivate people working within that system. Rewards can be designed to appreciate performance of individuals and for team effort. Rewards should also be in public, or in the presence of others, so that it is known to people at large.

In government, monetary rewards are difficult to come by. However, appreciation of the work of an individual or a team can be expressed in many ways. A note on the file by a superior which says, 'excellent note', 'good work', 'keep it up', and the like provide tremendous encouragement and motivation to subordinates. Such expressions on file are public in nature since they are seen by superiors and subordinates. A reward can also be in the form of sending an employee for training within the country or abroad. The training would not only enhance the skills of a person but would further refresh him/her when they return to work.

Though not related directly to my experience as a civil servant, I would like to share an innovative and novel experience of a reward system from my school days. In the 1950s I was studying in a boarding school at Nainital. The school had no swimming pool. Some boys from the school used to sneak into the Raj Bhawan premises and swim there, when the Governor was not residing there. One day, our Principal received a call from the Raj Bhawan Secretariat complaining of this. The Principal made a general announcement asking all the boys who have been going to the Raj Bhawan swimming pool to meet him in his office in the afternoon. To his surprise, as many as about 90 boys, out of a total student strength of about 350, lined up outside his office door. Of course, as a matter of routine, each student received four strokes of the cane as a punishment! However, this incident gave the Principal an idea that the school needed a swimming pool. It also established that the students were imbibing the rare quality of owning up to their mistake and being ready to receive punishment for the same. Since the school did not have all the financial resources, he decided that the material cost would be provided by the school while the labour would be done by the students. The labour task was not compulsory but the reward system which he built into the effort provided the motivation and incentive to the students. There was an individual reward in terms of the student getting an extra town leave every month if he did a given number of man hours of work. The collective reward was to the House to which the student belonged in terms of points earned by the House in proportion to the man hours put in by each student belonging to that House. These points were valuable because each of the four Houses strongly competed for the school Efficiency Cup which was a prized cup and the points earned from this effort were added to the points that the House earned from their performance in other spheres of school activity. Therefore, the House Captain and the House Master of each House encouraged more and more students to work at the pool.

The two swimming pools were thus built in about 18 months. The Principal achieved his objective, the students were happy that they got their swimming pool, and along the way there were rewards for individual students and for the team effort. Willy-nilly, the students were instilled with the concept of dignity of labour. It was a win–win situation for everyone.

This experience, in my view, is also a classic example of doing what you can, where you are, with what you have. Many times civil servants complain about inadequate resources and make this an alibi for non-performance. They do not look around their environment to utilize all available resources. This is, in fact, the first thing that they must do when they plan to take up a new project.

Postings and Tenures

This is a big issue in the civil service. There is criticism both from within and outside that this is purely on a political basis and that no consideration is given to the qualifications, aptitude and experience of officers. This is partly true, but it is also true that within the service itself there is the unfortunate perception that some posts are coveted while others are not so. Therefore, it is not unknown to find some officers trying for certain posts and others who are in so-called non-coveted posts trying for the coveted posts. This vicious circle creates the problem.

As mentioned earlier, all posts in government provide challenges and opportunities, provided one is willing to stay on and work. In this regard, I would like to give the example of an interaction I recently had with a young official from one of the central services. He had been in this service for one year. Prior to this he had been a clerk in the Social Welfare Department of a neighbouring state for about six years. The interaction revealed to me how he, even at the clerical level, was able to convert a challenge into an opportunity. In that state there was a blind school with 50 vacancies, all of which were full. In the course of his work he received a representation made to the Chief Minister of that state on which the Chief Minister had recorded that the applicant may be given admission to the blind school. The clerk had three options. One was to accept the order and let the child be admitted but this would have resulted in further similar orders and the administration at the school level would have gone haywire. The second was to resubmit the matter saying this was not possible as there was no vacancy. The third option was to say that the representation indicated that there was need to increase capacity at the institution since there was an increasing demand. He followed the course of the third option which was finally agreed to. The child got admission and the capacity of students was increased form 50 to 100. To me, this is clearly a case of converting a challenge into an opportunity.

When I look back at my own career over 35 years (excluding the two years as a probationer), I find that the number of postings I have had have been 16, of which two were in Jaipur during one tenure in the early 1990s. This is not too bad with an average tenure of about 2 years and 2 months. Of these postings I do know that in the case of 7, without my involvement in any manner, there was a request/selection process which resulted in my posting. In one case, where the post was certainly one which was much sought after, though I was not inclined to move there, the final argument given to me was that in public service one sometimes has to make some sacrifices. This argument, coming from a political leader, indicated a considerable level of maturity and I obviously had to give in. In the case of another coveted post, a few persons who were keen on that post got excluded only because they were showing eagerness for that particular post. This again indicates that the problem lies, to some extent, at the level of the civil servant, rather than at the level of the politician.

In conclusion, on this issue of postings and tenure, it can be said that the blame lies equally with the politician and the civil servant. There are good persons in both groups, but their number is dwindling. The effort has to be towards postings based on the qualifications, aptitude and experience of officers with tenures of at least three years on each post.

Institution Building

During one's career, one may occasionally be required to set up new institutions/organizations. Also, on every post one joins, one wants to improve the institution/organization. Institution building is, therefore, a challenge for every civil servant throughout his career. In this context, I would like to share an experience which I have had while on deputation from government to the Indian Institute of Management, Ahmedabad (IIM-A) for two years as a Visiting Professor from 1981 to 1983.

Prof Ravi Mathai (Ravi to his friends) was the first full-time Director of the IIM-A. I came to know him from July 1975 onwards when he along with Professors Udai Pareek and T.V. Rao initiated a project with weavers and tanners in Jawaja block of Ajmer district. IIM-A faculty working in the rural areas with village folk was not conventional, but then nor was Ravi.

He left a very promising career in the private sector in the mid-sixties to join as a faculty at IIM-A. Soon thereafter, he took over as the first full-time Director. Many of the conventions, traditions as they exist today at the institute were established by him. While the institute was set up to train young boys and girls to take up work in industry he realized that management systems within government should not be excluded from the institute's sphere of work. That is how, the Centre for Management in Agriculture (CMA) and the Public Systems Group (PSG) came to be set up. His leadership, dedication, innovative instincts all led to good practices being established at the institute. On completion of a term of five years as Director, and while still in his early forties, Ravi took the very unusual decision to step down as Director. Obviously, he took the Board, the faculty and the staff by surprise. He did not give in to pressure to continue as Director but rather continued as a faculty member till his untimely death in 1984. His decision of stepping down was based on the firm belief that the institution would stagnate if leadership did not change. At the same time, subsequently, as a faculty member, he kept aloof from matters relating to the management of the institute. Such a tradition has continued at the institute and has been responsible for its premier position and status as a management institute.

Coming back to the Jawaja experiment, or the Rural University as he called it, Ravi and his colleagues spent days without number in the villages of Jawaja block. They provided new technological skills to the weavers and tanners and also helped them in improving their managerial and accounting skills. In doing so, they were also experiencing and learning new things which they were taking back and using in their teaching efforts at the institute. While doing so, Ravi was not only enjoying himself but also advising others. Telco was probably considering the export of 5 ton trucks to desert areas in the Middle East. Ravi was loaned a truck by Telco, to advise on its suitability in desert areas. For a year Ravi himself frequently drove one such truck from Ahmedabad to Jawaja, interior areas and back. I do not know what advice he gave or whether such trucks were exported, but such action of his indicated the seriousness of his response to any situation. I also saw him often riding a Vicky (two-wheeler) around the institute's campus.

Another very important trait of this institution builder was his humane and generous approach. An example of his response would make this clear. I once sent Ravi a note requesting for the use of the matador vehicle for my tour to Udaipur. The matador was probably within the ambit of the Jawaja project. Normal consent could have come in one of two ways—'approved', which would have been somewhat stiff, or 'yes' which would have been milder. The reply, however, that I got was 'its my pleasure'. What a different, humane and generous response. One typical only of a multi-faceted person like Ravi.

Ravi left us more than 23 years ago but his spirit lives on both at the institute in terms of its work and also in the lives of those fortunate enough to have known him. He was truly a great institution builder who, by his example, established that it is not the individual but rather the institution which is above all else. Civil servants must learn from such examples.

The Invisible Hand

Some people may disagree, but I firmly believe that the invisible hand has a role to play in what we are able, or sometimes, not able to do. Some call it destiny. Let me take the example of the setting up LNMIIT at Jaipur. In September 2000 the International Rajasthani Conclave (IRC) was held in Jaipur. Acknowledging the absence of an IIT or an IIM in the state and responding to the demand from the participants at the IRC, the state government announced the setting up of a Centre of Excellence in public-private partnership mode. The decision was to establish an Institute of Information Technology. Thereafter, 15 months went by where our efforts with some interested parties did not fructify. It had so happened that in the last week of December 2000, Shri Dewang Mehta, the President of NASSCOM had met me at the Chief Minister's residence and indicated that Shri L.N. Mittal had asked him to pursue this matter. Unfortunately, Shri Mehta passed away in March 2001 and there was no contact from or with Shri L.N. Mittal. By December 2001 it appeared that all efforts in trying to set up this Centre of Excellence were not succeeding. In the second week of January 2002, I received a telephone call from Shri L.N. Mittal informing that the President of Kazakasthan was visiting India in February and the visit would include a short stay in Jaipur. At the end of this conversation I had asked whether his interest in setting up this institute was still there. His reply was very positive. Thereafter, he made two or three quick trips to Jaipur, details were sorted out, the foundation stone was laid in September 2002, and the institute started functioning from July 2003. Not only was a state government commitment fulfilled, though with some initial disappointments, but the invisible hand seemed to be evident here.

Mid-Day Meal Programme

Around 2002, the Supreme Court passed an order in a Public Interest Litigation (PIL) that a scheme of providing mid-day meals to children in primary schools should be introduced throughout the country. Such a scheme had been introduced in the state of Tamil Nadu many years before. It was estimated that the introduction of such scheme in Rajasthan would cost the exchequer more than Rs 100 crore annually. I had favoured the immediate introduction of the scheme, not only because the Supreme Court order required to be complied with but because it was in the interest of children at that level for two reasons—the children would get at least one square meal a day, and thereby better nourishment, and the provision of such a meal would attract more children to primary school and the enrolment would go up. There was resistance at the level of the bureaucracy and the Finance Department but I was surprised to find resistance in this case also at the ministerial level. Some of the ministers even wanted that the state government to file a review application before the Supreme Court. Fortunately, the Chief Minister realized the significance of the Supreme Court order and supported my views. Rajasthan was probably one of the first states to start implementation of the mid-day meal programme in primary schools after the Supreme Court judgment.

"Boond-Boond Se Ghara Bharta Hai"

Sometime in 1994 when I was Secretary of the University Grants Commission (UGC) we had invited the then Union Finance Minister, Dr Manmohan Singh to our office for a function. I had escorted the Finance Minister from his office in North Block to UGC, a distance of about 5 km. After the function when I was about to escort him back from UGC to the North Block the Finance Minister remarked that this was not necessary as I had already done my duty by escorting him from North Block to UGC. When I attempted to persist, he politely gave me two reasons why this was not necessary. He said that the time taken for me to escort him to North Block and come back to office would take about 45 minutes and surely I had enough work pending in my office to dispose of the same rather than spend time in escorting him. Secondly, he said that by my not escorting him the government would save about one litre of petrol. Such thoughts, small as they may appear to some, can only come from a great and visionary man who not only has an eye for detail but a real concern for government's work and the people. I may mention that about 29.5 per cent of the country's import bill (First three quarters of fiscal year 2007–08) is on account of oil import bill and this amounted to Rs 1,92,974 crore in April-December 2007. Annually, the oil import bill would be over Rs 2,50,000 crore. If each one of us was conscious of the need to conserve and economize on the use of petrol, and other scarce resources like water and power, many of our country's problems would be considerably reduced. If only all politicians and government servants could think along these lines what a different country we would be living in.

Presentation to the Prime Minister

One of my most challenging situations was a presentation made to the Prime Minister at less than 24 hours notice. In 1990, I was working as Joint Secretary in the Ministry of Rural Development, Government of India. Since 1988 we had been working on a constitutional amendment relating to Panchayati Raj Institutions (PRIs). In the late evening of Sunday, 15th April, 1990 I received a telephone call from the Private Secretary to the Cabinet Secretary that we were required to make a presentation to the Prime Minister the next morning at 10:30 am on the proposed constitutional amendment. I telephoned the Cabinet Secretary to confirm this and then informed him that our minister was on tour. He said that if the minister could be contacted, he may be requested to be present but the presentation had to be made in any case. However, late at night I was able to contact the Secretary and requested him to be in office by 9 am when I would first make the presentation to him for any suggestions. He enquired whether this was possible and I told him that we would manage. Through the night I worked on the presentation with just a pencil and a paper. Reaching office at 7 am and till 9 am the slides were prepared for use in an overhead projector. The Secretary was pleased, though somewhat taken aback that it could be done so soon. Against the allotted time of 30 minutes the presentation took 45 minutes. Besides the Prime Minister, the Cabinet Secretary, Additional Secretary and Deputy Secretary in PMO were present. On our side it was just the Secretary and myself. The Prime Minister heard us very patiently, shared his thoughts and heard our views. It was a challenging experience and one that made me realize the importance of being prepared for emergencies at all times.

The Way Ahead

In this third and last section I would like to briefly develop on how the civil service should be responding to the changing scenario in India. It is clear that over the last nearly 60 years the image of the civil service has been on the decline. This is more so in the last 40 years, notwithstanding the fact that the environment is such where the role of the government seems to be increasing and money in the hands of the civil servants, in terms of development programmes, has multiplied manifold. Quite obviously, therefore, the civil servant and the civil service must pull up their socks and improve their performance. While much of the effort has to come from within the civil service, there is no doubt that the effort can only bear results if there is support and good leadership from the political leaders.

The XI Plan document correctly states that some of the values which the civil servant should be mandated to reflect and follow are objectivity, integrity, neutrality, dedication to public service, transparency, exemplary conduct, accessibility and efficiency. Each value is necessary, but it is only the sum total of these values which will make a difference. I recall a conversation with the Chief Secretary of a state some 10 years ago. Reflecting on the quality of officers working with him, he said that he had three types of officers working with him. Some officers who were intelligent but with doubtful integrity, some others with integrity but with no initiative and only a few who had both integrity and were doing hard work. Some may wish to question this somewhat simplified analysis, but in the overall it is not far from the truth today.

Corruption, as I have mentioned, is a disease which has infected the system. One has to deal with this swiftly and firmly in all cases. It is easy to slide down the slippery path of unethical behaviour simply because it seems advantageous. The climb up is certainly more difficult. Moreover, one must constantly keep in mind that the measure of a man's character is what he would do if he knew he would never be found out. As I mentioned in the opening part of the section on professional experiences, during our training at the Academy it was emphasized to us that we must not only be honest and fair in our dealings but also appear to be honest and fair. This is the approach all members of the civil service must follow.

While one cannot do without government, one must find ways and means to bring about systemic changes which reduce the requirements of an interface between the government functionary and the common man. In large measure this will reduce the possibility of harassment and automatically eliminate possibilities of corruption.

The basic objective of governance is to provide well-being, comfort and happiness to the people. This can be done when those who are entrusted with the responsibility to govern, do so with a sense of responsibility, in a spirit of transparency, exhibiting a culture of accountability, and as a people with integrity.

In terms of the nuts and bolts of administration, it may be emphasized that the process of change must begin at the recruitment stage and end only at retirement. Recruitment has to be based on merit, and young persons who can be groomed through a rigorous training process should be placed according to their academic qualifications, aptitude and experience. They must be made to specialize in one or two areas and then their expertise used accordingly. During their career, they must receive appropriate encouragement, guidance and motivation from their superiors who must set a good example through impeccable standards. Individual civil servants, on their part, must learn to do what they can, where they are, with what they have.

A piece of advice that I would like to give to the young officers. For their personal work, they should themselves regularly visit government offices like the municipality, urban authority, electricity office, water works, transport office, passport office, the hospital/dispensary, bank, etc., and experience real-life situations. This should be incognito. Only then will they realize what difficulties a common man has to face. Hopefully, then, they will respond differently to people.

Today, if I were to be asked which career I would chose if I was to start once again, I would still opt for the civil service. The reason is that it provides innumerable challenges and thereby opportunities for job satisfaction. In this way it also provides opportunity for helping and serving fellow citizens through a constructive approach. However, I must hasten to add that work in the civil service places on one's shoulders a heavy and great responsibility during one's long career.

Today, there is a lot of talk about a global vision. This is undeniable and necessary but it has to be marked by compassion for the individual, particularly the poor, the downtrodden and the powerless.

I would conclude by quoting Gandhiji: "There is enough in this world for everyone's need, but not enough for everyone's greed. Let us work towards a society where we would do unto others what we would have others do unto us".

7

I.C. SRIVASTAVA

Memorable and Useful Experiences

Administration may be termed as "an art of the possible". Very few readymade or scientific solutions can be found or discovered to be handed down to succeeding generations of administrators who have to devise or improvise their own solutions and methods to achieve their goals and objectives—both short-term and long-term. Management, simply defined as "getting things done" or making people do their duties towards desired goals and objectives, when applied to public administration implies, to my mind, in short, as follows: management of public and state affairs by political masters assisted by senior bureaucrats and supported down the line by a vast bureaucracy.

I have penned down a few memorable experiences which may be as interesting and rewarding to readers, especially trainee administrative officers, as to me by hindsight and also useful to those who might recall, with edifying pleasure, to take them into account while being confronted with or going through similar or more challenging situations.

As an IAS officer, one gets a chance, rather a host of opportunities to come face to face with numerous problems in the field, to begin with, as Sub-Divisional Officer and early in career as Collector and District Magistrate. Thereafter, the officer is either posted as Deputy Secretary in the State Secretariat or as Head of the Department (HoD) in a state cadre unless one is seconded to a Central Government assignment quite early in career. In Secretariat and HoD postings, the officer gets to know the processes of policy formulation and the role players therein. Broadly, following this career graph I have culled some rich and intense experiences and others not so rich or deep but nevertheless rewarding and worth reporting. However, since quite a few events and situations including experiences of three districts, namely, Barmer (1970–72), Sri Ganganagar (1976–77) and Bharatpur (1977–78) as Collector and District Magistrate have been dealt with and narrated at length in two of my books: *Challenge and Change in Administrative System* (1999) and *Bhartiya Prashasan: Parivartan Ki Chunotiyan* (Hindi) (2004), the latter being an enlarged, revised and updated version of the earlier one. I have concentrated on experiences not already narrated in the two books.

Initial Training

It is with immense satisfaction and a modicum of pride I would like to state and clarify that having to migrate with my eldest brother way back in June 1955, from Allahabad, the day my High School results were out, I virtually became a 'Rajasthan' citizen at the early age of 12 years. After completing my studies with a Master's degree in English Literature in the year 1961 from the then premier Maharaja's (P.G.) College, Jaipur I had to wait in the wings as a lecturer at two government and three private colleges including BITS, Pilani before I was allowed to write papers for the Combined Civil Services Examination of October 1965, which was held immediately after our getting over the trauma of the Indo-Pak War of 1965, not to speak of the black-outs at night and my gruelling teaching task in day time at Government College, Tonk. However, IAS examination results in April 1966 did not belie my expectations.

Joining the National Academy of Administration (now called L.B.S. Academy of Administration) at Mussoorie with great hopes and fears, I found myself managing and coping with baffling variety in curricular and co-curricular activities including oft varying timings of morning PT and afternoon horse-riding classes. Looking back, to say the least, and to sum up my experiences of institutional training which, so to say, suffused our being and personality to the core ingrained and inculcated a unique sense of rigorous discipline, punctuality and high morale emanating from values of civil service neutrality coupled with objectivity and, what goes with that, transparency and sensitivity. Recalling two incidents would suffice to illustrate the lessons. I vividly recall Nikhilesh Prasad (nick name 'Nixie'), an IFS (Indian Foreign Service) fellow probationer leisurely walking up from his Happy Valley Club room to join the PT Group at 6.20 a.m. (varied timings were set for various groups for the whole week to inculcate punctuality). The moment 'Nixie' was going to join the PT square, he was stopped short by a horse-rider and 'lo and behold' our Director, the legendary Mr M.G. Pimputkar, probably from the last batch of ICS surviving, first halted his galloping horse and then yelled, "Stop. You are late. You cannot join this Group. See me in my office at 3 p.m. in the afternoon". He did not stop to ask the name of the officer and trotted away to his morning round. 'Nixi' thought that probably he did not commit any mistake, but was given the necessary dressing down by the Director, and also extraordinary leave on the second day of the entry in service, which became not only a talking point among probationers but also an object lesson for everyone to be punctual for all classes including lunch and dinner timings—for the latter ten minutes were given for entry and 20–30 minutes to finish. Punctuality wore a mantle of sanctity so much so that once our Deputy Director Senior (who rose to be Chief Secretary, Uttar Pradesh and later Secretary, Steel, Government of India) was shut out by the doorman who punctually closed the doors of our classroom and politely conveyed his inability to the senior officer. In another incident, the awesome and haloed person of Mr Pimputkar conveyed to our group to wait outside his home between 5.15 p.m. and 5.30 p.m. when he himself opened the door punctually to welcome us for a 'formal' afternoon tea with him. Of course, once inside, we were at home and relaxed with his own sense of humour and jokes.

However, despite the near puritan atmosphere and Spartan lifestyle, we smelt the air of romance which prompted a few probationers to go walking as duo and pairing by choice, which finally led to announcement of engagements a little before the training was over and also made the farewell dinner a gala and memorable event. I can still recall the speech made by the President, Mess Committee proposing a toast to the Director and the engaged couples beginning with "Despite you and your rigorous discipline some of us managed to fall in love and therefore, it is with pleasure, I announce the engagement of three couples". His speech was received with a thunderous applause and laughter. Mr Pimputkar's hilarious congratulations to the couples over, his final remarks still resonate in my mind, "As you leave the precincts of this training institution, one final word of advice I would like to give based on my own experience. I have seen 26 transfers in 27 years of service by now and I have never hankered after places or postings. Remember, if three of you can withstand the political pressures by resisting the temptation of postings and good places, the fourth colleague of yours will not be victimized". Alas, I could never count myself as the fourth officer having been made to resist political pressure on my own, which resulted into a mixed bag of 29 bad, good, better and so called best postings at various stages of my career with little or no regret—regret only on account of having to undergo five postings in a period of two years, during the years 1976–78.

Academy training over, two of us (total being four) landed in Jaipur in the second week of July 1967 with a renewed vigour after spending two weeks with an army unit near Naushera (Jammu) on the borders with Pakistan. We made the mandatory calls on the Chief Secretary who spent forty minutes instead of ten and other Senior Secretaries to Government, one of whom, a *shikari* himself, desperately short of time while rushing out of his room for a formal meeting advised us to "eat what we killed in the district" to which we were posted for field training. Strange but not true, an advice we hardly ever followed. As a coincidence, I found in my second trainer-collector at Ajmer, a *shikari* by hobby, who found time to go shooting in jungles close to places of his tour which occasionally was fixed with an eye on hunting. He asked me to join him on 'shoot' or enjoy myself during probation, a period which one always recalls with nostalgia later on and also receive training with other senior officers posted in the district during his absence. Obviously, I found the latter more satisfying and edifying too. My first collector and mentor Shri B. Hooja was an outgoing, effusive and affectionate person who always enthused both of us (Shri Anil Kumar, a senior trainee officer of 1965 batch) and made it a point to pick us from Dak Bungalow or residence to join him on tour. On one of the tours, he announced to us that he had conveyed to SDO concerned to get a good lunch prepared for his two 'Rajkumars'. We felt elated and enthralled at his gesture. To our dismay, he had to leave Ajmer after nearly two months, to take charge as Commissioner and Secretary, State Enterprises, Government of Rajasthan, certainly a prestigious posting even in those times.

Although the sheen, aura and ardour of academic training did not wear off easily, the field training did present an interesting contrast. My first day experience on arriving at Collectorate after one kilometre walk from the picturesquely located Circuit House, overlooking Ana Sagar Lake was somewhat like a jolt to the mind and memory. A lone, turbaned sweeper clad in *khadi* uniform was sweeping the floor at 10 a.m. while I entered the building. Looking around, I saw a burly, rather heavy bodied, bespectacled officious looking person walking into the room across Collector's chamber. He was the Office Superintendent who timely advised me to go to the senior trainee officer's quarter located behind Collector's residence nearly a kilometre away from Collectorate. Apparently, Shri Anil Kumar my senior who was already aware of my arrival at Ajmer welcomed me with open arms. Though fully groomed by Mr Pimputkar at the Academy, he gave me hints enough to be at ease and peace with myself. Friendship with him developed over the years, has lasted beyond our service career. 'Jhandewali' small room court below the high flying tri-colour national flag beckoned me from a distance and became my prize possession for more than a year after he was posted out as Sub-Divisional Officer. I went through the intensive block, tehsil and nominal settlement training besides disposing off court cases as Assistant Collector and Magistrate. Apart from a few revenue cases, I devoted time and energy mainly to learn the trial and disposal of criminal cases under Gambling, Motor Vehicles, Excise and Police Acts. Collectorate training also included functioning as sub-officer and officer-in-charge of various sections including Revenue, Transport, General, Nazarat, Record, Famine, Accounts, Development, etc. I was posted as SDO, Bharatpur in October 1968.

Interface with and Interference by Political Masters

Bharatpur, one of the first three erstwhile states of Rajputana to join Matsya Union which merged with Greater Rajasthan had a chequered history of Jat warrior kings who plundered Delhi infrequently and joined Marathas in their campaigns against the Moghul rulers of Delhi in the eighteenth century. In the nineteenth century, Lord Lake could not defeat the hardy Jats and was nearly tired out by laying siege of Bharatpur for nearly 26 months before overwhelming them. Bharatpur people with a "bee in ones bonnet" nature, always opposed their rulers for one reason or the other during feudal times, which habit sustained their protestations even after the formation of Rajasthan.

The whining and growling of complainants against perceived administrative injustices, at times, turned into shouting bouts when faced with obdurate officers with a keen eye to see through their contrived complaint to get a Patwari or Land Records (LR) Inspector transferred out of a Circle. Patwari, with his "*Oopar Kartar Neeche Patwar*" image of dare devilry to manipulate records to the undoing of many required joint public effort to oust him or to retain the favourable one. If a Patwari was suspended, farmers would approach the political cadre fellows or even Union Deputy Minister at Delhi, an MP from the district to throw weight for his reinstatement. One such case cropped up on Land Records Section File, of which SDO Sadar (headquarters) was officer-in-charge. A strip of paper pinned on a file contained the Minister's desire as endorsed by the Collector. The wily LR Assistant dropped no hints to the new SDO or 'Chhote' Collector as I came to be called later on. With prying eyes he gauged my temper and temperament. I asked him to explain. He suggested that I should better discuss the matter with the Collector who would clarify everything. Collector without mincing words politely asked me to prepare a note for reinstating the Patwari against whom a preliminary enquiry was already under way on the basis of serious allegations and charges. In sheer desperation, I told the Collector, "how is it possible to justify reinstatement?" He calmly stated, "You can suspend him again after a fortnight. After all he is your subordinate but for once let the Minister's desire be carried out". I remained unconvinced. I sent up the file with factual position. Even so, Collector reinstated the Patwari. Thereafter, he never asked to me to do something similar to this. Nonetheless, he would transfer Patwaris frequently mostly at the request or desire of politicians who always took sides resulting in cancellation of transfer orders being issued more than once in the case of the same notorious Patwari. My pleadings more often failed. But I was satisfied that I could keep myself above board.

Here is another instance of a political desire, in this case, by the then Revenue Minister who conveyed on phone that a particular Patwari should be transferred to an indicated place when I was functioning as Collector, Barmer. On my submission that I would check back facts and speak to him, he thundered, "When Revenue Minister speaks, it is a government order", to which I submitted 'Yes Sir'. Eventually, I looked into the facts and did what was desirable and certainly not the 'desired' posting indicated by the Minister. Needless to add, he never phoned me again and surprisingly became an ardent supporter of my administrative style of functioning which resulted into a bonhomie between us during Indo-Pak war of December 1971 when he announced himself as Commander-in-Chief of Civilian Forces in the desert districts of Barmer and Jaisalmer. He gave full support to our war effort. Later when I was posted as Director, Rehabilitation of Kadana and Mahi Projects at Banswara, I had several opportunities to interact with him. He had the courage of conviction also to praise the Chief Minister Shri Harideo Joshi in his face for posting me as a Deputy Secretary, GAD and Cabinet during the infamous emergency in July 1975.

Memories of interface with political leaders and powers that be crowd into the "mind's eyes". But some incidents and anecdotes can be recalled vividly, being sharply etched in memory. A great leader and Chief Minister, Rajasthan for 17 long years, Shri M.L. Sukhadia left an indelible impression on my personality with his inimitable candour in conduct, vision of future and insight into the ground realities and need of the hour. A few months into my first assignment as Collector and District Magistrate of Barmer district early in 1971 before he resigned to make way for

Shri Barkatullah Khan, Shri Sukhadia came to inaugurate Talwara Cattle Fair near Balotra sub-divisional headquarters. After receiving him on the outskirts of the town, we escorted him to Dak Bungalow from where he proceeded directly to the fair ground. I was taken aback when he beckoned to me to come close to him immediately after alighting from the car. Looking into my eyes, he asked a simple question, "Collector Sahib, *Aap ko mujhse alag se kuch kehna hai? Sab theek hai*". "Yes, Sir, everything is all right. I joined here two months back and am still studying the problems of the district". He called the then SP Shri Dulhe Singh and asked him the same question which he had asked me, followed by another query, "*Aap dono ko kuch saath me kehna hai*?" Formalities over, he proceeded with graceful gait and joined the waiting crowd of Pradhan, members of Panchayat Samiti and the irrepressible lady MLA Mrs Madan Kaur. It was obvious that he was a true leader of people and knew their moods and needs too closely, free from any doubt, narrow and grooved thinking. He seated the Pradhan of Panchayat Samiti on his right side alongwith members (he knew too well how and when to keep appropriate people on the right side) and the local MLA and other leaders on his left. He addressed the gathered crowd with aplomb, grace and dignity par excellence. People nodded and responded with measured clapping. As it was the pre-election period of parliamentary elections due in March 1971 (later postponed to April 1971), Shri Sukhadia proceeded to Siwana and did not pick me up as was his wont to take Collector in his car for a discussion about the district's problems on the way. Probably, seventeen long years as CM had given him enough feedback and food for thought leaving little scope for a newly arrived officer like me to brief him further. Addressing some meetings on the way, he arrived late in the afternoon at Siwana and went for a brisk walk in the big courtyard behind the Dak Bungalow. After a cup of tea, he went to address the big election meeting organized on the crossing, right opposite tehsil office and Dak Bungalow. Surprisingly, he made the Sarpanch of Siwana, go with him. Siwana, though a tehsil headquarters had not graduated to an urban status. Here he had forgot all about us who waited in the wings of the Dak Bungalow, literally as protocol required and maintained our civil service neutrality from a safe distance.

Shri Sukhadia's grace and greatness blended well with his essential humility when he came to visit Barmer in the month following his resignation as CM, in a black party car without the grandiose of security and frills of power. He was required to supervise civil defence arrangements alongwith Shri M.D. Mathur, his erstwhile Finance Minister, who was declared Secretary General, Civil Defence Council, Government of India.

Needless to add, his visit boosted the morale of the people before the impending war which loomed large on the horizon. However, he was all humility when we went to call on him at the Dak Bungalow. He was visibly pleased as we had gone to see him on our own out of sheer courtesy without any hint or call from him or his local followers and party cadre.

A tall leader and a great persona who overshadowed all state leaders for a long time, richly deserves a sharply etched, unique niche in the history of Rajasthan for his visionary zeal and astute management of politics. His famous smile and cool composure helped him win over multitudes of common people who reposed full faith in his stewardship of the state's affairs. The industrialization of the state received a great fillip during his tenure besides all-round development under a stable government. Kota was declared the first industrial town of the state which slowly and steadily also developed as a tourist destination under his able leadership.

Two other Congress leaders with whom I came in contact, stand out as great political stalwarts. If one goes by the adage, some are born great, some achieve greatness and some others have greatness thrust upon them, while Shri Sukhadia was a great achiever Shri Barkatullah Khan had the greatness thrust upon him. He was called upon by the then Prime Minister Indira Gandhi to assume the mantle of Chief Ministership immediately on his return from a visit to Middle East when Shri Sukhadia was asked to step down ostensibly for his supporting Congress (O) leaders Morarji Desai and others who had split the Congress Party (The other was Shri C.M. Baid, the then Finance Minister under Shri Barkatullah Khan and Shri Harideo Joshi).

Shri Barkatullah Khan with his buxom demeanour and heavy gait gave the impression of an easy going person but on a close contact he revealed the essential human and humane side of his personality. The imminent war with Pakistan arising from India's intervention in the ongoing war between Mukti Bahini of the erstwhile East Pakistan and Pakistan army provided opportunities to me as Collector, Barmer to come in contact directly with Shri Khan. His bearhug on alighting from the plane at Uttarlai or car besides generating warmth also kindled the right mood and spirit for interaction with him individually or during meeting with officers. An occasional pat on the shoulder was also in order to serve the same purpose. This warmth in relationship was clearly reflected in the following two episodes. In the last week of October 1971, an officers' meeting was convened in the Dak Bungalow under the chairmanship of Chief Minister to review and gear up the preparatory measures for the war which was considered a certainty in view of the assistance provided by Indian forces to Mukti Bahini. Just before the start of the meeting, sitting beside the Chief Minister, at the head of the table, hesitatingly I opened the ordinary non-official envelope containing the letter from my wife who had delivered a son on 15th September 1971. Before I could glance through the contents, the CM happened to notice the letter and asked me in whispers "Is it from your wife? Go ahead and read it". My gestures revealed all and in sheer excitement I told him in low tone and voice, "My wife wants to join me here urgently but I wish to tell her not to come over here due to imminent war as the child is barely a month and half". God only knows what inner voice prompted Shri Khan to exclaim, "You know, Gentlemen, Collector Sahib's wife wants to join him in his war effort alongwith a small child and Srivastavaji is going to tell her not to come to Barmer. I think Collector's wife is more brave. I am asking him here and now not to prevent her from coming here as it will give a good boost to the morale of the officers' families and to others as well". I was flabbergasted and speechless for a while and then everyone had a hearty laugh as I gave a nod in agreement with CM's suggestion which left no scope for any further thinking. I telephoned Archana to come post haste as the clouds of war were gathering and threatening to burst before long. Needless to add, her arrival not only set the house in order but raised the spirits of the members of officers' families living in the Government Colony located behind the Collector's bungalow.

The other episode relates to the aftermath of the bombing of Railway Station of Barmer on the night of 8th-9th December 1971 by Pakistani fighter planes. CM was visiting Jaisalmer on the 9th December and was scheduled to come to Barmer on the 10th December. Shri Bhim Singh, the then Border Commissioner, discussed the situation in the wake of bombing as aforesaid. After I explained to him, at some length, the situation especially the departure of some traders' families in panic and also about the efforts we were making to keep up the sagging morale of the people by addressing them on the microphone network address system and by convening Citizens' Council meeting, Shri Bhim Singh, a highly experienced but a flamboyant officer initially did not agree with my advice to CM (to be conveyed through him) to postpone his visit to Barmer on the 10th December 1971 as scheduled, by a few days so that we could bring the situation under control especially by making urgent and earnest request to Air Commodore at Jodhpur to provide night cover to Barmer town by deploying MIGs at Uttarlai. When the arrival of MIGs was announced by a loud bang of their crossing the sound barrier, people sighed with great relief. Shri Bhim Singh telephoned again to say that CM had expressed a desire to come despite my advice. With complete composure and in a clear tone I insisted that my advice, given on grounds of security should be accepted. The Chief Minister graciously relented and decided not to come for a few more days. When CM did come later, after his usual affectionate bearhug, he gave me a pat on the back for handling the situation well.

Shri C.M. Baid who had also served as a Minister in Sukhadiaji's ministry was another remarkable political personality who inspired confidence and respect among officers of the State. In a way he was one of the longest surviving senior ministers in various Congress ministries. I had met him on a few occasions during my short tenure as Deputy Secretary, Education in 1973, when he had the education portfolio besides being Finance Minister. But, during my eventful tenure in 1976–77 as Collector, Sri Ganganagar, Shri Baid visited the district as minister-in-charge of Prime Minister's Twenty-Point Programme implementation, a number of times. During these meetings and otherwise too, his frank, forthright advice and direction helped me in gearing and toning up the administrative machinery for a variety of tasks especially the Family Welfare Camps and the National Savings Campaign, the latter resulting in the declaration of the District as number one in the state while the efficient management of the former, symptomatic of the emergency measures, however, saved the district from going the 'excesses' way leading to Shah Commission Enquiry. Shri Baid had strong views on Twenty-Point Programme and had the courage of conviction not to mince words when it came to pointing out the weaknesses in implementation. His loud and clear voice and appreciation of problems faced by field officers, set the tone and pace of implementation of the programme and enthused the officers across all the departments which enabled them to achieve the tasks assigned to them.

With the change of government in 1977, I was again posted out of Jaipur, after a short stint as Director, National Savings, as Collector Bharatpur. However, within one year, I received two posting orders viz., Excise Commissioner (lasting 4–5 months) and Secretary to Governor (lasting eight months). Finally, I went on deputation to Government of India and was posted as Director, Census Operations for Rajasthan with headquarters at Jaipur. In this capacity, I had a chance meeting with or rather ran into Shri C.M. Baid at Raj Bhawan 'at home' hosted by the then H.E. the Governor on 15th August 1979. Of course, Shri Baid was still an MLA and one of the few erstwhile ministers to retain their seats in post-emergency scenario. He hugged me warmly, and spoke high of my work done as Collector, Sri Ganganagar adding a remark: "*Jaise kisi bahut achhi cheej ko kahin rakhkar bhool jaate hain, sarkar aapko janganana mein bhejkar bhool gayee hai*". What could I say? Tables were turned against Congress. I was also enjoying my new assignment, free from the fever and fret of state administration, which turned out to be one of the best and most satisfying in my career and lasting for four years, of which nine months were spent on training in development administration at the University of Manchester, UK. An account of my experience of census work under the title "We count every one and every one counts for us" is already included in the book, *Challenge and Change in Administrative System.*

I must also pay tribute to Shri B.S. Shekhawat, another towering political personality and leader of Rajasthan, considered and acclaimed as next only to Shri M.L. Sukhadia in political acumen, sagacity and wisdom gained by his long innings in politics of the state. He was elected Chief Minister three times but completed only one full spell of five years from 1993 to 1998. As I can recall, my first face to face meeting with Shri Bhairon Singh Ji (as he was normally addressed) took place when I called on him after my posting as Collector, Bharatpur in July 1977. I was rather on the horns of a dilemma (having faced three transfers since August 1976 as already mentioned above) whether to go to Bharatpur or remain at Jaipur by making a request to CM directly. A warm hand on the shoulder and a pat on my back by Shri Shekhawat overwhelmed me and I could not utter anything when he said, "*Mere kahne se chale jaiye*". A revolutionary change in government on 'Janata Party' wave had brought him to power and position of Chief Ministership for the first time and the whiff of rising expectations of people also filled me with a new zeal to work in my 'old' district which was already familiar to me, having worked as Sub-Divisional Officer headquarters at Bharatpur for more than two years. Probably, Shri Shekhawat was quite confident that I would be able to face floods and provide relief to people with my earlier experience because he visited Bharatpur the same day but left before my arrival in the evening by the last train which I had taken to travel with family for taking charge there in the midst of swirling flood waters. Surrounded by floods on the outskirts on almost all sides, Bharatpur people were facing 'deluge', so to say, and I, therefore, plunged myself into my duties and rounds of the city without taking formal charge after being briefed by the officers for about half an hour.

After about ten months, Shri Shekhawat, however, had to transfer me reportedly, under great pressure, from his erstwhile Emergency Jail co-inmates of Bharatpur, who wanted to play favour based 'transfer' politics with me. But with my reputation and earlier stint in their mind they knew that they could not get Patwaris and ILRs transferred by making polite requests to me or even on the basis of complaints, unless I was satisfied about the genuineness of requests/complaints. That "transfer is no punishment" is an oft-cited adage in government, conveniently recited to suit the convenience of the person and the occasion. Thus, I had to undergo 27 transfers in 37 years of my career in the IAS. But I was never disheartened with the "strange but true" ways of government. However, the then Chief Secretary Shri Bhanot was courteous and gracious enough to have called me to Jaipur to explain the background. He almost apologetically asked me to go for next posting as Excise Commissioner at Udaipur where my brothers and parents were also living, which fact was also cited by him additionally to smoothen my ruffled feelings.

However, Shri Shekhawat never lost the confidence he had reposed in me and time and again it showed in the course of my working relationship with him during his second and third spell as Chief Minister. I was posted as Secretary, Education, Irrigation, CAD, Food and Civil Supplies and Revenue by him and finally as Chairman, Board of Revenue, Ajmer in September 1998 before the Assembly elections in November in which BJP was defeated. He did give me some advice not only in a friendly manner but also as an elderly leader. Once he remarked, "*Srivastava ji, aap seedhe hee 'yes', 'n' kar dete hain, hamare liye kuch kahne ko rahne dijiye. Kuch kagaj kuch samay rakhiye. Jaldi mein jawab mat dijiye*". As Principal Secretary, Revenue, I had told a delegation of representatives, mostly Sarpanchas, that Karauli during that year would not be notified as a district for various reasons, although Kumat Committee set up to examine this matter, had given a favourable recommendation in this regard. They, then, approached CM, who could not contradict me in their presence nor could he give any definite answer. Hence, his above mentioned friendly advice.

Shri Shekhawat was a self-made leader. He had imbibed some leadership qualities of Shri M.L. Sukhadia who was reportedly his 'mentor' in private and opponent in public, being leaders of rival political parties. Humility, wit, patience, perseverance and persuasive skills were hallmark of his personality which reflected his qualities in all places and on all occasions. An incident affecting my promotion and career would illustrate it better. As I had enjoyed his confidence, there was no reason to think otherwise despite some of my transfers necessitated by exigencies of situations, political or otherwise. But when I was promoted in the grade of Principal Secretary and posted in January 1994 as Chairman, Rajasthan Tax Tribunal at Ajmer, I lost my patience and called on him to represent that both my daughter and son were studying in the final year of M.A. and engineering courses respectively and I could not shift to Ajmer my family for obvious reasons. He was all courtesy and with great humility and grace, he said, "*Mujh se galti ho gayee. Mujhe dhyan nahin tha. Main aaj, aur abhi aapke Jaipur posting ke order kar deta hoon*". On my further submission and query whether I had committed any mistake and was, therefore, no longer in his good books, his forthright reply was "*Aap ki nishtha, karya, kshmta aur mehnat ke bare mein mujhe kabhi sandeh nahin raha*". The same day orders posting me as Principal Secretary, Revenue, Colonisation and Devasthan were issued. I remained in that position for more than three years and this gave me great satisfaction in formulating two sets of new draft legislation namely the Rajasthan Tenancy Bill 1996 and Rajasthan Land Revenue Bill 1996. Drafted in consultation with a legislative committee headed by Revenue Minister himself, both the bills were introduced in the State Assembly with delay and thus could not be passed as the general elections were looming the large on the horizon in 1998 and no political party was willing to put its stakes on the passing of these bills.

To my mind, Shri Shekhawat will go down in history as a great visionary leader who indefatigably worked for an all-round development of the state with an emphasis in education and empowerment of women which received a great fillip during his Chief Ministership. He proved to be a tall stalwart in the national and regional politics. Finally, he showed his sharp mettle and deep political wisdom in steering, for five years, the proceedings of Rajya Sabha as Chairman and Vice-President of India. He has rightly earned a unique niche for himself in national history and politics.

So far I have dwelt on my interface and support with the top political leaders of the state. Coming to interference part, I can recall three-four illustrative cases/incidents which would bring forth, hopefully, the nature and purpose of uncalled for direction nearly always oral, at times subtle, and rarely blunt and sharp edged. An administrative adage, "reputation of the officer travels before him" always helped me overcome my apprehensions about the fallout of my transparent and clear decisions based on ground realities and the human side of the comprehensive picture. An administrator has to appreciate and appraise not only the facts of each case or situation but his keen insight into the human problem implicit or embedded therein should nearly always throw up correct decisions to make him a successful officer for "nothing succeeds like success" is the oft-repeated and accepted bureaucratic cliche.

I came across the first case of political settlement by intervention at the top level when I was asked to negotiate as Director, Kadana and Mahi Bajaj Sagar Rehabilitation (of oustees) Project in a series of meetings with officers of Gujarat Government and members of Mahi Control Board. A detailed account of the divergence between the norms approved for rehabilitation of oustees of Gujarat and Rajasthan by their respective governments resulting into protracted negotiations at administrative levels has been given in the case study, "The Belated Agreement" included in the book *Challenge and Change in Administrative System* as aforesaid. However, the point to be emphasized here is that Rajasthan State lost time and opportunity for resettling the predominantly tribal oustees of the two dams, living in Banswara and Dungarpur districts due to sheer lack of political will and obduracy at the bureaucratic levels resulting from exaggerated norms which were not agreed to by Gujarat Government for a long time. Matters came to a head just before Emergency was declared in the country as it dawned upon the State Government that time was running out both for agreement with Gujarat and execution of rehabilitation work which had already been completed in Gujarat side long back. As against the initial amount of over Rs 16 crore, Rajasthan Government under people's pressure wanted to strike a compromise at Rs 12 crore against which Gujarat offered Rs 4 crore. Finally, on May 29, 1975, Shri Jagjivan Ram, the then Union Minister of Irrigation presided over a meeting attended by the then Chief Minister Shri Harideo Joshi and Shri H.C. Sarin, the then Governor of Gujarat which was, then, under President's rule. After a three hour discussion preceded by the presentation and exposition of the problem by me as Director, Resettlement, an agreement was signed on that 'fateful' day—fateful because it scaled the fate of 7,000 families who had been living till then only on promise of a bright future. A bargain was settled at Rs 8.10 crore and this amount excluded the cost of Ring Wall for the Muslim Shrine at Galiakot, which was additionally, to be borne by Gujarat. It may be recalled that an unclear agreement barely outlining the principles and terms for future action had been signed between Irrigation Ministers of the two states in 1966. Both agreements signed at the political level illustrate the uncharted course of protracted negotiations to solve an inter-state problem resulting into inordinate delay and loss of time for both sides. Lives of thousands of simple, tribal people remained in 'suspended animation' for nine long years due to lack of political and administrative will to settle a human problem expeditiously. Finally, sheer strong political will at Chief Minister's level alone clinched the issues. This political intervention did not come too soon but when it did it took only three hours to bring about the long awaited compromise and agreement. The pivotal role of sagacious Shri Jagjivan Ram, the then Union Minister cannot be overemphasized for it was he who insisted that agreement should be reached then and there in that one meeting: The object lesson for administrative officers seems to lie in assessing the popular upsurge based on felt needs, which in turn, would engender political will of a high order and for which a lot of home work was called for on the part of administrators.

The second episode relates to a politico-cum-protocol issue arising from a well-publicized, high-profile visit of Sanjay Gandhi to Bikaner early in 1976. The VVIP treatment he had received a few days earlier in Haryana had set senior police officers' ears on alert and alarm. The curious rural crowd was expected to turn up in large numbers to attend the public meeting scheduled to be addressed by him with his new found 'mantra'—"*Batain Kum Kaam Jyada*". He had already begun to be addressed as the new leader of young India, an icon for the surging crowds.

Briefly, the security issues for the State CID were reduced to two demands: provision of two white Ambassador cars from the State Garage and a temporary telephone connection below the rostrum generally provided for Prime Minister on official visit. Being Deputy Secretary of General Administration Department (GAD) I also functioned ex-officio as State Protocol Officer and in that capacity I was required to maintain and observe protocol. For the Youth Congress leader that he was, there was no priority in the order of precedence or the State Guest list dignitaries. In fact, his position did not figure in either list. When the then DIG, CID rang up as a follow up to the letter of requisition for two cars and a temporary telephone as aforesaid, my initial reaction was a point blank 'no'. But the then IGP Shri Ganesh Singh also tried to contact me. Little realizing how to duck the issue, I made myself unavailable for a while. But, Mr O.P. Tandon, DIG came to Secretariat personally looking for my location. I, then, decided to seek the guidance from the Chief Secretary, Shri M. Mukerji, who was also ex-officio Secretary, GAD. As he could be available at 6 p.m., I requested Mr Tandon to contact me at 6.30 p.m. on the eve of the so called VVIPs' visit. Shri Mukerji, a highly experienced bureaucrat found an easy administrative solution to a political-protocol problem, situation for which could not be found at my level.

"Yes, Srivastava! What is it that is bothering you?" he asked.

On my explaining to him the problem as precisely and briefly as possible, he exclaimed, "It is not a big problem! You see the Police Department has sent you the requisition. Allot to Police Department vehicles as well as temporary telephone for security duties. While the vehicles will be on security deployment Police Department will be responsible for paying the bills to Telephone Department for installation and call charges of telephone from their own budget, as GAD only allots telephones even otherwise".

What a great relief it was to me to have found a quick solution to a troublesome problem.

Even though press censorship had been relaxed by then, the Fourth Estate would not have taken notice of VVIP facilities provided to Sanjay Gandhi as he had grown larger than life in stature and estimation. But I was on my bureaucratic guarded fence and wished to maintain strict neutrality in relation to Congress Party programmes. However, with extra expenditure Circuit House was spruced up and extra facilities were provided, which added to the comfort of stay for senior officers and ministers later on. I remember vividly how the then Collector, Bikaner walking into my room with a proposal for extra budget provision for Circuit House made a personal request to forward the same immediately to Finance Commissioner who was waiting after office hours to approve the same so that purchases made that day could be backed up by government sanction of necessary funds. All is well that ends well also found application in this episode which brings forth and confirms my view that administration is an art of the possible and cannot be hide bound in a set of unimplementable rules, for they are formulated for the management of men and matters and their enforcement can be an end itself only to serve public interest which has to be gauged every hour day in and day out.

Another episode relates to my first tenure as Secretary to Government in the Department of Tourism, Culture and Sports in the period 1984–86. As a part of new Tourism Policy on the anvil we had decided to launch a publicity campaign estimated to cost about Rs 5 lakh to project the newly identified tourist circuits of Marwar and Mewar regions. Four firms were short-listed based on their two-in-one technical and financial bids as was the practice in that period. One of the firms came out as the brightest and the best during deliberations in the Selection Committee headed by me as Secretary, Tourism. While the Committee's recommendations were under process in the office of Director, Tourism for submission to Minister, I got a call from the office of the Minister, Tourism and Culture who appeared to be not only close to the then Prime Minister, Shri Rajiv Gandhi having studied in the same school or college as PM did but was also acclaimed as a dilettante of fine arts and a culture wizard in the public eye claiming as he did his descent from royalty, which probably ensured flow of such knowledge by inheritance, upbringing and some interest developed thereby. His overbearing personality reflected in the swagger of his shoulder at times was scary enough for the coterie surrounding him but not for your humble writer who was, then, as now proud to be a disciple of the great disciplinarian Director of training at the National Academy, Mr M.G. Pimputkar.

The Minister knew from his own sources that the committee had finalized its recommendations in favour of the best among the four publicity firms. He did not broach the subject straightway. Instead, he took out from his drawer and showed me the resignation letter of the then Chairman, RTDC, a political appointee whose primary qualification was to be a Kashmiri Brahman who had managed an access to Mrs Indira Gandhi's office-at-home thanks to his proximity to one of the private secretaries to the Prime Minister. Both the Minister and the Chairman, RTDC had an inflated ego and hence those coming in contact with them had to take extra care to satisfy their ego and in the Chairman's case, his egotism too had to be pacified by patient listening.

"Mr Srivastava, do you know I had obtained this resignation letter from Mr Kak the day I had become Minister. But today I have conveyed my acceptance which you must have read in newspapers" (Mum was the word besides a non-nonchalant nod from me). "Now about the publicity campaign: I understand you are in the process of finalizing your recommendations for submission to me".

"Yes, Sir, we have already finalized and selected the best among the four building firms. The file will reach your office by this evening or tomorrow at the latest".

"Mr Srivastava, I want to tell you that there is a reference from PM's house about the firm … (name forgotten obviously for good). Therefore, this firm should be given order, you know!" The Minister blurted out in one flow.

To this my reply was, "Sir this firm has no experience at all, nor even worth the name. In presentation, its representative showed a small poster for a shoe company and an invitation card printed by it! Obviously I can not go against committee's findings and recommendations".

"You can go Mr Srivastava. I think we have to part company also". A loud and clear message from the "horse's mouth" so to say and thus I got the hint that I should be prepared to move to another department as soon as possible.

However, my transfer and exit from Tourism and Culture Department was effected in a rather unexpected manner. Shortly after my encounter with the Minister, I was deputed for one month Training on Policy in Government at Indian Institute of Public Administration, New Delhi, which had been notified earlier. But towards the end of this training, i.e., in the last week of December 1985, I received a call from the then Chief Secretary who in his rather mellow, sweet and almost muffled voice told me, I suggest you should take some leave in continuation of your present training as your Minister wants a change. I know it is not your fault, "*Par woh peeche pad gaye hain kya karun*".

I replied, "I would not like to waste my earned leave for this, Sir! I was expecting this change already. Hence you may like to post me in any department for which you consider me suitable".

"You know, Srivastava, in that case I have to send the file to Bombay for the approval of CM who is attending the Plenary Session of Congress there. I don't want to bother the CM there, you know".

"Alright, Sir. As you wish, I will comply with for I do not want to put you to inconvenience for this purpose", was my unpremeditated reply.

I applied for a fortnight's leave and before this was over, the newspaper announced the change by posting another officer. A few days later I was transferred and posted as Desert Development Commissioner at Jodhpur. But before the end of another fortnight, the Chief Minister announced in a Press Conference that he had dropped the Minister and his resignation had been forwarded to Governor for acceptance. My unceremonious exit from my first department as Secretary which I came to like, because of my background and study of history and monuments of Rajasthan was followed by the Minister's removal by the Chief Minister which reflected a crude contrast to the claim he had made to me about his proximity to PM's house. God alone, or the two political masters themselves would know the real reason for his being dropped from the Council of Ministers.

I joined my duties at Jodhpur leaving behind, at Jaipur, my family for the first time in my career. Before that I met the CM to represent my case.. But he maintained a stiff upper lip silence. Of course, the Chief Secretary had assured me that he would get me posted as soon as possible after the ensuing Assembly session was over. My luck again seemed to run out, for the Chief Secretary Shri Naresh Chandra was sent to Jammu and Kashmir as Adviser to Governor. But I did not lose heart and spoke to Shri V.B.L. Mathur, the new Chief Secretary who assured me that I would be posted back to Jaipur after the Assembly session. It seemed, he knew the whole case from his own sources or his predecessor who must have briefed him. I came back to Jaipur after 90 days (of which 46 days were spent on tour of desert and other districts) and took over charge as Secretary, Social Welfare, Women and Child Development in the last week of May 1986.

I remained in the Secretariat for nearly three years from May 1986 to January 1989. In January 1989, I was transferred as Chairman, Rajasthan Civil Services Tribunal and the same year in July, I was again, transferred as Divisional Commissioner, Jaipur. During this period July 1989 to 1991, Jaipur witnessed two major riots the first one in Shastri Nagar and the other in Ram Ganj area—the latter spread to Johari Bazar and other areas too. Fatehpur, in Sikar District, witnessed communal riots as a result of slogan shouting and stone pelting by miscreants on Moharrum procession from roof top of a temple. As a result of this, some shops were damaged. This incident has been recorded in detail in the book *Challenge and Change in Administrative System* under the title "The Communal Conflicts: A Challenge for Administration". Riots were mainly the result of build up of heightened tension arising from Ramshila Pujan i.e., the purification of bricks made for new Ram Temple proposed to be built at Ayodhya before they were to be despatched for construction.

A one-man Enquiry Commission headed by Justice N.L. Tibrewal was appointed to enquire into the riots that took place in Jaipur. A number of measures were recommended by the Commission for action by government as well as officers. The interaction and nexus between political cadre and communal elements has been a subject of study by many authors and in the reminiscences of this nature, it is neither necessary nor possible to throw light on this matter.

Transfer as a Weapon of Authority and Interference

As Secretary to Government, an officer has an interface with political bodies of various parties functioning or operating from panchayat, block, district, region and state levels. Numerous problems of individual and public nature are dealt with and decisions are taken after consultations and deliberations in committees constituted at various levels and even otherwise in informal meetings held at the request of political representatives. Efforts are made to get matters expedited or decided in favour of an individual or group of workers. This political interaction with bureaucracy cannot be termed as 'interference' in most cases. However, when government takes a conscious decision even though not recorded in writing to reinforce political authority over bureaucratic echelons by using the weapon of transfer of officers and subordinates at the behest (not request as was the case earlier) of MLAs especially, the objectivity and impartiality required for this purpose are thrown out of the window. This results in erosion of the concept of neutrality of civil services in the perception of public mind leading to the assumption, that MLAs could call the shots in their constituency or area of operation. In Rajasthan, this erosion has taken place slowly and steadily over the years as compared to other states like UP, Bihar and Gujarat where officers' cadres especially in the IAS and IPS are polarized into main political camps of ruling and other parties. Officers face nemesis with the change in government. They believe in the principle "make hay while the sun shines" and do not mind being dumped or sent on deputation by the powers that be. They can afford to wait in the wings for the favourable wind to blow.

There was a time when a polite request for transfers was made by the local MLA or Pradhan for individual transfers of Patwaris, Inspectors of Land Record, by SDOs/Collectors and of Sub-Inspectors and other ranks by DIG and SP. At times, groups of farmers would come to meet Collector, SP or other senior officers at district, division or state levels with a complaint or even for informal request with a slip of paper from MLAs. However, it evolved into a system of 'desire' by MLAs over a number of years and Bihar was probably the first state to adopt a 'yellow slip' method by which request of MLAs and others was allowed to percolate in the files of Secretariat for issue of necessary orders. The administrative function of issuing transfer order after review of work of those who had completed three years in a post was handed down by the British rulers who devised this to keep Indians on leash and at their beck and call as they, generally, had a deep distrust of Indian officers down the line. However, they trusted Indian ICS and IPS officers who were recruited by them to maintain their grip on the steel frame of administration. Senior officers like DMs and SPs were, therefore, given choice of postings at two-three places and were told in advance to be prepared to move. As most of the officers enjoyed good salary and perks including provision of domestic servants, they moved from district to district in the British India or came to State Secretariat at a fairly senior level with their experience which only served well to maintain the so-called 'steel-frame'.

In the nineties of the last century the erosion of the 'steel-frame' took place at a faster pace as a parallel to formation of coalition governments at the union and state levels. The political parties joining the coalition government clamoured for authority and looked at the ways and openings for obtaining and scouting more powers for their ministers. However, in Rajasthan (where coalition existed for a names namesake), the past decades have witnessed a steady decline in administrative authority as a result of conscious decision taken a few months before elections in 1998. In

Rajasthan, MLAs of the ruling party were given a free hand to choose and change SDOs, Deputy SP, Tehsildars, SHOs and even teachers of their area so that such chosen ones could help them, or at least they thought so, come back to power. Transfer thus became an 'industry' at the hands of the MLAs and Ministers who set a precedent for the next ruling party namely the Congress Party. In year 2000, the ruling party backed by a strong majority at the hustings decided to go whole-hog about the business of organizing transfers at various levels. MLAs were reportedly allocated informal transfer-quotas by Ministers of Education and Panchayati Raj Department. Other departments followed suit and MLAs ruled the roost with the help of henchmen and camp followers. Ministers became the epitome and centres of power and authority. Feudal Rajputana tendencies crept in with sycophants and hangers-on operating and manipulating transfers and postings on a graded scale and range of good, better and best. 'Malai' and 'Baraf' postings represented 'earning' for the favourites and non-earning ones for the cold-shouldered officers and workers. Secretaries and Heads of Departments meekly surrendered their judgement and competence to the sweet-will of the powers that be who bartered government orders and favours for money and gifts at rates fixed by themselves in their private offices.

In most cases Rules of Business and Work Distribution chart between Heads of Departments and administrative Secretaries were amended to provide for powers to Ministers, even to deal with cases of Class III and IV of government employees in addition to transfers and postings of officers both at HoD headquarters and in the field. Opaque corruption became translucent if not transparent.

As Chairman, Board of Revenue I was confronted with 'desire-transfer list' of Tehsildars, Sub-Registrars and Naib Tehsildars received informally from the office of the then Revenue Minister. Registrar, who was the declared Head of Department for Revenue Staff under the control of Board of Revenue, obtained Chairman's approval invariably on the final list which had been processed within laid down norms set by the government. As the Minister's Office did not have the record, it had simply passed on the Minister's wish-list. Registrar put up the list informally for discussion. On my instructions to ignore the cases not covered by the norms and go ahead within the framework of criteria laid down, he acted accordingly and obtained my approval before issuing the orders. Obviously, the matters did not rest there. He was summoned by the Minister at home and given dressing down for not complying with the 'informal' list sent by her office. He informed the Minister about the instructions to process all cases as per government guidelines. Minister being adamant to get all informal orders executed, Registrar felt helpless and bewildered. I talked on phone to the then Secretary to Chief Minister, who did explain somewhat apologetically that indeed the matter had been discussed in Cabinet informally and the decision was to allow the MLAs and ministers to have their 'say' in the matter of postings and transfers. Finally, I called on the then CM who told me politely but clearly that the previous government had set a precedent in that context and, therefore, for once he had given his approval to Ministers' desire. This one time measure opened a flood gate of transfers as an 'industry' which led to the 'deluge' of democratic malfunctioning of our polity. Norms were thrown to winds and MLAs dominated in their area transforming themselves into feudal lords of pre-independence Rajputana for their constituency-fiefdom in which they could command all that they could survey and descry. Of course, in keeping with my career-long characteristic of outspokenness and forthright manners, I did submit to the then CM that this policy and practice of transfers would not serve the Government well and might be viewed adversely later on. "*Yeh theek nahin hoga*", I had stated.

Meanwhile, Revenue Minister had sent for me and in a similar vein I told her in no uncertain terms my point of view. She only said transfers are a prerogative of the government of the day and I could also figure in the list of transfers some day. That day was not too far off and I was posted as Chairman, Civil Services Tribunal (RAPT), a position I had occupied in the year 1989. Less than three years before my superannuation, my exit from the post of Chairman, Board of Revenue, regarded as equivalent and next only to that of Chief Secretary of the State, was a big 'come down' in public eye with a 'repeat posting', an unusual phenomenon to happen even in these turbulent times.

I called on the Chief Minister to give vent to my feelings and also to register my protest-request. He was gracious enough to post me as Chairman, RSMM and CMD, RSMDC—the two minerals corporations of the state. My mandate was to bring about amalgamation of the two corporations which were doing business in the same minerals in competition with each other creating piquant situations more often than not. The merger was achieved with a lot of teething troubles. Besides, it was also immensely satisfying that a record turnover for both corporations was attained during my tenure. These positions, as it turned out, augured well for my future after superannuation. Based on the experience in this last assignment I was appointed Director, on the Board of one GoI corporation and three disinvested/private limited enterprises companies. I also served for three years as Member of MoU Task Force constituted to examine the overall performance of GoI corporations and enterprises in a financial year as also to finalize an MoU of targets of performance for the subsequent year for the Corporation to be signed by CMD and Secretary of the concerned ministry in Government of India. Needless to add, I have thoroughly enjoyed these positions besides receiving well earned remuneration.

Conclusion

To conclude, expectations of citizens from government always remain high, unlike customer satisfaction in goods and services and thus it will be difficult to bridge the chasm between people's expectations and experience in the public services rendered by civil servants. Nonetheless, of late, public service delivery systems of governments have been thrown wide open for fresh winds of New Public Management to blow in transparency, accountability and responsiveness so as to bring about necessary change in paradigm and dynamics of public administration in order to enable it to meet new challenges posed by liberalization, competitiveness and the need for public private partnership in the new emerging scenario.

II

Remembering District Tenures

SECTIONAL INTRODUCTION

Administering a District

Rakesh Hooja

The first district posting as Collector has always been something special for each IAS officer and has invariably been looked back upon later in life with fond memories of challenges overcome, special initiatives undertaken and specific events which helped to forge ones administrative capacities and future career, as also with some regrets about what could have been done but did not prove possible at that time and place.

For citizens also, the Collector represents the coordinated or unified, if not integrated, administration in the district. He is the face of the government, a more than primus inter pares, still often referred to locally as 'Annadata' or 'Mai Baap'. Thus, accounts about working in the district tend to fascinate all and sundry.

First created in 1772 by the East India Company, the Collectors post was unlike anything that existed in the preceding Mugha1 or pre-Mughal administrations. The office of Collector (referred to as Deputy Commissioner or District Magistrate in some States of the country) was initially assigned a prime position in local administration in India by the Court of Directors of the East India Company in 1786. His role changed following the taking over of British rule in India by the Crown in the wake of the events of 1857; following the Montague-Chelmsford Reforms of 1919 which brought about provincial autonomy and dyarchy; following the advent of democracy in independent India; following the introduction of statutory Panchayati Raj; following the separation of executive and judicial functions as per the revised Criminal Procedure Code; and following the 73rd Constitutional Amendment and constitutionalized Panchayati Raj. Changes have also come due to technological advancements, as well as in the wake of economic liberalization, and due to increased political interference resulting inter-alia in the dramatic shortening of tenures of postings of Collectors.

In fact, one commentator has gone as far as to state that the Collector has been reduced to the role of a "target-chaser and a fire fighter on behalf of the government" and "a flunkey of Chief Ministers" being dependant upon their good will.

However, the Collector's central position as the kingpin of general administration in the field has remained unchallenged. His law and order related role is facing increasing challenges as incidents of breaching of law and order have grown in variety and frequency, as also at times in magnitude. He has virtually become the leader of the development team in the district. He is a coordinator amongst various departments, monitoring the progress of development schemes, removing bottlenecks in their implementation, maintaining constant direct touch with Government departments in the State Secretariat, as well as making frequent visits in the field "to the spot", and striving for the achievement of public peace, sustainable development and efficient provision of public services in the district.

Though the role of the Collector differs somewhat from State to State; broadly speaking todays Collector is directly responsible for, or has a significant coordinating role at the district level, in the following spheres (not listed in order of priority): (1) public order, law and order and crime related administration, (2) land record administration and land revenue court work, land reforms, as well as land acquisition, (3) supervision of the district treasury, (4) civil supplies and public distribution, (5) protocol, (6) disaster management and drought/flood relief, (7) district development, (8) conduct of elections, (9) urban and municipal affairs, (10) social welfare and social security, (11) industries and attracting investment, (12) agriculture, (13) cooperatives, (14) district planning and district statistics, (15) registration and stamps, (16) excise, (17) consumer affairs, (18) redressal of public grievances, (19) conduct of census—human, livestock, agricultural, industrial, etc., (20) coordination with banks, (21) supervision of jails, (22) supervision of prosecution staff, (23) MP/MLA Local Area Development Programmes, (24) procurement of agriculture produce, (25) conduct of special campaigns of government, (26) heading special project agencies and trying out new initiatives in various sectors, (27) arms licensing, (28) cinema licensing, (29) regulation of fairs and festivals, (30) e-governance, (31) public relations, (32) various miscellaneous or residual matters which can be grouped under a category of general administration. In some States the Collectors are also being associated with programmes related to health, education, water management, etc.

The seven pieces that comprise this section range from district postings in the late 1950s and 60s to the mid-1980s (They include essays by my father and my wife with more than twenty year's separating the district experiences described by them. My own district assignments were at the beginning and then at the end of the 1980s). The earlier recollections were of a time when the Collectors dependence on horse-back touring had ended, and the jeep had replaced it (by the 1980s, Collectors had been provided the standard white Ambassador cars). But vehicles were few in the district, pucca roads and electrified villages were scarce, the telephone had made its way down to the district headquarters town but rarely to the rest of the district, and despite the Collectors right (and that of State Government officers) to book 'lightening' trunk calls, communication between State headquarters and the district could take much time. Communication between the grassroots and the district town was still relatively primitive. If a situation developed, the Collector had normally to handle it locally with his team and could only then report about it to the State Government. Thus, freedom to act as per ones own initiative was almost thrust upon the Collectors (as David Gilmore has written about the ICS and HEICS "ultimately officials in India had to live on their own resources, their lives determined by individual temperaments, environment and experience and by the eternal problems of human relationship").

The numbers of development schemes to be implemented in the district and funding for them were both comparatively limited compared to today.

As a recently retired Chief Secretary (not a contributor to this volume) has been known to comment that in the good old days officers worked at their own pace as per their own conscience, since neither the populace, nor the politicians had grand expectations or demands from the government system nor was the media and the citizenry running after officials for quick and immediate actions and solutions. This writer feels that earlier, a more reflective style of administration could be followed which allowed more time to be responsive to various views and viewpoints, while today everyone both in the State Secretariat and more so in the districts is always working against time constraints. Spending long hours in office every day and often having to put in work on holidays has always been the fate of an IAS officer.

In the 1950s and 60s, the earlier tendency of ICS officers wanting to spend the bulk of their service careers in the districts rather than in the Secretariat still prevailed among a large number of IAS officers who tended to serve in 3, 4, 5 or even more districts; though some had started thinking of doing a district or two and then moving on to the State Capital which provided creature comforts, better education for the children, a role in policy making, and eventual postings as Secretaries to State Government, or even assignments in Government of India.

Most Collectors loved touring in villages and dealing directly with villagers. However, the earlier emphasis of night halts in the district has disappeared and many tours today have become day tours with officers returning to their homes by late night. Interacting with local politicians was normally not looked forward to but considered necessary, and the politicians have tended to become more aggressive over the years.

The dealing with a natural disaster while in the district, and the sense of satisfaction that a Collector had in having faced the challenge, was one that invariably left a mark on ones memories, and one of the pieces in this section concentrates on dealing with a flood in an urban setting (this editor was at that time undergoing district training there and got totally involved in the flood relief work), while others have also referred to dealing with natural disasters including droughts. In those days there was no emphasis on keeping district, city, block and village disaster management plans ready for such an eventuality, nor did District Disaster Management Agencies chaired by Collectors exist. However one still managed, and normally managed well.

The computer, internet and mobile phones, or the police wireless network now a mainstay of district administration, communications and monitoring—were not known to those Collectors (in fact many served when there was no intercom system in their offices and the creaking civil defence phone system was limited to only some district headquarters)—and we will have to wait for the present crop of Collectors to write their reminiscences to get a feel about the working style of the Collectors of the first decade of the 21st century—though many of the situations and problems that todays Collectors face are similar to those described in this volume.

This section, most of whose contents were penned in the late 1980s and only one after 2000, provides a flavour of the life of a Collector and the problems that could confront the district officer in India between 1950 and 1990, and even later.

8 T.N. CHATURVEDI

A Time to Remember

When one looks back to his posting or work as the District Officer or Collector and District Magistrate, one finds it difficult to pick and choose from the incidents or activities with which one happened to be connected or the events in which one participated. The basic factor that one finds is that the job of the Collector in the district is not only of variegated nature but also in a sense, personalized one. It is true that there are some basic functions which one has to perform in the official capacity but they always bear the imprint of the personality of the Collector and there are many things which are taken up only as the Collector takes interest in them. Thus, while drawing on one's memory, even to narrate a few instances, one cannot avoid the use of the word "I" very frequently. It is not that one necessarily wants to project oneself but it is inherent in the very nature of the job itself. It may however be worthwhile to keep it in view that the success of the Collector depends upon the team spirit that he/she is able to generate and the way he/she gets the best out of his/her colleagues. To that extent the Collector is only the symbol of success and failure, and others have also to take equally the credit and the blame. Further, while mentioning some event or incident, one is apt to forget that the way one handled a particular situation may not necessarily be ideal in certain other circumstances. It will be, therefore, not correct to say that every incident mentioned in one's recollections certainly holds a lesson for others.

I worked in the district under reference below more than a few decades ago and I am well aware of the changed political and social context and the more complex working environment. It is therefore worth repeating that my reflections do not have any didactic purpose and the element of ego as may be evident is something which cannot be avoided.

A Town with Awareness

I was fortunate to be posted as the Collector and District Magistrate of Ajmer in July 1960. Till 1956, Ajmer happened to be a Part 'C' State with its own political paraphernalia and administrative structure. Even in history, Ajmer has been an important political, administrative and cultural centre. The people of Ajmer have always felt that they had much wider awareness than was either possible or existed in the neighbouring princely states which had constituted Rajasthan. The seat of the representative of Central Government in Ajmer during the British times also made substantial difference. After the merger of Ajmer in Rajasthan, the then Chief Minister, Mohan Lal Sukhadia was always anxious that the new district of Ajmer should have good official set-up with a senior officer as Collector in charge so that the people may not have a feeling that they had lost in terms of good administration after their lot was cast with Rajasthan; instead, they should feel that their opportunities and identity had expanded in a wider setting. That is why, since the merger, Ajmer had a series of very distinguished Collectors; my immediate predecessor was Mohan Mukerji. I took over as Collector of Ajmer on my return from the World Bank where I had gone on a fellowship to study the problems of development.

Coping with the Crisis

Hardly had I finished acquainting myself with the problems and people of the city, when the Central government servants' country-wide strike took place. Ajmer has a Railway Workshop and is a very important centre from the viewpoint of rail and road communications. I did not realize till quite late as to why there were frequent enquiries from my friends in the Rajasthan Secretariat about the arrangements that were being made to cope with the strike situation. I thought I had taken adequate note of the changed situation, discussed the likely problems with my Magistrates and the Superintendent of Police alongwith the senior officials of the various Central government department including the Railways. The precautions that we had taken and the arrangements that we had taken and the arrangements that we had made to meet any emergent situation had been brought to the notice of the Commissioner of the Division, M.U. Menon, whose headquarters also happened to be at Ajmer, and of the Range Deputy Inspector General of Police, Shri Sultan Singh. It was only later that I learnt from one of my friends that they were not sure that as one in the Secretariat for five years and having returned from the United States just before joining the district if I was realistic and comprehensive enough in the understanding of the problems that the strike situation might pose in Ajmer. Fortunately for me, apart from the good advice from the Commissioner and cooperation of all the officers, I had the advantage of getting many things done easily since I had known all the senior Heads of Departments at Jaipur during my placement in the Secretariat. Another fortunate thing was that following my taking over as Collector, Shri Mohan Mukerji also happened to come back and stay with me at Ajmer for a few days for purposes of packing up. He was of great help to me in telling me about places and persons about whom I had no first-hand knowledge. He was good enough even to go along with me to strategic locations in the city during the night as I wanted myself to assess the situation. We had a few restless nights. I must say that this was my first independent experience in the district of a crisis situation. I feel I could evoke the cooperation of my colleagues and I subsequently wrote letters of commendation to a large number of them. My existence and identity also came to be known much more prominently and comparatively in a short time so far as local people were concerned. Probably, they had some kind of a measure of me and thought that I would not let them down.

Links with the Intellectuals

A few days later I was invited to preside over the Tulsi Jayanti celebration and though I was initially unwilling, yet because of the insistence of the organizers I went to the function in the Municipal Hall. I found myself at the centre of curiosity of the elite of the city represented in the function. This also helped me, when I look back, to forge my first link with the academic and intellectual community. I also feel that it was good for me to get identified with the cultural activities of the district. I increasingly participated in such functions organized by voluntary organizations and different communities or religious groups, thereby earning not only certain amount of satisfaction but also goodwill for the district administration.

Development through Goodwill

Later on I decided to have a quick visit to the sub-divisional and tehsil headquarters. Fortunately, Ajmer is well connected by road and that was a great advantage. Within a fortnight or so I could visit all the important places and meet a large number of officials and non-officials. Besides Ajmer city itself, the district of Ajmer has some important towns, particularly Kekri, Beawar and Kishangarh, the last being one of the former small princely states. Each of these places is also famous for one reason or the other. During my visit I found some kind of murmuring or reservation about the development problems, especially when I met MLAs and Panchayat Samiti leaders. The reason as I realized was that Ajmer as Part 'C' State had a separate Five-Year Plan and at the time of merger, the assurance was given to the people that all the allocations of this specific plan would be spent in the Ajmer district itself. Somehow, many of the schemes relating to minor irrigation, education, expansion etc., were conceived in haste and naturally were being scrutinized afresh by the Planning Department in the State Secretariat.

There was hardly a year and a half left for the Second Plan to end. This gave me the idea that I should better discuss the problems with all officials as well as non-officials, including the Zila Parishad members, and try to see that reordering the priorities or revision of schemes is carried out with the cooperation of concerned departments. This turned out for me an exceedingly satisfying experience. Not only I got to know more about the people and their problems but I came to have a much better idea of the complexity of the planning process also. Somehow it was possible with the help of my colleagues to work out new schemes and persuade the State Government to sanction them. This was a pleasant surprise for the people. Many of the earlier schemes were given up or radically revised but many new schemes were also taken up and even diversion of funds from one major head to another was made with the approval of the government. Many institutions, schools, colleges and hospitals got a number of additional facilities. Besides, a number of schemes could be initiated in the realm of social welfare. Thus, it was by and large possible for us to ensure that the planned allotment of the former Part 'C' State of Ajmer was actually spent in the area as originally envisaged. I managed to get the approval of some of the schemes only on phone at the fag end of March and drew the money from the State Bank whose Manager was cooperative and who kept the bank open till late in the night on the 31st March. In some cases I even arranged to have the funds brought from the distant treasuries under police escort during the night. All this could not have been done without the very willing cooperation of my officers and the confidence that the authorities in the State Government were good enough to place in me.

The Municipal Obligation

Ajmer has a very well established Municipal Council dating from the beginning of the local self-government experiment in the country. It has had also very eminent and capable chairmen. When I joined as Collector, I met some of the former chairmen who were thorough gentlemen and were deeply motivated for public good. Unfortunately, however, the municipal politics and wranglings had badly affected the working of the civic body. Very often I received complaints about its functioning. Eventually, the State Government decided to supersede the elected civic body. The State Minister for Local-Self Government was good enough to aks me whether I would agree to become the Administrator of the Municipal Council as well. My initial reaction was not favourable: firstly, due to my own work as Collector, and secondly, because under the provision of the Municipal Act, certain matters of the Municipal Council would have to be put up to the Collector for consideration and approval. Further, by this time, the post of the Divisional Commissioner had been abolished and I had to act as the Commissioner, though only notionally, for almost 10 months with the limited aim to wind up the office. Somehow, the Minister persisted and observed that in view of the special position of Ajmer, the Chief Minister would like that the Collector himself should become the Administrator of the Municipal Council and the elections to the Council be held as early as possible. I felt I had no choice. Moreover, I thought it would be a good experience to function in an area which was quite important to the people. Somehow I decided that in order to avoid delay in conduct of business it would be better if the State Government delegates the powers of the Collector under the Ajmer Municipal Act and other related regulations to the Additional Collector of the district. Thus, interestingly, the appeals for revision against some of my orders as Municipal Administrator went to an officer who was otherwise subordinate to me in my capacity as the Collector. I can honestly say that I never interfered with the discretion of the Additional Collector.

Reaching the People

Sometime after I had become the Administrator of the civic body, I found that there was substantial public relations and public contact involved. I had to devote my time between the Collector's office and the Municipal Council. An important problem was to know well the staff of the Municipal Council which was virtually permanent in nature and had their own network of contacts, connections and vested interests. I spoke to the members of the municipal staff in small groups and gave a bit of my mind as to how I wanted them to function. In order to keep myself better informed I posted two additional posts for them. I found that the cooperation from the staff was also forthcoming in full measure when they realized that I meant business. Thus, we worked out schemes for cleaning up the city, broadening of roads, tree plantations, digging up of new wells, giving permanent structures to *pheriwallahs* (hand carts), providing house sites, shops, etc. Once I got involved, I found that all this was a terrific official and personal strain. There were vested interests, and besides, there were goondas in possession of certain land, and strangely enough some politicians never wanted that even the displaced persons coming from Sindh and Punjab who had only temporary shops etc., should get permanent allotments as then their influence would wane. The municipal employees obviously also had their interest if the temporary allotments continued. So, whether it was a question of allotments or removal of encroachments, legal and political hurdles generally cropped up: questions were asked in the State Assembly; veiled threats were conveyed; and agitations and demonstrations were organized. But, the Chief Minister and other members of the Cabinet were fully supportive of the Collector's actions. I decided to go with my officers both from the district and the municipal office from mohalla to mohalla in the city, hold street-corner meetings, explain our projects, take decisions on-the-spot, face the disgruntled and try to persuade the reasonable ones. Still, there were legal notices and even the contempt notices though none did really fructify. I tried that our actions should be according to law and we should act in a manner that would make a moral impact; only then we hoped that most of the people would cooperate with us and the small centres of opposition would get dissolved. The people of Ajmer even today fondly remember that the road going to Dargah Sharif was broadened by removing overnight the encroachments existing for fifty to sixty years. No doubt, considerable thinking and organization had gone into such matters.

My association with the Municipal Council also enabled me to promote the cultural activities and even organize the centenary celebration of eminent leaders such as Rabindra Nath Tagore, Madan Mohan Malviya and Pandit Moti Lal Nehru. The functions was of a massive scale. It was inaugurated by the then Union Education Minister, Humayun Kabir and presided over by then Chief Minister, Mohan Lal Sukhadia. Ajmer was naturally elated. Two other functions were presided over by Prof. Narlikar, formerly distinguished Professor of Mathematics from BHU and the Cambridge Wranglar, who had come to Rajasthan as the Chairman of the State Public Service Commission. Moreover, under the renovation plan, new parks were erected, roads were named and statues of freedom fighters or illustrious Indians installed at various important points in the city, and the first Teacher's Day was organized on a massive scale with very wide participation.

Facilitating Development

It was also my effort to see that the resources of the Municipal Council were realized and properly spent on specified schemes. I tried to build permanent assets for the Council. This was an extremely satisfying experience. It seems strange now that I had to issue notices for the realization of taxes, among others, to a former Speaker of the Ajmer State Assembly and even to the then Finance Minister for compounding charges for unauthorized constructions. I must say we did succeed. It was a genuine effort on my part that no discrimination or pressure was allowed to creep in. Care was taken to see that genuine grievances of all the sections and not just of the articulate groups were promptly heard and corrective action taken. When certain unauthorized portion of a hotel was ordered to be demolished, a good deal of high level pressure was brought in, but very quietly I resisted it. What had transpired in absolute confidence, as I had thought, was immediately the hot news in the city. This also gained respect as well as trust for the district and the municipal administration.

I may also mention that my predecessor, Mohan Mukerji had already finalized the arrangements for the setting up of the Urban Improvement Trust (UIT) for Ajmer in accordance with the legislation on the subject that had only been passed recently. It was left to my lot to build on it, get the people nominated as members and draw the schemes for urban development and housing. Some of my municipal work had brought me nearer to some distinguished people in the city. A few senior citizens whom I nominated as members of the Trust, gave me useful suggestions for city improvement, apprized me of what had been attempted earlier at different times and also mobilized efforts for the schemes of the Trust. In my capacity as the Chairman of the Trust and as Administrator of the Municipal Council, I discussed with the office bearers of several registered societies and institutions ways and means to strengthen their activity and resources base.

The election of the Municipal Council could be arranged after about one and a half years or so. The newly elected Chairman, who had also held the position earlier, lent all support to the district administration and UIT.

During the period I was in the district, the Chinese aggression had taken place. With the help of local leaders throughout the district, we organized meetings and money and material were collected for defence purposes. Certain areas in Ajmer provided a good number of recruits to the Army. Nasirabad is an old Brigade headquarters. There was a remarkable awakening in the public in the countryside when we organized meetings. Some of them were addressed by even the Central and State

Ministers. Whenever I had a programme to attend the meetings, I found that my new Superintendent of Police, G.P. Pilania was keen to join me. Later on, he also began to accompany me occasionally to several meetings of Panchayat Samitis and other development agencies where he would talk of the need and methods for village improvement, proper functioning of village institutions, character building etc. This had two very distinct advantages. The magistracy and the police came closer and police also became more responsive to the public grievances.

At the Grassroots

Ajmer had a very alert Zila Parishad and equally active Panchayat Samitis. As Collector I was only a member of the Zila Parishad. But, my presence was helpful in smoothening many difficulties of Panchayat Samitis and provide an opportunity to the public representatives to ventilate their grievances, have clarifications or even seek redressal. The district administration had also opportunity to convey its viewpoints in an effective manner. I regularly attended the meetings of the Zila Parishad and so did the development officials of the district. Likewise, I attended a few meetings and functions organized by the Panchayat Samitis and interacted with people at the local level. I realized at the fag end of my stay in the district that this was really exhilarating. When I was leaving the district, the amount of affection that was showered on me—and literally there were roses and roses all the way from the Collector's house to the last milestone of the district—was something that could not be imagined. But for my intimate association with Zila Parishad and Panchayat Samitis I would never have known the rural India and the people.

An Imperative Firmness

While reminiscencing I would like to mention one or two more incidents—one relating to the General Elections in 1962 as these had assumed some importance. Principal J.T.M. Gibson of Mayo College, a very distinguished academician though an Englishman, had for long identified himself with public education system in the country. As Collector, I was a member of the Governing Board of the Mayo College. Gibson with all his amiability would at times behave in a peculiar manner which could not be easily explained. As is usual, during the elections, one polling booth had to be set up in the Mayo College for the area. But, when the District Election Officer, the City Magistrate and the Returning Officer went to see the exact spot, Gibson turned up and rudely asked them to leave as he would not permit the polling in his college. My officers naturally felt insulted. When it was reported to me, I realized that if Gibson was allowed to have his way, similar situations could arise in other places as well. Gibson later on met me and tried to explain the position. I told him however, that it was difficult for me to do anything unless he could satisfy the officers concerned that he had meant no disrespect to them and that he was only anxious about his college annual function which was to take place shortly. It seems amusing now that he approached the late Maharaja of Jaipur, the Chief Minister, the Chief Secretary, some former princes, some senior members of the Revenue Board residing in Ajmer, Dr Nagendra Singh and many other distinguished people in different walks of life. Somehow, though most of them in their own way did speak to me for extricating Gibson from his dilemma as he was a dedicated person, but each one of them practically told Gibson that only the Collector under the election law could help him. For one week, Gibson came to see me daily and apologized profusely. I was really in a fix but somehow I had made up my mind that organizing election was only one periodical function in a Collector's work but if rightful authority was allowed to be flouted with impunity, not only would the officers concerned get demoralized, the authority in general in the district even in day-to-day matters would get denigrated. I therefore refused to make any change and insisted that the polling booth be set up as previously decided by the officers. Suddenly, my colleague G.K. Bhanot, then the Chief Electoral Officer of the State, rang me up to say that the Chief Election Commissioner of the Government of India wanted to speak to me while I was on tour in the interior to press me for a change in my decision regarding setting up a polling booth in Mayo College.

Hardly half an hour later, a lighting call was received from Delhi and the Chief Election Commissioner, Centaurium spoke to me emphasizing that I should accommodate Gibson's wishes. I naturally was a bit agitated and enquired of him if it was an order or a request. If it was an order of the Chief Election Commissioner, I would carry it out by publicly making it clear, but if it was a suggestion then I would give utmost respect to his word if Gibson made amends to officers who were only doing their duty and whom he had needlessly offended. I added that I would like him (Chief Election Commissioner) to know that I had to run the district with the help of my subordinates and colleagues and organizing elections was only one part of it and hence if I could not protect my officers in the due discharge of their duties, how could I expect them to help me to run the district? I must say that Sundaram could realize my viewpoint. He remarked at once that it was only a suggestion as he had been approached by many eminent persons, and it was absolutely for me to decide what to do, though he could feel happy if some adjustment could be made.

However, there was a happy ending to this needless controversy. Gibson came to see me the same day shortly afterwards and conveyed apologies to me for all that had happened. He assured me that there was no disrespect intended by him to my officers. I assured him that I would try to persuade my officers so that some mutually satisfactory solution could be found. After a short while, Gibson turned up with his letter of regret for the incident and while I was reading the letter, the concerned officers also came to my residence to report to me about the progress of the election arrangements in the district. Somehow, my officers were so cut up seeing Gibson that they wanted to return and when I asked them to stay they kept their reserve. The atmosphere was really chilly. Gibson however took initiative. He walked upto the officers, mumbled his apology and shook their hands. After he left I showed the officers his letter and persuaded them that as responsible officers we should accept the apology as it may not be proper for us to humiliate anybody further and that this agonizing chapter should be closed. I suggested that a slight adjustment about the polling booth could be made while it would remain within the college premises. All this was fully known in the college and the city and the district administration was commended for its firmness and fairness in the local press. My colleagues also got a feeling that whatever may be the pressure, the Collector would not let them down.

Rajaji's Visit

During the elections, C. Rajagopalachari, the former Governor General of India, came on an election tour to Ajmer as a leader of the Swatantra Party. I ensured that the he was accorded all necessary courtesies and protection during his stay. Rajaji was staying with the local Swatantra Party chief, Raja Sahib of Bhinai, a very cultured but embittered person, who gave a small private tea party in Rajaji's honour. To avoid any misunderstanding I advised then Superintendent of Police, who was a Rajput and also related to Raja Bhinai, that he should excuse himself since already needless allegations had been levelled against him. But, I along with the local DIG of CRPF (later IG of the Force), went to attend the reception in Rajaji's honour. Others present were surprised but were happy. I spent some very pleasant time in Rajaji's company listening to his scintillating conversation. While I took leave of him, he said, "So you were not afraid to come". I politely replied, "Sir, the Government does want me to be polite as Collector, I have come to see a distinguished leader and pay regards to our former Home Minister and the Governor General". He gave his well-known smile and affectionately patted me. Raja Bhinai rang me up in the night to thank me and said he would send some photographs taken at the reception. But that was not to be as Bhinai had a sudden and premature death very shortly thereafter.

A Gratifying Experience

One can go on mentioning many more incidents and events, some pleasant and others not so. I would like to mention that district is a viable area where an officer can leave an impact. If a Collector, with a minimum of competence, is fair, firm and sympathetic, he can mobilize public cooperation and also catch the imagination of the people. It is always worthwhile if he can identify himself with cultural life and social activities in the district.

For a Collector it becomes easy to play his coordinating role effectively if he attends to problems of other departmental officers not having any direct access to the government. The district provides variegated experience of life and governmental activity. It is as Collector, that an officer finds often in the course of his multifarious duties that how appreciative and grateful people in general feel for small things done for them, even though these may be their due. Common people are the real hope of our democracy. In a district, a vigilant Collector can ensure that benefits go to those for whom they are intended and that development proceeds with justice. In spite of the existence of many powerful politicians in the district, I had no real problem of political harassment, for I had found that people had great confidence in me. Truly, people have their own yardstick to judge their officers.

Public confidence has proved to be my patron and my guardian. Even after the passage of twenty-four years, people from Ajmer write to me, send greetings and invitations and remind me of my association with the district. Many write to me on the basis that they belong to the district where I worked as Collector as if they have special claims. This speaks eloquently that for their Collector, they have a long memory and store of affection as well as goodwill. At different stages of my career I would receive congratulatory telegrams or letters and greetings. Even my wife cherishes fond memories of our stay at Ajmer, though I wonder if I had much time to spare for her. She made good friends among ladies who were associated with social work. I recall with pleasure that I developed an affinity for 'my' district. The period I worked there as Collector was indeed amply rewarding in human terms and from the viewpoint of administrative experience and insight, it enriched by understanding of men and affairs. It provided as sense of fulfilment. If I had my time again, I can say without hesitation and with a sense of pride, that once again I would like to work as a Collector in the district of Ajmer.

9

BHUPENDRA HOOJA

A District Odyssey

There is something memorable about one's first district assignment, something in the nature of a first love that even after decades one can recall quite vividly, the varied impressions and experiences of the district life. This was in the erstwhile district of Mahasu in the then Union Territory (UT) of Himachal Pradesh in the early 1960s.

My posting (or deputation) to Mahasu district in Himachal had come to me as a surprise. Perhaps, in those days, there was no established practice of consulting a prospective deputationist before he was sent out of his parent state to a different state or UT or on an assignment under the Government of India. Somehow, I had not been consulted nor forewarned, though in the early summer months of 1962, I had a vague feeling or premonition that I would soon be shifted from my assignment as Secretary to the Chief Minister of Rajasthan. The orders came and I set out for new adventures amidst unknown frontiers.

I had a quick run through the length and breadth of the district stretching along the Sutlej river almost immediately after my arrival because there was a message awaiting me from the Lt. Governor that after assuming charge, I should proceed towards the Indo-Tibet border along the duly laid out road to meet him while he was on tour. So, the very next day, after my arrival, I got into the jeep and started on my journey.

When I met him, the Lt. Governor, Raja Bhadri, was on his way back from a visit to the border posts at Shipkila and the border district of Kalpa along with his entourage which consisted of most of the senior officers of the UT, both in the Secretariat as well as in the Administrative Departments, particularly those connected with police or law and order, roads, PWD, forests, electrification, etc., from the rank of Chief or Director or Chief Conservator, etc., down to the operative officers at the district level. There is no doubt that considerable government work can be speedily transacted on the spot and mutual differences of interest sorted out through this strategy.

Dealing with Detractors

I remember fairly well one of the first such missions on which Lt. Governor deputed me. I had to go and survey the possible alternate alignment of a proposed all-weather road between Nashanda-Thanedar hill feature and Kotgarh ridge at a height of 5,000 feet against the existing road at 7,000–8,000 feet. Naturally, there were many opponents, especially whose orchards were likely to be curtailed. For me it became a test of physical endurance as well as negotiating skill as I climbed up and down steep paths on foot or horseback, met hundreds of people at their homesteads every day. The scheme was shelved but I got experience of strong lobbies of elite farmers who were very shrewd and highly educated but wanted to be left alone. In this context, the government orders, or may say the wishes of the Lt. Governor, were very clear (at least they came to be pronounced very soon following reports of rapid erosion in various parts of the land) that whenever any mountain slope or hill surface was disturbed during the road construction operations or otherwise, and wherever due to the blasting or road-cutting operations, the hill sides shifted or caved in, suitable protective and soil conservation measures should be taken up immediately. Thus, the concern for protection of the forest wealth and the natural environment was emphasized along with the stress on development activities, particularly road making, etc.

The raising of potato seed as a cash crop had become a widespread agricultural activity in Himachal Pradesh. It so happened that my district, Mahasu, was the key area for the production of potato seed in ideal and almost disease-free conditions. But, the farming practices and techniques had to be explained to the people, and ultimately their product had to be gathered, transported and marketed in the face of stiff competition and almost market monopoly conditions imposed by the traders, some of whom were known as 'potato kings'. Substantial time and attention of the district administrative officials, particularly those connected with transport, cooperative marketing, agricultural operations and general bandobast, had to be given to the supervision of various stages and facets of these large-scale and widely spread out operations. And, all these things had to be done in the face of inclement weather, when keeping the roads and the *kutcha* hill tracks open was the biggest worry for all of us. The district administration remained on alert round the clock for these few crucial weeks but the preparations had to be done well in advance. In two seasons of my involvement, both as District Collector-cum-District Magistrate and Member (later Chairman) of the District Cooperative Federation, matched every move of the private traders and managed to channelize 40 per cent produce through the cooperative, thus breaking the monopoly of the private traders.

Simple People, Strong Hopes

Next to economic activities came various social services, particularly arrangements for safe drinking water so that various hill streams were tagged and harnessed through rubber pipes and the places or sources of drinking water were protected or so located as to keep them free from pollution. Electrification through micro hydel sets as well as by taking the newly available Bhakra power to the high mountain tops and deep valleys, the provision of educational facilities along with incentives, and the expanding of medical services, were some of the other important items on the development agenda.

It was indeed an atmosphere of upsurge, hope, self-confidence and determination. The people were hard working, self-dependent and peace-loving but still very much within the old traditional social folds of brotherhood and village loyalties and not much infested with the fever of competition and aquisitiveness. Most were simple and straight-forward, honest and trusting. Their local disputes or problems with each other or with the village and area officials were not too complex. They had their complaints and grievances but none so involved and complicated as to result in long-lasting litigations or court battles or even tensions. The overall result as far as the district authorities were concerned was that it was a district which was easy to administer, if the logistics of physical distance could be managed.

Apart from the involvement in various development activities on many fronts, every visit, every tour into the interior became a pleasant experience, a friendly meeting with the local people without any apparent complications, almost like an invigorating restful picnic, the joy and beauty of which was heightened by the natural environment, the endless folds of mountains, sloping curves of the green hills, deep gorges, mountain paths along slopes covered with pine and fir trees with winds swirling and swishing through them. However, there was work aplenty, from fire-fighting on one occasion to the spot enquiries into the total accidents, from supervising civil supplies and the drudgery of court work and office routine to the ceremonials and receptions of VIPs and inspections. Since the district was so close to the UT headquarters, there were numerous calls from the Lt. Governor or the Chief Secretary for meetings or discussions. However, as departmental supervisory officers were also close at hand, there were less of district level coordination meetings.

Knotty Problem of Land Reforms

The introduction of land reforms and resumption of *jagirs* became an interesting and instructive experience for most of us in district administration in states as well as in the UT administrations. The Ministry of Home Affairs, Government of India had been pressing the Himachal Administration to go ahead and expedite the work and with this end in view, a few months before I went to Shimla, the post of Land Reforms Commissioner had also been created and was filled up by a very senior and seasoned officer who had spent most of his working life in the area in different positions and was otherwise also held in high esteem. A few years ago, he had worked as Deputy Commissioner, Mahasu and hence he knew the district quite intimately. Because of close physical proximity and because Mahasu happened to be the main district of the UT, it was but natural that the district should have been selected for the detailed preliminary exercise and implementation of the Act in the first round.

We started a series of discussions with each one of us going through the letter and spirit of the Act and the rules made thereunder so as to properly appreciate and grasp the implications as well as the procedures to be followed. A round table discussion was also organized both at the level of the Land Reforms Commissioner and at the district level, so as to have some idea of the nature and type of problems or complications which may have to be faced. Thus, all along the line in the hierarchy of the district revenue administration, proper orientation was facilitated.

If I remember correctly, there was a rather strange provision in the original Act, which laid down that on the prescribed date (to be notified in due course of time through the official gazette etc.), all lands in excess of the ceiling would stand resumed by the government, and there was no provision for a prior notice to be given to the affected *jagirdars* or landholders whose surplus or excess lands were to be resumed. In other words, all that was required to be done was to identify these lands and their *khasra* numbers etc., and bring about the necessary amendments or corrections in the records of rights. Yet another clear anomaly was there which enabled the government to take over almost all the lands surrounding a residential building (or a palace in case of erstwhile *rajas* and chiefs) right up to the building site itself or its approach road. However, there were some lacunae as well, since there was no system or arrangement by which lands of the same *jagirdar* or landholder lying in different villages or in different tehsils and districts could be taken together. The utmost we could do by way of some short-cut device was to arrange for data or notes to be compared between the field level revenue officials, the *patwaris* or at the most at the tehsil or sub-divisional level so that in many cases it was possible to identify persons holding land in different parts of the district (sub-division and tehsils).

Taking the Plunge

In a nutshell, after preparatory detailed examination of the law and the legal procedures and after a mock trial or a simulated rehearsal in respect of some holdings on duplicate copies of the land records, it was decided to take the plunge. Within a couple of weeks, necessary corrections were incorporated in the records of rights. However, to play it safe and not to go against the spirit of the law or of natural justice, we had taken the precaution of informing in advance the various affected parties and also given them notices that the records were being corrected in the light of the Land Reforms and Resumption of Jagirs Act so that before the final entries were made, both in the revenue papers and in the field maps, they could raise their objection or offer valid and acceptable proofs or evidence on the basis of which they sought exemption or objected to the entries being made in favour of the government. I also remember the concrete case of one or two important persons (VIPs, ex-rulers) in whose case all the land of their residence/palace right up to the plinth of the foundation level came under the axe of resumption.

Naturally, there was a big hue and cry with representations and deputations being sent to the Lt. Governor and the Union Home Ministry, the ex-rulers leading the *jagirdars* or owners of large orchards and large holdings, as well as political leaders of various shades of opinion rushing to and fro. I think, ultimately, the Union Ministry of Home Affairs had to issue a directive to stay the proceedings on the ground that the existing law would be suitably amended. I do not remember exactly what followed next because soon after these operations, I fell ill and was transferred from the UT.

Smooth Administration

Meanwhile, there was a change in the administrative set-up as well, after elections to the Territory Council and by about middle of 1963, a new popular representative government had taken over. But I can make bold to say that in the process of implementing the law, the entire administrative machinery had moved in unison almost like one man and the manner in which the whole exercise was conducted, hardly left any scope for outside and undue influence or pressures or even occasions for corruption and such other social evils which are usually laid at the doorsteps of revenue administration. In fact, whatever little I could see of the functioning of the revenue machinery as well as other district or sub-divisional and tehsil level officials, whether in revenue matters or in connection with the provision of civil supplies and other multifarious functions, it can be said unhesitatingly that at least until then the administration had a fairly clean image. Here and there, village loyalties, caste considerations, political influences or pressures might have influenced some decisions or certain allocation or distribution of concessions and facilities, but what goes under the name of bribery or corruption was not there, at least not in a big way. I would not say that temptations or the opportunities were not there or that there were no parties like various contractors connected with road, building or transportation activities or those connected with marketing etc., but the manner in which the administration had evolved and was then functioning, the frequent tours for routine inspections or surprise check even by the Lt. Governor and his team of senior colleagues moving around in the area, rapport with the local people and their representatives, the ease and the confidence with which the common citizens or the aggrieved person could approach the local authorities as well as the supervisors and the seniors—all these factors contributed and supported each other in creating a very favourable atmosphere for a clean and welfare-oriented and helpful administration. Much of the credit for this image as well as for the real picture should go to the then Lt. Governor and the group of senior dedicated officers, the secretaries or the heads of the departments who were brought together to forge new directions.

But one could almost feel some undercurrents of vaguely expressed protest against the heavy presence or intrusion of outsiders. The Himachali people, even the ordinary citizens, were then quite sensitive, somewhat hurt and wary, about the manner in which the outsiders, be they army officers or the bureaucrats and their minions who used to immigrate to Shimla in the past, or be they Punjabi businessmen or traders, who had made Shimla their temporary capital from the British days and later after 1947, their home. Somehow or the other there was a general feeling that all these outsiders were there to exploit the Himachalis and to deprive at least the growing younger generations of their rightful claims and opportunities. When the UT administration came to be run or managed by more and more senior officers from outside, from Punjab or Uttar Pradesh or

Delhi and Rajasthan, naturally, there was some increase in the simmering feeling of resentment. Even, the slightest slip of default on the part of the lowest functionary was brought out into sharp focus as a possible ground for grievance and a grouse against the existing administrative set-up.

Escorting the Eminent

During my two years' stay in the district, I had an opportunity and pleasure of looking after, escorting and entertaining a number of interesting and important visitors, particularly in respect of those who were extended official hospitality or were treated as state guests—ministers and senior officials from Government of India, ministers from the neighbouring states, especially when some inter-state or zonal meetings were held, teams of army officers who would come out for establishing contacts with the civilians, one or two well-known writers and painters, and a host of others with a variety of interests and presenting a wide spectrum of professions. Some of these VIP visits or contacts somehow still stand out in my memory. In a crowded and colourful atmosphere, the visit of late President, Dr Zakir Hussain, who was then holding the high office of Vice-President, remains in my mind for a number of reasons. First, because of his very pleasant and benign nature, his polished, yet very simple manner, his dignity in every movement and in his speech, his command over North Indian Urdu or Hindustani, his sense of humour and his capacity to make the other person feel at home—all these personal attributes made it a very pleasant assignment for me when I had to accompany him on his visit to various places of interest near about Shimla. Dr Hussain was very keen on gardening, horticulture and besides he was a lover of animals.

Another visit worth remembering was that of His Holiness Dalai Lama, who had come to Shimla as a guest of the Punjab government. In any case, he had to stay in a building under the control of the Punjab government (Public Works Department) and apart from visiting a couple of Tibetan centres and other institutions where Tibetans were residing in or near about Shimla, his itinerary included visits deep into the Himachal territory, where hundred of Tibetan men and women were living in camps and were engaged mostly in road building operations. For the Tibetans, Dalai Lama was and remains a living God, a highly exalted personage at whose smiling, friendly, youthful and intelligent face they dared not look. Escorted by senior civil and police officers of the Himachal Pradesh government and the district officers, His Holiness went out to meet his people to give them solace and comfort and to rekindle their faith in their future. His visit seems to have acted as a miracle, one sign of which was that all the camps which only a couple of days earlier appeared to be in shambles and were like hovels, were all cleaned, polished and decorated so that it became a very pleasant experience to walk through the areas or even to approach the camp sites with flutter of flags and buntings high up on poles touching the skies, while drums were being beaten. There were holy dances to strange melodies as if the Himalayan rocks had begun to sing. There were incence-carriers preceding Dalai Lama and on both sides of bridle paths or the roadside. Men and women in their colourful costumes, bright and cheerful, full of emotions, yet controlled with their heads bowed, had joined the ceremony for exchange of scarves or for offering their scarves to His Holiness.

Dalai Lama spent almost two days in the Himachal area where I had the good fortune and privilege of being physically very close to him and 'feeling' the simplicity of his nature and his direct friendly approach and the curiosity or the depth in the range of his mind. He would ask about the welfare of his people, their wages, and medical facilities available for them, particularly about and education of the younger generation who were all being looked after and educated in centres away from the camps and were getting the best that was then possible. He would also enquire about the flora and fauna, the forest produce, the agricultural and horticultural developments and the life of the Himachali people. One query made by him still rings in my mind. He had asked us how soon or when the road works would be ready for traffic up to the Tibetan border. Did he have a premonition of the coming events? His visit preceded the Chinese aggression in 1962 by a few weeks only.

The Challenge from China

The Chinese intrusion into the north-eastern frontier areas of India came as a sudden and unexpected bolt from the blue. Its shocks were felt in Himachal Pradesh as much as anywhere else in the country. Suddenly, the administration was jolted into action and the emotions of the common people were electrified. But, there is no doubt that we were not prepared for such an eventuality. Though slowly over the years the new all-weather and motorable Indo-Tibet road was being laid, the slowness of these preparations and their inadequacy suddenly became apparent.

The challenge before the Himachal Pradesh Administration as well as the Western Command of the Indian Army was to keep up the morale of the people and the army units of the border posts, inculcate among them a fighting spirit and build up the supply lines for provisions, stores, etc.

Vigilant action was also necessary against any possible anti-national or anti-social elements. An idea of how sudden and unexpected these developments were can be realized from the fact that at the headquarters of the Himachal Pradesh Administration, there were no previous records or precedents or detailed worked out instructions and procedures for internal/external security. I am not suggesting that nothing had been done in this respect but somehow the various pieces of the jig-saw puzzle had never been put together to present a coordinated or comprehensive picture of the steps and measures to be taken in the event of a national crisis or calamity. I remember having returned to my office from a discussion at the Secretariat and mentioned to my colleagues about this problem (what appeared to be a dilemma at that time) when the Superintendent of the Deputy Commissioner's office who mentioned to me that perhaps in the English Record Room (room in which records or documents in English were kept) there would be some references. Curiously, I asked him how he could say that. His explanation was quite simple that during the Second World War years, he was working in the office of the Political Agent as a junior hand and recently while checking up the record room of the Deputy Commissioner's office in the course of routine annual inspection, he had noted that there was a *basta* (heaps of papers properly filed) or two, which had some reference to the war-time instructions. Within an hour or two, we were able to report to the Himachal Pradesh Administration in Shimla (few miles from Kusimti) that we had come across some war-time reference and guidelines.

Managing Scarcity

Daily meetings and conferences, mostly business-like and to the point, followed by issue of instructions or inspection and field visits and such other frantic activities became the order of the day. The more the Himachal Administration or the district authorities looked at the problems and the likely challenges or threats, the more we learnt that we were not at all prepared for or attuned to this task. All the sub-divisional magistrates in the interior even near the Indo-Tibetan border were not mobile and had to depend upon the public transport system which was also not very well managed. There were no fire-fighting arrangements, even arrangements or facilities for first aid. However, within a few days, it was possible to make reasonably satisfactory arrangements all through the district (as in other neighbouring districts) even though the machinery was constantly under constraint and had to be spread out in a rather thin manner. But, whatever little show of the arrangements could be made was perhaps enough to keep up the spirits of the local people and warn any possible anti-social or criminal elements. Yet another problem was to somehow keep the roads open and safe so that army vehicles going up and down had an uninterrupted flow of traffic. This was also the time when the gathering and marketing of apple crop was just coming to a close but the potato seed crop had to be collected and transported to the main rail head at Shimla. Thus, there were dangers of traffic congestion and jamming up at various crucial and vulnerable points but with the PWD gangs constantly in attendance, the district or police authorities being very vigilant about the matter and the local sub-divisional officers also being alive to the situation, there were no unnecessary jamming or hold-ups anywhere.

We had another problem to cope with when hundreds of soldiers not used to the heights and not even properly clad or equipped for the local environment started moving up towards the border posts. The local people, particularly citizens of important towns on the way, wanted to display their support and sympathy with the soldiers and they started organizing way-side rest and recreation or refreshment points for the moving convoys where tea or coffee or milk, sweets, biscuits, food, etc., used to be served with scores of local people—old and young men and women—on duty round the clock. Their enthusiasm was really remarkable and overwhelming and one could see hundreds of soldiers from the plains being overwhelmed by the attention and keenness they were receiving. However, our job as local administrators was also to see that there were no unnecessary hold-ups at these points or that the soldiers were not repeatedly fed or fettered time and again. It did take some time to bring about some sort of system and organization in the whole affair. A message was received that not only soldiers but the gangs of PWD workers or labourers, who had to keep the roads open or to keep on shovelling snow or loose soil or debris from the roadside were also in need of woollen clothes or protective cloth against the on-setting cold wave. The Lt. Governor, being a man of innovations, experience and ingenuity, suddenly thought of cotton-padded jackets and trousers as a possible protective wear for such workers as well as others on duty in the border areas. The local citizens also came out with whatever little help and cooperation they could offer.

Thus, within a very short time, it appeared that not only the administration, but also the people were ready for any eventuality. It is indeed fortunate that no serious threat or challenge arose in that area so that our preparations were never put to a severe test.

Preparing the People

At the outset of the emergency, one of the first steps taken was to send senior officers out into the interior for a quick survey or appraisal of the mood of the people and to acquaint and brief them about the impending threat, stressing the need for discipline and preparedness. I remember covering hundreds of miles up and down the district, meeting my field colleagues and others as well as leading citizens, teachers and lecturers of the schools and colleges, doctors at the hospitals and dispensaries, various officers, engineers and traders. This mass contact programme perhaps set up the tone and created suitable conditions for mutual trust and confidence and subsequent cooperation. In the process, I happened to visit almost all the parts of the district which were not easily approachable by road including *kutcha* tracks or forest roads. I remember hearing from the local people I met that mine was the first visit of the Deputy Commissioner in quite sometime. Also, these visits revealed to me the general attitude of respect for law or government machinery amongst the common people and their capacity to function on their own even.

By way of people's support and contribution, efforts to collect National Defence Fund or contributions of gold and silver ornaments by the people had also been initiated. Though perhaps Himachali people did not have much ready cash or gold and silver to offer, their response was quite good in terms of the number of people who came forward with their small contributions. Suitable instructions had been issued to all the field-level officers of the district to exercise proper care and direction in handling such donations and in keeping proper record and bringing the funds to the UT headquarters.

Tragedy around the Treasury

It so happened that some important temples in the country as also in Mahasu district had a lot of collection of gold and silver received over the centuries by way of offerings to the presiding deity. Far away from Shimla and even Rampur Bushahar on the old Indo-Tibet road, there is the famous Hima Kali temple at Sarahun. On a visit to the area, I was told that a lot of temple treasure, consisting of gold and silver ornaments, coins, jewel-studded daggers, silver trophies, etc., which had been offered to the deity, had been donated for the national war effort. In any case, it was considered prudent to remove most of these treasures from the temple premises for protective custody. With the help of the local Sub-Divisional Magistrate (SDM) and the Citizens Committee as well as the temple management, we drew up lists of possessions, properly sealed the various boxes and brought the chest to the treasury at Rampur Bushahar. Some of the collection was of historic value. But it really broke my heart when I saw that in their eagerness or carelessness, the local people had tried to fold together a beautiful silver plated umbrella so as to place it within a small box. Somebody in our party seemed to murmur that this action would highly displease the goddess. We did not pay any attention to this mild protest based on local tradition or superstition. But when after depositing the treasure at Rampur Bushahar treasury, I proceeded towards Shimla and reached the Narkanda Rest House, I got the message that the local SDM had suddenly collapsed, a victim to heart attack. Though I did not believe in local superstition, for a moment, however I thought that perhaps Goddess Bhima Kali had claimed her first victim for the desecration of the temple or the removal of the temple treasure. A few days later, the treasure chest had been brought to Shimla and displayed in the Raj Bhawan. Even the Lt. Governor and Chief Secretary present were really amazed at the collection of its grandeur and variety. The Lt. Governor decided to take a few specimen pieces like old Mughal coins or jewel-studded daggers, etc., to show to the Prime Minister so that these might be placed in the National Museum. But that was long after the dust raised by the Chinese intrusion had settled down and the conditions appeared to be somewhat clearer.

Au Revoir

But perhaps, there is an interesting end to this episode as far as I was personally concerned. In the months of June-July 1963, due to the strain of the previous months and may be my own negligence, I suddenly fell ill. Unfortunately, I took my illness rather lightly and continued to work as before until suddenly it was discovered that the infection (some sort of measles that I got from my neighbours) had affected my heart and damage seemed to have been done because at the early stage of my illness, I had kept up my usual routine. There was no choice before the doctors but to advise me complete rest. It was true that I had to cope with the pressure of hectic touring because the Lt. Governor was going away after about a decade of service in the Union Territory and very detailed and comprehensive programme of his field visits and farewell had been planned. I remember that the day I was advised complete bed rest, I was expected to proceed with a fairly high-powered team of senior army officers on an uphill journey into the interior to select and identify a suitable site for high altitude training and firing practice by the army jawans. That might have happened if instead of medical check-up and the bed rest, I had proceeded on this visit.

Thus came an abrupt end to my very interesting though short but eventful stay in Himachal as Deputy Commissioner, Mahasu. I seem to have been so much carried away by my experiences that after a few months' rest in the plains, I was once again willing and ready to go back to Shimla and resume my charge. But my well-wishers and senior colleagues from Rajasthan, who had come to serve the Government of India, advised me, while I was on my way to Shimla, that I should not proceed there and take unnecessary risk. Thus, in a way, I withdrew or retreated from my karmabhoomi of a sort, and returned to further service in Rajasthan without even saying the usual goodbyes to the people with and for whom I worked in an interesting period of my career.

10

V. NATH

District Administration in Rajasthan in the 1960s: Reminiscences of a Former Collector

Although written mainly for personal use, these reminiscences of my two-year tenure as Collector of two districts, viz., Sawai Madhopur and Pali, in Rajasthan describe and comment on the major social, economic and institutional reforms, the development programmes and the socio-economic changes that the rural areas of the state witnessed during the 1950s and the early 1960s. These contain observation also on the administration during the period, in which under the outstanding leadership provided by the Prime Minister Pandit Jawahar Lal Nehru at the centre and the Chief Minister Shri Mohan Lal Sukhadia in the state, there was political and economic stability and it was possible to undertake far-reaching institutional and administrative reforms, including abolition of the feudal tenurial system of *jagirdari* and conferment of permanent and heritable rights in land on the cultivators and introduction of a planning process aimed at achieving rapid rural development and social change. The administration experienced a progressive increase in its role of initiating and leading the process without suffering serious conflict or cleavages. At the same time, its efficiency and effectiveness increased steadily.

There was much scope for conflict within the administration because it was led and dominated by officers of the former princely states, for the great majority of whom implementing programmes of economic development and social change was a new and daunting experience. Furthermore, all officers, old and young, had to maintain good working and personal relations with elected representatives of the people and to meet their demands, as far as possible, within the laws of the state and administrative rules and procedures. They had to understand and appreciate the fact that the elected representatives might make demands on them under pressure from the people, who had elected them and on whose continued support they depended to remain in office, and that the representatives would often ask the officers to bend the rules in order to meet the demands. These had to be refused politely without offending the representatives.

This paper narrates my experiences in Sawai Madhopur district only since most of the time (20 months) of my two years' tenure was spent in it.

Sawai Madhopur

My wife and I recall our stay in Sawai Madhopur with fondness mixed with nostalgia. I had requested the then Chief Secretary, Shri B.S. Mehta, for being posted in a district in preference to being posted in the secretariat in Jaipur. This was a somewhat unusual request as most IAS officers preferred then (and perhaps do so now) to be posted in the secretariat. But I wanted a district posting for reasons explained below and I have never regretted the choice. My wife and I learnt more about rural life and rural development in Rajasthan (and to an extent also in India) through my district postings, than we would have ever done otherwise.

I had joined the IAS in 1958 after spending eight years on the staff of the Planning Commission, five of which had been with the Programme Evaluation Organization (PEO) of the Commission. The PEO had been established to evaluate the effect of the community development and other rural development programmes of the government on the life of rural people. It carried out its duties through:

(a) concurrent, independent evaluation of the working of programmes by its own Project Evaluation Officers posted in community projects and blocks located in different states and regions of the country; and
(b) survey and studies designed to measure the social and economic effects of the programmes on rural people.

After completing my 15-month training for the IAS in Simla and Jodhpur, I had spent a year (1959–60) as Vice Principal and Director of Research of the newly established Central Institute of Community Development, Mussoorie, UP.[1]

After all these years of study and research on rural development programmes, I was keen to acquire first-hand knowledge of their working in the field, and felt that it would be obtained best through a district posting. The then Rajasthan government was keen on the Collectors giving first priority in their duties to direction and overall supervision of community development and other rural development programmes in their districts. The government considered Collector's duties as a District Development Officer to be the most important. It had implemented the community development programme with great enthusiasm and success, and had been the first government in the country to establish in October 1959, the 3-tier structure of Panchayati Raj Institutions (PRIs) consisting of village-level Gram Panchayats, block-level Panchayat Samitis and district-level Zilla Parishads, which had been recommended by the Balwantrai Mehta Team.[2]

The District

Sawai Madhopur is a medium-sized district which had an area of about 5,000 sq km and a population of 8,75,000 in 1991. It is situated south-east of Jaipur and Tonk districts in eastern Rajasthan and borders Madhya Pradesh to his east. It had formed part of the former Jaipur State and had the reputation of being a peaceful, almost somnolent district, where "nothing much ever happened". There was no city in the district. Sawai Madhopur itself and the sub-divisional headquarters town of Gangapur were small towns with population around 20,000 in 1961.

Sawai Madhopur's only claim to distinction within Rajasthan was that a large cement factory was located near its suburb Maantown, in which the offices of the Collector and other officers were located, and its railway station was the meeting point of the broad gauge Delhi-Mumbai railway line of the Western Railways and its metre gauge branch line to Jaipur, located about 130 km away. The factory has now been closed for more than a decade. Sawai Madhopur and Gangapur were connected in 1961 by a metalled road and also by the railway.

Sawai Madhopur town and Maantown are located at the southern end of the district. River Banas, about 20 km north of Maantown, has to be crossed for going both to Jaipur and to Gangapur. The crossing was not a problem during the dry months of January to June when water level in the river was low and it could be crossed by jeep. But, during July to December, the water level was too high for the crossing. During these months, the bridge on the river at Tonk, about 60 km west of Sawai Modhopur, had to be used for going to Jaipur. Gangapur could be reached during these months only by the Delhi-Mumbai line of the Western Railways.

Almost two-thirds of the district is a plain from which small hillocks, each topped by a fortress, emerge as islands out of a sea. The fortress housed the residence of a former Jagirdar with the principal village of his *jagir* spread around the base of the hillock. The eastern third of the district is hilly and has extensive thorn forests in which there is much wildlife. The historic Ranathambhore Fort is located about 15 km from both Maantown and Sawai Madhopur. The Ranathambhore Wild Life Sanctuary and Tiger Reserve are located in the forest surrounding the fort.

Sawai Madhopur is not a dry district. Average annual rainfall of 63 cms is adequate and reliable enough for growing the *kharif* (monsoon) crops of sorghum, millets, groundnut and cotton without irrigation. The *rabi* (post-monsoon) crops of wheat, mustard, barley and gram (chick-peas) can also by produced without irrigation because the heavy block soil retains moisture. They do best however under irrigation. Wells, powered by diesel-operated pumps, and tanks, are the principal sources of irrigation. Less than 10 per cent of the cropped area of the district in 1961 was irrigated; the proportion had increased to 60 per cent in Sawai Madhopur tehsil by 2001 because of widespread use of diesel-operated pumps on the wells. The increase in yield per hectare of dwarf high-yielding variety of wheat and mustard—the principal cash crops—justified the high expense on diesel oil for operating the pumps.

The irrigated fields on which vegetables and fruits are grown, are heavily manured, intensively cultivated and are also surrounded by 2 to 3 feet high mud walls for protection against dry summer winds, soil erosion and damage by animals. In case of tanks, both the areas below them and those in their beds, which become dry during the dry season, are cultivated.

In 1961, however, the district was twice its present size. It had an area of 10,000 sq km and a population of just over one million. Karauli and Hindaun sub-divisions of the district were constituted into a separate district during the 1980s. It is much more compact now than it was in 1961. It would take me six hours by train to reach Hindaun and a similar time to reach Karauli: four hours by train and up to two hours by jeep. It would take up to seven hours to reach the tehsil (now district) headquarters town Dausa, located about 100 miles north of Sawai Madhopur. Dausa was closer to Jaipur than to Sawai Madhopur.

It was convenient to tour the district by road during January to June when the Banas would be crossed by jeep. In the rainy season, the roads were so bad that one tehsil headquarters of Sawai Madhopur sub-division and most of those of the other sub-divisions were almost unapproachable.

I visited Dausa only twice during my entire stay in Sawai Madhopur: once at the time of panchayat elections in January 1961 and again on general elections of 1962. The first visit was to get a feel of the district and see the arrangements for the elections. The second was to reassure myself that the arrangements for the general elections had been made strictly in accordance with the instructions issued by the Chief Electoral Officer. I was somewhat surprised to find that in contrast to the other tehsils, where most of the farmers were Meenas, in Dausa, they were Gujjars and Jats. They could become violent if any officer tried to interfere with the decisions of their caste panchayats. I was lucky that both elections went off peacefully and there was no untoward incident anywhere. My successor was not so lucky, however. There was some violence in Dausa. He was blamed for not being able to prevent it and was transferred soon after the elections. Such transfers, rare in those days in Rajasthan, are perhaps more frequent now.

The People

More than 90 per cent of the population of Sawai Madhopur was rural in 1961. The proportion was reduced to 83 per cent in 1991. For most of it, agriculture was the principal or secondary means of livelihood. The principal castes were (and are) the Meenas, the Malis, the Jats and the Gujjars among the cultivators and the Jatavas (Chamars) among the Scheduled Castes (SCs). Sawai Madhopur is often called a Meena district because the Meenas constitute majority of the cultivators in it. They and the Jats are classic, dryland farmers. The Malis, originally vegetable growers, specialize in intensive cultivation of irrigated lands in which they produce wheat, mustard, sugarcane, vegetable and fruits (guava, papaya and banana). The Gujjars are also dry land farmers. But, their inclination is towards pastoral pursuits; they depend mainly on sale of milk of cattle and meat of sheep and goat that they graze in the forests.

The Jatavas, called Chamars earlier, are petty cultivators-cum-agricultural or non-agricultural labourers. Large numbers of them used to migrate until the mid-1950s to forests of Madhya Pradesh during the dry season to make wood charcoal there. But, the migration had stopped by the end of the 1950s. Most of the rural Jatavas had become cultivators-cum-labourers. They had been allotted small plots of land for cultivation which had become available after the abolition of *jagirdari.* They supplemented their income from cultivation with working as agricultural labourers or as workers on construction works located at short distances (up to 19 km) of their villages. In a bid to raise their ritual and social status, they had stopped their traditional practices of lifting dead cattle, flaying their hides and eating their meat. Large numbers among them had become vegetarians. The Jatavas of the hamlet that I had selected for my study were mainly cultivators-cum-labourers. Most of those whom my wife studied, worked as unskilled workers for contractors for the factory because their village was located close to the factory, or in the factory itself.

Employees in the factory had much higher incomes than others, and this was reflected in their more diversified and urbanized consumption. Consumption of milk, vegetables, fruits, meat, sugar, tea and oil was much higher among them than other villagers. One reason for this was that they bought most of their food, whereas the farmers produced most of it themselves. The educated sons of factory workers wore western style clothes (bush shirts and trousers) outside their homes and had become quite assertive of their rights and privileges, such as award by the Government of Rajasthan of scholarships for attending schools and colleges, reservations of jobs in government service, and of seats in the state legislature and the parliament for them. Some of them had become clerks and school teachers and many more were aspiring to get such white-collar jobs.

The Meenas, who were classified as a Scheduled Tribe (ST), were also entitled to these privileges. But they rarely mentioned them in our discussions with them because the privileges meant little to them. They were much more interested in the opportunities for employment on various construction works, located within cycling distance of their villages, which had opened up since the mid-1950s. In the Meena village, located closest (4 km) to Sawai Madhopur railway station, which we had selected for study, one or more young men from every household worked on public works, which included periodic repair of the road connecting the village with the railway station and keeping the railway station and the double line track of the Delhi-Mumbai railway line and the metre gauge railway line to Jaipur in good repair. Wages from labour on these works provided a useful supplement to their meagre income from agriculture.

The Period

Institutional and Socio-economic Reforms, Development Programmes and Social Changes

The two years (1960–62) of our stay in the districts came towards the end of the Nehru era. During the 1950s the country had enjoyed political stability, after the trauma of the partition of former British India into India and Pakistan in 1947. Political integration of the country was achieved between 1946 and 1948 through accession of almost 600 former princely states to the Indian Union. Organization of cadres of all-India, central and state services during 1948–49 provided the administrative infrastructure for orderly government and social and economic progress.

The decade of the 1950s was also a period of major institutional, political and social reforms and steady economic growth. The Constitution of India, which provided for parliamentary democracy and separation of the legislative, executive and judicial wings of government, was adopted in January 1950. It was followed by establishment in March 1952 of an elected, bicameral parliament at the centre and legislative assemblies in all the states. Orderly and efficient conduct of the election in 1952 as well as the two that followed it in 1957 and 1962 had demonstrated to the world, India's capacity to conduct this major operation in the democratic process peacefully and efficiently despite the handicaps of extreme poverty and low literacy of its predominantly rural electorate.

Among the socio-economic reforms, abolition of *zamindari* and *jagirdari*[3] was perhaps the most important. Others related to statutory abolition of untouchability, and special measures for uplift of the SCs, STs and OBCs. Rapid economic development and social change were perceived to be the most important national goals to be achieved through national development plans. Two Five-Year Plans had been implemented during the 1950s and the Third Plan (1961–66) was launched in April 1961.

Rajasthan was among the states, most affected by the political changes and social and economic reforms. It had been formed in 1948–49 by integration of about 20 former princely states and the British administered district of Ajmer. This was followed by organization of cadres of the IAS, the Rajasthan Administrative Service (RAS) and various technical or developmental services. The services were manned at the beginning almost exclusively by officers of former princely states, who had the qualifications and experience needed for absorption in the services. Even in the early 1960s most of the officers in many services belonged to this category. The senior-most positions in all the services—almost 20 per cent in the IAS—were occupied by them. Their number and proportion in the services would go down rapidly, however, during the 1950s as a result of their retirement and increase in number of young direct recruits to the services.

The principal political and socio-economic reforms, and development programmes undertaken in Rajasthan during the 1950s, were the following:

(i) establishment of the state legislature followed by orderly and peaceful conduct of the general elections in 1952 and 1957;
(ii) abolition of *jagirdari* which had been the dominant system of land tenure in former princely states;
(iii) establishment of village panchayats in the early 1950s after elections based on the principle of adult suffrage, and of nyaya (judicial) panchayats. The village (or multi-village) panchayats became part of the 3-tier structure of PRIs from October 1959; and
(iv) implementation of the community development and other rural development programmes.

Abolition of *jagirdari* was accompanied by conferment of full and heritage rights in cultivated land on the actual cultivators. Furthermore, large areas of cultivable lands, which had been retained by the Jagirdars as their *khud-kasht* (self-cultivation) or *shikar* (hunting preserve) lands, became available for allotment to the landless, belonging mainly to the SCs or the artisans. The area which a Jagirdar could retain for self-cultivation was limited by ceiling on it.

The village panchayats were entrusted with important administrative and developmental functions, as also the right to levy taxes and other duties. They also had responsibility for management of the common lands of the village, which included woodlots, pastures and other uncultivated lands and the small but very valuable area on which the village *abadi* (inhabited area) stood and that reserved for extension of the *abadi* in future. Their responsibilities related to maintenance of sanitation within the villages, periodic repair of village tanks and approach roads. They had responsibility also of construction or repair of drinking water wells, construction of buildings for schools, *panchayat ghars* (building in which the panchayats met), and offices of cooperative societies. They had to make contributions towards construction of these works to match the grants given by the state government or to undertake the construction with their own funds. This role became very important under the community development programme through which large grants became available for construction of the works from the state government. The panchayats were expected to make matching contribution in money, labour and locally available materials. The three high castes, namely, Brahmin, Rajput and Mahajan (traders), contributed money where as the contributions of the farmers and the SCs were in labour or locally available materials.

The judicial panchayats had powers of hearing and deciding complaints about petty crimes, intra-family quarrels and disputes relating to land or other property among the villagers. Appeals against their decisions could be made to the law courts or to the Collector.

The principal effect of the community development programme, launched in 1953, was to extend to the villages a network of developmental and welfare services, provided either by the government itself or by institutions like the cooperatives. Extension services for agriculture, animal husbandry, cottage industries and handicrafts, veterinary services, primary and secondary schools and primary health centres were the principal services/facilities provided by the state government. The government also gave grants for construction or repair of roads, reclamation of wastelands, construction/repair/improvement of drinking water sources (wells and tanks) and land improvement measures. Short and medium-term credit, supplies of improved seed, chemical fertilizers and other inputs of improved agriculture and facilities for marketing and processing the crops were provided by cooperative institutions. The community development and other programmes also provided funds for welfare of the disadvantaged sections of the rural community, particularly the SCs, STs and women.

Implementation of development programmes and extension of basic services to the rural people had been started by the state government immediately after the formation of Rajasthan. The process received great impetus, however, with the start of the community development programme. By the end of the1950s the network of services was almost complete. The 1960s and later decades would see further extension of the network, improvement in functioning of some services and provision of specialized services relating especially to agriculture.

Political Stability

The background to this steady progress and emphasis on implementation of development programmes was provided by political stability under the leadership of Shri M.L. Sukhadia, who was the Chief Minister of Rajasthan during most of the 1950s and the 1960s. He and the Chief Secretary, Shri Mehta, led an administration marked by stability and progress in all directions.

These, in turn major factors in fostering among all concerned—ministers, legislators, officials and the people—the feeling of belonging to Rajasthan, instead of to the princely states of which they had been officials or subjects earlier. This was perhaps the greatest achievement of the two men.

I cannot help recalling a remark made to me during his visit to Sawai Madhopur by Shri Barkatullah Khan, then Minister of Forests (and Chief Minister in the early 1970s) which showed the intensity of the parochial feelings among the older residents of former states. He was a native of Jodhpur and had gone to live in Jaipur only after he joined the Rajasthan cabinet. He told me that his old mother had never visited him in Jaipur because she considered it to be a city of a ruler, Sawai Man Singh I, who had betrayed the Rajput cause by giving his sister in marriage to the Mughal emperor, Akbar. The rulers of Jodhpur who had submitted to the emperor much later considered themselves superior to them. Those of Udaipur considered themselves superior to all others because their forebear—Rana Pratap—had never submitted to the emperor.

Village Studies

Our 20 months in Sawai Madhopur were uneventful. My work at the office was quite light and I had plenty of time to devote to study of three villages located 3 to 8 km from my office which I had selected for the purpose of study. My wife joined me in the studies when she saw abject poverty of the Meena women in one village.

They would thank their stars if they could get enough cereals to eat through the year and avoid hunger during the lean season (July-September) before the monsoon season crop of sorghum or millet was harvested. They could not afford to keep milch animals—buffaloes to provide milk for their children or themselves. They worked hard in the fields; they did more work in the fields than the men. They bathed in the pond located next to the village in which their livestock bathed also. They were too poor to afford use of soap or hair oil. As a result, they were not much cleaner after the bath, than they were before it. They neglected their children and household duties because they were busy in the fields. As a result, infant and maternal mortality was so high that they could never think of family planning.

There had been dramatic change in these respects by 2001. Now, they bathed in two wells located in the village, or with water which is piped in many houses. They can afford to drink water which is piped in many houses. They can afford to drink milk and have vegetables and fruits as part of their diet. Maternal and child mortality has gone down so much that many couples in the reproductive age group practise family planning. Advice for it is given by an auxiliary nurse midwife living in a village or by nurses in a multi-facility hospital with 40 beds located in a suburb of Maantown.

During my 20-month stay in the district, I had to conduct election to the panchayats based on adult suffrage in January 1961 and the general elections of March 1962. Detailed instructions for conducting the elections were given by the Chief Electoral Officer in Jaipur. The polls were peaceful. We were surprised so see that the villagers—both men and women—came out in large numbers, dressed in their best clothes and singing and dancing, to exercise their votes for election of members of the panchayats. But, few people bothered to vote for elections of the MLAs and MPs. The villagers concluded, correctly, that the decisions of members of village panchayats would affect their welfare far more than those of MLAs or MPs. Jaipur was 130 km away and Delhi might as well be in an another country as far as they were concerned.

Visit of Queen Elizabeth II and Prince Philip Mountbatten

The only other notable event of my stay was the visit of Queen Elizabeth II and her husband Prince Philip Mountbatten for a tiger shoot in the forest of the Ranthambhore Game Sanctuary. Invitation for the visit had been extended by the former Maharaja of Jaipur, without reference to but with the concurrence of the governments of Rajasthan and India. All arrangements for the stay of the royal couple and the shoot were made also by the Maharaja. The royal couple went away satisfied because the Duke shot a tiger and his secretary shot a tigress. My only contribution to the visit was to make foolproof arrangements for their security. I had to relocate about 40 shops located at the junction station where the railway lines connecting Sawai Madhopur with Mumbai and Jaipur met. This mini-market of 40 odd shops in 1961 had about 800 shops in 2001. Plots for location of additional shops were sold for later by the Nagar Palika (Municipal Committee) of Maantown at prices which made a handsome contribution to their budgets.

One of the secrets of Shri Sukhadia's success as a Chief Minister was that he did not interfere with day-to-day work of the Collectors. During my 20-month stay in Sawai Madhopur, I received only one telephone call from him at the time of a strike by workers in the cement factory. He enquired whether everything was under control. When I replied that it was, he said no more.

Shri Mehta was superb as a trainer of young recruits to the service. Most of them belonged to other states, viz., Uttar Pradesh, Punjab, Tamil Nadu or West Bengal. Yet, by the time they had finished their one-year probation, and were posted to the secretariat or a district, they would forget their native states and would have a feeling of belonging to Rajasthan.

Training of IAS Officers

New Recruits as Bridegrooms

The new recruits would be treated like bridegrooms at the welcome dinner given by senior officers which include Secretaries and Deputy Secretaries to various departments of the government, the Commissioner, the Collector, the Deputy Collectors, and the City Magistrate of Jaipur. Before the dinner, they would be introduced to the senior officers including the Chief Secretary. After the dinner they would be regaled with music by the best musicians of Jaipur. On their next day, they would call on the Chief Secretary and senior officers in the secretariat as well as the Commissioner, the Collector and the City Magistrate of Jaipur. They would not meet them again until after their nine-month training in a district when they would come back to Jaipur for their first posting in the secretariat but preferably in a district as Assistant Collector or Sub-Divisional Magistrate. They would be posted to the district in which they had been trained, unless they had any problems in staying in a district too far from Jaipur.

Annual Conferences of Collectors and Commissioners

These conferences, which were held in March, were another occasion when all the Collectors, Commissioners and many Secretaries and Deputy Secretaries would met young officers. The conference would be inaugurated by the Chief Minister and addressed by the Ministers of Planning and Development, Finance, Health, Education and Welfare. Every Collector had to make a presentation of about one hour to explain working of development programmes in his/her district and the problems that he/she faced. The Ministers and Secretaries and Heads of Department would take measures to solve the problems. In both evenings of these meetings, there would be dinner parties attended by the Chief Secretary and other senior officers stationed in Jaipur, besides the Collectors and Commissioners. The dinner meetings were held invariably in some historic buildings, the architecture of which was of particular interest for the invitees.

Shri Mehta would compare favourably with any British officer of the ICS in his capacity for training of young officers. Whenever he was in Jaipur, about 20 young officers posted in the secretariat or visiting Jaipur would gather at his home in the evening. He would take two drinks (no more) over 2 to 2.5 hours at which he would be joined by the young officers present. The young officers would seek his advice on any problems that they faced. The subjects discussed ranged over a wide area, even personal problems that they faced would be discussed also. However, even the gossip was never malicious.

The 'training' given by Shri Mehta through these evening meetings has been so effective that two officers of the cadre have held posts of Secretary to the Government of India with much distinction. One went on to become the Governor of Tamil Nadu, while the other was until recently the Ambassador of India to the United States. The number of those who went on to become chairmen or directors of public sector undertakings after serving as secretaries to the Government of India would be two dozen or more.

Notes

1. The institute, now called the National Institute of Rural Development, is located in Rajendra Nagar, Hyderabad in Andhra Pradesh.
2. A committee to evaluate progress of Community Development and National Extension Service Programme, Ministry of Community Development and Cooperation, New Delhi, 1957.
3. Jagirdars in former princely states were intermediary tenure holders. Their principal duties included collection of land revenue from the tenant-farmers, preservation of law and order and other duties specified by the prince. A large proportion of the land revenue had to be deposited by them into the treasury of the state.

11 R.S. KUMAT

The Flood

It was *kawwali* night. On the occasion of Urs fair in Ajmer, held in the memory of Sufi Saint Khwaja Moinuddin Chishti, *kawwals* (devotional singers) come from near and far places and sing *kawwalis* in the Dargah (the religious place where the tomb of Khwaja Moinuddin Chishti lies). They also hold public and private sessions. The district administration had arranged a public function of *kawwali* on the evening of 17 July, 1976 and famous kawwals gave their performance almost throughout the night. In the early hours of 18 July, after the *kawwali* programme was over, the S.P. (Superintendent of Police) and myself took a round of the Dargah bazar where the mas Friday prayer would take place next morning to look at the arrangements and ensure that everything was set for the next day. At about 5 o'clock in the morning I went to bed and just after two hours, got up to see that it had started raining.

It was the month of rains and it was not unusual to have rains. Normally such rains last for about an hour or so and as the rains started, one hoped that the temperature would cool down and weather would become fine for the *namaz* (mass prayer), which would take place at 2.00 p.m. However, the rains did not stop; on the contrary the intensity increased and by about 10 o'clock a number of phone calls started coming in with a message that certain low lying areas had been flooded and there was lot of water everywhere. The number of telephone calls started going up and even before I could organize the relief parties, the phone went out of order. I tried to contact the S.P. through wireless, only to know that even his house had been flooded.

Other staff could not move out because of rains and whoever had tried to take out his vehicle, got stuck in the waters gushing through the roads.

Communicational Impediments

Realizing that contact through phone or wireless was not possible, I moved out myself in a jeep, but even the jeep could not negotiate through the flood waters on the road. Hence, I got down and looked for a heavy vehicle. A truck passed through that side and I asked its driver to take me to the telephone exchange. Moving in this truck and negotiating my way to the telephone exchange, I realized the immensity of the situation and therefore contacted Army authorities and State headquarters to seek help. It however came to notice later that no help from outside was possible because the road and rail communications had been damaged and no vehicular traffic could come to Ajmer except from Jaipur side.

Having contacted the State capital, I went to the Ana Sagar, the historic lake of Ajmer where from emerges the Luni river, carrier of large quantities of water through the desert and ending in the Rann of Kutch. Not surprisingly, Luni was overflowing and all its surplus water was moving through a small *nala* across the city. The capacity of the *nala* had been greatly reduced as a result of population pressure and lack of annual cleaning arrangements. The original size of the *nala* had been reduced by making it a *pucca nala* and the area so reclaimed was used for developing colonies. This *nala* was good enough to carry only the normal sewage, and not the flood waters which were unprecedented.

The Devastating Downpour

In the living memory of the people, this was the first ever flood Ajmer had experienced and the main reason was the downpour of about 275 mm. (11 inches) in three hours between 7.00 a.m. and 10.00 a.m. whereas the average annual rainfall for the city was only 350 mm (14 inches). It naturally meant that at any time the normal precipitation would not be more than 50 mm to 75 mm (2 to 3 inches) and the *nala* was sufficient to carry that much water. But now the precipitation was so intense that no drain could carry this amount of water. On the one hand the rainfall had not yet stopped and on the other the Ana Sagar was releasing as much as 3,000 cusecs of water. All the colonies that had been constructed in the downstream of the *nala* experienced heavy flood and people had five to six feet of water in their houses and all their belongings were either swept away or damaged and *kutcha* houses were completely washed away. Immediate need was to rescue the people and take them to safe shelters.

Normal population of Ajmer at that time was around 3.5 lacs and it increased then by about another 2 lacs as a result of pilgrims coming for the Urs, from all over India and neighbouring countries like Pakistan. The

Dargah of Khwaja Moinuddin Chishti is located in a most congested place right at the foothill of the Taragarh fort, the towering feature of Ajmer as a part of the Aravalis. It is difficult to accommodate this increased population in that area. Almost all the pilgrims who come by rail make their own stay arrangement, but those who come by chartered buses, have to be provided with a parking place and other sanitary facilities. Ajmer is surrounded from all sides by hills and as such the nearest place that the administration could locate was on the banks of the Ana Sagar. In the previous ten years, Ana Sagar never got filled to its capacity and no wonder, the upper reaches of the Sagar were considered as a safe place for parking and provision of camp facilities for the pilgrims. This place, popularly known as Vishram Sthal had more than 400 buses parked in this area and the pilgrims would normally keep their belongings in the buses and sleep in the shelters near and around it, while during the day, they went to the Dargah for paying their homage. Fortunately, the rains took place in the morning and so almost all pilgrims had left the buses for safe place apprehending the danger of increased waters in the lake, but the buses could not move out and about 100 buses got submerged in the flooded Ana Sagar. Thus, the emergency for rescue and relief had been created both for the normal population living in the town and in the downstream of the nala sa also the pilgrims in Vishram Sthal. In the Dargah bazar area, water coming from the hills passes through the Nala Bazar (the original nala or drain for carrying flood waters had become a bazar and so named as Nala Bazar) and as the velocity was very high, some people were swept away. The local people however rescued them through ropes, etc.

At Vishram Sthal the buses had been submerged, but their was no casualty and all the people had taken shelter in the upper reaches of the Vishram Sthal. The bus owners had engaged some trucks to pull the buses out of waters. This course was a matter which could take time and accordingly I decided to leave that spot and go to the area in the downstream of the nala carrying the surplus water of Ana Sagar. On the way, I met the Additional S.P. and ADM (Additional District Magistrate). They were trying to do whatever little they could on their own, but the organized effort could not be started because of lack of communications. Only by about 12.00 noon we got organized and took a round of the area. The most affected area was a slum known as Jadugar Basti. Most of its inhabitants were employees of the Railway workshop. Their houses and belongings had been completely washed away, but fortunately there was no casualty in this basti. Later, as we took stock of the casualty situation, we found that only three persons had died as a result of being swept away in a *nala* or due to house collapse. The major problem now was the provision of shelter and food.

Managing Relief through Concerned Action

Finding that the area of operation was near Jadugar Basti, we all operated from the office of Ajanta Cinema which was the nearest point from the *basti* and the only place where we got a telephone in working order. Parties were sent to different areas for reconnaissance and provisions for food. We purchased some dry ration and got it distributed. The local inhabitants had also prepared food and brought it for distribution to the flood affected families. Soon they found that whatever they had brought was precious little and hence were being mobbed. It was also evident that people were distributing food items time and again in certain areas, while in some other areas none had visited. We, therefore, decided to coordinate all the private relief efforts and asked all the people to bring their food articles to a central place from where they would be directed by the district administration for distribution. In all about 25,000 people had been affected and so nearby schools, *dharamshalas* and some houses constructed by the Rajasthan Housing Board were occupied. Besides, kitchens were opened for preparing food.

On 18 July, we could only distribute dry ration, coordinate activities of the voluntary agencies and provide immediate shelter. Other necessary measures like disconnecting of power, lest there should be short-circuiting and cases of electrocution, and deployment of police force to keep a watch throughout the night, were taken. Moreover, full-scale measures were planned from the morning of 19 July, onwards.

On the second day we shifted our office to the nearest Railway building which was normally used for arranging club activities, and opened our camp office for relief operations. The City Magistrate was made incharge of the entire affair and all voluntary agencies and philanthropic groups were requested not to distribute any article directly to the people. They were asked either to deposit the articles if these were in small quantity or distribute them under the guidance and supervision of the district administration. This was done mainly to avoid overlapping and confusion. The voluntary agencies also felt happy that they were able to reach the needy areas and their effort was not being wasted.

We opened government kitchens in different localities. However, we found to our dismay that the flood-affected families were coming to the kitchen only to receive ready-made food and the kitchen managers were finding it difficult to feed two to three thousand persons at a time. The flood-affected people were requested to help in preparing the food, but they declined to help for they did not consider it was a part of their duty; instead, in their view the government was duty-bound to provide everything. I took a round of the kitchens and found that the flood-affected people were sitting and waiting for the food as if they were the guests and were complaining whenever they did not get the food in time. I had no alternative but to ask them firmly and politely to provide help in cooking or else they would not get the food. Some people refused and even tried to question my decision, but persuasion and arousing of their self-respect helped ease the situation. I exhorted them not to rely on charity and instead earn their bread in this calamity by joining hands. A direct talk with the people helped the situation and we could manage the kitchens without employing extra labour. This arrangement continued for about a week and then we put the people on their own and withdrew the relief arrangements gradually. They needed help in providing clothing, utensils, food and shelter. All this had to be planned quickly and the administration had to normalize the situation so that the people did not remain on charity for long.

The response of philanthropic institutions was substantial and we received donations in cash and kind from all quarters. The donations in kind were not kept in Government store. We encouraged the voluntary agencies to distribute the articles with their own hands under our supervision. This promoted motivation and confidence among the voluntary agencies for they could see that whatever had been donated by them was reaching the needy hand and was not being stored in the government stores. Full lists of affected families with notings of assistance provided by each voluntary agency helped us to ensure equitable distribution of articles.

The government assistance was limited to food ration, some cash assistance and temporary shelter. There was no provision for clothing, utensils, blankets, etc. This could be done only through voluntary agencies and it came in good measure. This was further fully proved in the unprecedented floods of Jaipur in 1981. I had the opportunity of organizing voluntary effort in that critical situation as well and the experience of Ajmer stood in good stead. Tremendous response of voluntary agencies was responsible for providing permanent shelter, rehabilitation and reclamation of flooded agricultural land. This could not have been achieved by mere government effort.

Arranging Rehabilitation

Timely relief was not enough and steps were needed for permanent rehabilitation. An assurance against repetition of similar calamity was called for, as unfounded rumours three days after floods created panic and all began to run for safe places. The basic problem of the flood affected victims was that they were living in *katcha* houses and could not have permanent houses for various reasons, namely (a) land on which they were squatting was not their own, (b) it was too congested to accommodate all of them, and yet none wanted to move out of that area, (c) lack of finance in low income groups, (d) reluctance even to replan and regroup the houses in the existing locality. This had been experienced even when the programme of slum improvement was launched much before floods and the inhabitants were asked to have a replanned locality.

Floods enabled us to acquire some additional land and replace the old sites. Effort was made to adjust all the affected people in the same locality by giving to each family 50 sq yds plots. Finance for making *pucca* houses was obtained from Life Insurance Corporation and the Urban Improvement Trust was involved in providing all the necessary facilities like road, drains, water and electricity. Plans were prepared after consultation with the inhabitants, and the development of the *bastis* was initiated. This was not a small effort by any means, because even one person in the locality could hinder the entire development. Besides persuasion, use of local leaders was made to expedite the work and the recalcitrants were dealt with sternly. This resulted not only in rehabilitation, but also in the improvement of slum areas. Six months earlier, efforts made to replan the houses in these very slums had failed. But the floods provided a blessing in disguise and facilitated us to replan the houses in the slums. The experience gained here was used later in replanning the *katchi bastis* of Jaipur.

The Moral

The story of handling this calamity holds out some important lessons, which can be summarized as follows:

1. When communications fail in a crisis situation, it is better to move out and collect all those who are available for organizing the effort.
2. Government resources are not enough to handle a calamity and therefore voluntary support should be encouraged and properly directed.

3. Keeping up the morale of affected families during the crisis is a requisite to effective handling of a crisis.
4. Calamities bring blessings in disguise and one should always see the opportunity to seize the challenge.

The District Collector has multifarious duties and is expected to do everything under the Sun but his office attains crucial importance in times of crisis. It is a great challenge and a time of real test of leadership. It is not a routine job, nor are there precedents or blue books to tackle crises. One has to rely on one's own resourcefulness, but more than that, on the cooperation from colleagues, political leaders and people at large. The test of leadership lies in the measure of cooperation the Collector can obtain from the various sections of society.

12 KUSUM PRASAD

A Certain Turbulence

An enduring memory of Tonk is that of two cobras who kindly shared the garden of my decrepit house on the hilltop, their hoods raised enquiringly, swivelling this way and that like periscopes, or sunning themselves on the steps to the house but slithering away politely when any one approached, for all the world like pet dogs. They were company to me in that otherwise empty house—my husband and daughters being back in Delhi. In retrospect it seems that I must have frequently discussed with them, the development of the fifteen eventful months I spent in Tonk.

It seems to me that no other fifteen months in my or anybody else's life held so much experience. Anything that could possibly happen, happened: State-wide government servant's strike, students unrest, famine, industrial unrest and peculiar to Tonk, floods hard on the heels of draught and communal tensions erupting into a mini riot! To my jaundiced mind it also seemed that Tonk was the major battlefield for the faction fights for supremacy within the ruling party. Political interests were so tangled that it was impossible to unravel them and try to anticipate which way any political leader would pull in any situation. God, politics, people, all conspired to keep the cauldron that was Tonk, boiling.

Things were not improved by the local telephone system that was controlled from a central exchange where the operators with their inadequate knowledge of any national language such as Hindi or English, freely listened to all incoming conversations and served as misinformation bureaus based upon their peculiar understanding of anything they had heard. The town of Tonk always had the most far-fetched information on any local development which was built upon and embroidered in such a manner that it required the utmost self-confidence (not always available to the battered Collector that was me) to continue to assert the facts as I knew them directly from official sources.

In Search of Action

In retrospect, the government servants' strike was a cake walk. Long boring days, spent in the empty collectorate with my personal staff surreptitiously attending to my needs. There was the daily ritual of slogan-shouting, processions, and the employees ritually offering themselves for arrest and our equally formal arrests at the front gate of the collectorate and immediate release at the back. This was good so far as the district went, but frustrating both for the state government as well as the state-level leaders of the agitation, nothing was happening: Papers elsewhere were screaming of *lathi* charges, hundreds in jail, fasts unto death, and in Tonk nothing!

The Chief Secretary, S.L. Khurana, made it a habit of calling me up after midnight every day and exhorting me to do something. Everyone's patience finally ran out and one fine day, agitators from other districts congregated in Tonk and there were fiery speeches, huge, processions, and a shower of stones! I struck lucky! The stone aimed at me knocked out a vociferous reporter, who till then was blaming me, that is the administration, for the 'contrived' riot. Thereafter, he was a staunch supporter of the administration.

Well, that day we had a *lathi*-charge that must have pleased all concerned and proper arrests, and the Chief Secretary rang up in the wee hours as usual and congratulated me. The nightly amazed query of the Chief Secretary, "Good Lord, Kusum, you weren't sleeping, were you?" still rankles. "I know Collectors are on duty round the clock, nevertheless..."

During the employees strike itself, we celebrated Independence Day. The usual pageants and processions were not possible. So the police brought out their old tattered bagpipes, drums in marching files and in tarnished, ragged cloaks, staged a rather doleful musical march-past to the jeers of the striking employees and pelting rain. The form had been maintained.

Allah Noor, my driver, really extended himself on these occasions. He would polish up the jeep and hang it with wreaths of leaves and flowers and many coloured bunting and make a slow and steady progress through the town to the parade ground with me feeling like an exposed and reluctant, and on this occasion, bedraggled bridegroom in the rain! (I wonder now why I did not resort to an umbrella—possibly for fear of looking even more like a bridegroom!)

Fury of the Flood

And then the heavens opened and the rains came and retaining walls of villages tanks, reservoirs and dams started popping like corks from fizzing champagne bottles all over the district. This kind of things is not too bad unless habitated areas are inundated. For one thing the area gets flood relief and you can mend all the walls whether affected by floods or not; affected families get individual relief, employment is provided on local works and the inundation prepares the land beautifully for the September sowing of crop such as gram and mustard—come January you have a bumper harvest. Flood or famine (or more correctly, the declaration thereof) is much in demand in a district, provided of course, no disasters occur and lives are not lost.

We came perilously close to disaster however, on one side the Uniara Dam threatened to give way and on the other, the old hardy bridge over the river Banas, which spanned the State highway linking Jaipur to Kota and on to Bombay, sagged on its piles, and was almost washed away.

The Uniara Dam outside Aligarh (yes, in Rajasthan) town and beside the Uniara Fort on a hill, was the largest in the district. Suddenly one morning, it developed breaches and instantly the Bundi Highway was under several feet of water which was moving rapidly towards Aligarh. Ajit Singh, the Assistant Engineer, Irrigation, was already there, buttressing the embankments with sand bags when Laxman Singh, the Superintendent of Police and I, set out on one and a half hour journey (under normal conditions) to the dam. The road and the surrounding countryside was a swirling sea of water. It was a miracle that our jeeps did not get washed off the road and embedded in the clay soil of the countryside. On reaching, we found the local police station in two feet of water. On the embankment, the labour force had done what they could. The last sand-bag had been placed and everyone had retreated to the Uniara Fort on the hill. There was just the weakened embankment, unending sheets of water, torrential rain, Ajit Singh, Laxman Singh, I and four or five others. It felt very lonely up there on the embankment. It was clear there was nothing further we could do. The breaches had been shored up for the moment; but it was touch and go whether the embankment would hold. Clearly there was nothing more for us but to get away while the going was good, which we did, except for Ajit Singh, who, with the foolhardy devotion of a mother, wanted to stay with the embankment "just a little longer" and would not be persuaded. We left with the vision of the tall young Sikh, alone in the deluge on that sheet of water; and almost rowed back to Tonk. The police station was now entirely under water—water was lapping our knees in the two jeeps and it could only have been some personal magnetism which kept the jeeps on the road and not overturned in the lakes of washed away land on either side.

One of the most difficult things that I ever had to do, was to telephone Ajit's wife to say that he had not returned with us but would follow. Fortunately, all remained well and Ajit returned to his plump and laughing wife who continued to entertain us, as always, with jokes and the choicest Punjabi food.

There was no shoring up that was possible for the ancient bridge over the Banas. It would either hold, or not, as God and the river waters below willed it. On the day however, when we battled to maintain our balance on its wildly swinging structure just two feet above the rising water, all of us, with one breath, cursed the state government for never having sanctioned the requisite funds for the replacement of this ancient relic, although in principle, the scheme had been sanctioned several years ago. One almost hoped that the bridge would go so that a new one could be constructed. In our anger and despair we were unmindful of the prospect of being cut off from the north completely. Looking back, I concede that my troubles, though legion, were mostly little ones. The bridge not only held but for all I know still exists to strike terror into the hearts of my successors.

One lingering memory of those days is that of a young friend, who along with her small daughter chose to break journey in Tonk and stay with me rather than continue the dangerous trip to Kota. There she would be, snug and dry in my hilltop home which I seldom used except to sleep in, if that, when I returned tired, hungry, despairing and drenched, and her opening remark invariably was "Kusum Didi, will I be safe?"

A late fallout of the flood was hilarious misunderstanding with a minor minion of the state government in the Secretariat at Jaipur, who found it impossible to understand why the irrigated crop in these areas failed the following spring for shortage of water! Never having been in the field, he failed to realize that floods break the retaining walls of reservoirs, and water flows away—it is not storable for use later!

A Concern for Identity

The city of Tonk derives its name from that of Tonkra Brahmins but was ceded by the British to the Pindaris for services rendered, and this paradox continues in a state of constant internal confrontation. The Hindus are aggressively Hindu with caste marks, beads, and taboos as to eating and drinking. The Muslims, similarly aggressive, sport, goatee beards, pathan hats and *sherwanis*. The Muslims have fallen on bad days, princely privileges of many of them having been abolished. They own huge ruined villas with no incomes to support them, or are rickshaw-pullers, *bidi* makers and such; but in the evening they all sport jasmine *gajras* on their wrists and *ittar* behind their ears. The Hindus are the traders, the owners of the rickshaws and the bidi factories. There is thus an economic, historical and cultural rift. The *Pindaries* had not endeared themselves to the locals. An honest administration has always to walk on the razor's edge of impartiality—but how many administrators are that demonstrably honest? Resultantly, the Muslims have an abiding sense of grievance. A shorthaired, modern, agnostic, married lady Collector living alone in the district and quite unmindful of the feminine modesties must have been an amazement and anathema to both communities. And thereby I achieved impartiality! I visited no religious places except to sight-see: I upset both the *mullahs* and the *pandits* by my heresies.

It was a continuing pain to me that women in large numbers came to me with their familial and social problems and I could do precious little to help them. The condition of the Muslim women was particularly pitiable—the protections given to them under their personal laws could only be enforced by the *mullahs* and *maulvis*, who were determined not to do so. My efforts at discussion and persuasion met stone walls. The Hindus were slightly better of because their personal laws had been amended and could be enforced by the courts of law. Besides, social pressure could be brought to bear upon the concerned persons who at least appear as 'enlightened'.

The ladies in any case were not interested in circuitous civil and social remedies. I was a woman and I enjoyed power, a *raja* in fact, I should understand and bring my power to bear upon an erring husband or cruel family and make them mend their ways! There was much muttering and caustic comment upon my unbelievable helplessness.

On Tenterhooks

The communal confrontation had us constantly on tenterhooks and people had all the time and inclination to get involved in every single issue. I recall the case of a Hindu girl of mature years who ran away to marry a Muslim teacher. The Hindus gathered in strength and canvassed every officer—the district education officer, the Superintendent of Police, the district health officer, the district forest officer and of course me—every time, me! The Muslims barricaded themselves in expectation of assault but would not surrender the newly wed bride.

And so I found myself surrounded by a large crowd in the garden of my house. I asked, reasonably, how they were concerned with the private lives of the boy and the girl. The crowd pushed forward a middle aged couple as the vociferous aunt and uncle of the girls. I enquired about parents and was told that the girl had been brought up by the aunt and uncle, the parents being dead. There was such a cacophony that I could barely hear myself think, and so more in self-defence than any considered plan of action, I stated that I was willing to discuss the matter with the girl's relatives but not the world in general and lapsed into silence. There was much consultation and confabulation, but finally the crowd melted away.

I asked the couple what they wanted and they said they wanted the girl back—consider the social stigma attached to them by the situation! I enquired and was told that the girl was not trained or competent to earn her living. What then did they plan to do with her, I asked? Were they hopeful of getting her remarried? This aspect of the situation had not occurred to them and not wishing to be landed with an unmarriageable niece for the rest of their lives, they also slipped away. And that was the end of that agitation.

Mini Riot

Our mini riot was another matter entirely. It was a second Saturday—much looked forward to off-day after a hectic month—and I was just settling down to a day of bridge and relaxation along with the Bandaris (the divisional forest officer and his wife) and Zameer Mia, a local teacher who made up the fourth in bridge and taught us billiards at the club, when there was a call from Dhabi, the Additional S.P. (the Superintendent of Police being away on leave). Some trouble had erupted around Barra Kuan in the main bazar. Dhabi feared that it was escalating. Our very small police force was distributed over the district, containing student unrest in Deoli and the industrial unrest in Malpur. There was nothing for it but to summon my jeep and proceed to Barra Kuan, not from the main bazar but from the back. There were just Allan Noor, the driver and I. Enroute we met a crowd of young men running towards Barra Kuan brandishing hockey sticks. I stopped them and enquired what they were up to. They said that the Hindus had attacked the Muslims and they were on their way to help their brethern. "Nonsense", I said, "No such thing had happened". I made them put their hockey sticks in my jeep and proceeded further—the crowd straggling after me. It was not that I felt courageous, but knew that this crowd of young men was afraid, not aggressive. It was always mutual fear, that led to these confrontations. At Barra Kuan, I found myself at the Muslim end of the melee. They immediately surrounded me, declared a temporary ceasefire so to speak, and ceremonially escorted me to the police party that was conducting holding operations between the two groups—providing a dividing line. Sixty odd constables keeping a crowd of several thousand people divided into two separate groups, not permitting them to mingle and exchange blows. The fact that from ten in the morning to six in the evening, the communities remained separate and did not break the meagre police cordon, is evidence that no one intended violence. They remained on either side shouting slogans and pelting stones. When verbal passions ran high, they named leaders of the opposing factions and described in graphic details what would be done to them.

Meanwhile, we had established general headquarters in a shop from where we telephoned Jaipur for police reinforcements. Rumours were rife, of people being stabbed to death, houses burnt and other atrocities, not in bazar, but elsewhere. Periodically when the showers of stones increased, leaders from both sides sought shelter in our and other neighbouring shops; then there would be a temporary lull. We were under severe pressure to open fire and disperse the crowd. I was new to this law and order situation and might have given such orders to the police had I been so advised by them, but Dhabi, the seasoned policeman that he was, kept his cool and kept the crowd contained until the evening when reinforcements arrived. By then everyone was tired out and hungry and dispersed in the face of armed police.

An impartial enquiry conducted by public men from outside the district assessed the total damage to 22 people having sustained minor injuries on account of stone throwing and Rs 5,000 worth of damage to buildings and property in the bazar.

The Political Drama

So far the situation had elements of a tragical force, but subsequently it took on sinister and malicious proportions. As outside armed police took charge of the town, politicians poured in from all directions, the rumour mills were in any case working overtime and everyone joined the fray for political gain, private revenue, pure sensationalism and countless mixed motives. Fear ruled the roost. Faces had been lost on that eventful Saturday and could only be regained by putting someone's head on the block, and whose could it possibly be except mine and Dhabis? We were really beleaguered.

The shops in the main bazar had necessarily to be closed on that Saturday and the following Sunday and then the trading community for some twisted logic of their own decided to go on indefinite *hartal* until amends were made. Expect what possible amends? Nothing very much had happened after all!

Obviously, the poor of Tonk who bought their daily provisions with their day's earnings would starve if shops remained closed. We therefore decided that the fair price and ration shops would have to remain open or suffer the punishment of having their licenses cancelled and enforced this order by giving each shop a police guard. This created a piquant situation because the leaders of the trading community who had instigated the *hartal*, were themselves in most cases, the license-holders of the fair price shops. Thus, while other shopkeepers lost out in the *hartal*, the leaders had a thriving business, though in this process, they lost credibility. Now, the other shopkeepers started looking for face-saving devices to enable them to open their shops. Finally, they prevailed upon a minister to come to Tonk to listen to their grievances, assure them of government protection and ritually ask them to open the bazar, which they did with evident relief.

The Tangled Web of Famine

Famine is another tangled web. In the district of western Rajasthan there is constant drought—cattle die and migrate and food and employment are scarce, while in eastern Rajasthan, the situation is not so bad. However, every time and rainfall is less than normal, any politician worth his salt ensures that his area is declared famine-stuck, for such a declaration would bring the benefits of famine works, food at subsidized rates, etc. That year in view of the straightened financial position of the state, the Chief Minister seemed determined not to declare famine unless genuinely called for. I was naive enough to believe that the government would be able to withstand pressure and in the face of shrewd advice to the contrary, continued to project the correct picture of my district. I made myself very unpopular and famine was, in any case, eventually declared, practically over my dead body.

As the famine works were set in motion, the Chief Minister decided to visit my district. Now started efforts to show the district administration of Tonk in a bad light, not because the district administration was disliked, but because it would reflect upon the Chief Minister who was facing heavy opposition from within his party, where different factions were angling for power. The local unit of the Food Corporation of India (FCI) was prevailed upon to slow down release of grain. This was easily handled. We merely showed the Assistant Manager of FCI various provisions of the Indian Penal Code read with the maintenance of the Essential Commodities Act and politely invited him to have a look at the jail. The Manager of the Tonk branch of a lead bank proved more recalcitrant. He continued to find excuses for not releasing the funds meant for payment of labour employed on the famine works. It would have gladdened many hearts, had the Chief Minister been faced with hundreds of labourers complaining of non-payment. Ash Karan Agarwal, my Additional Collector, discovered a little known provision in the Treasury Manual which enabled the Collector to take over a bank under certain conditions. I lost no time in serving notice on the bank which in turn immediately released the money. All ended well and the Chief Minister's visit passed off smoothly.

But I was verbally ticked off by the Finance Secretary on my next visit to Jaipur. Imagine threatening to take over a bank? Unheard of! How would I have managed it? I meekly replied that my bluff had not been called. The Chief Secretary, on the other hand, only laughed and refused to discuss the incident further. I was not always in trouble. There were comic interludes, fun and frolic and a great deal of satisfaction in working among the common people and in the beautiful verdant countryside.

Razia in Disguise?

There was the occasion when a small group in charge of a Moharram procession in a small town, took umbrage at some innocuous directions given by the Superintendent of Police, abandoned their tiny *tazia* in the middle of a small street and ran off to Jaipur to complain to the Chief Minister. In would have been laughable except that we were afraid that the half-starved cows wandering the street might take a bite from the gaily decorated *tazia* or a rickshaw collide with it. So we detailed four constables to guard it and sat around twiddling our thumbs and playing a waiting game. It is well known that *tazias* have to be buried within a certain period. Sure enough the complainants came back with a flea in their ears after four days and shamefacedly, picked up where they had left off.

It was great fun working for the common people. One of my brighter memories is the effort to revive the forgotten *Namdah* industry—beautifully embroidered rugs the sale of which I propagated in a small way, surprising my friends with gifts of these and then booking fresh orders. Mohan Mukerji, then Development Commissioner of the State, came on tour, saw and was conquered by the *Namdahs*, and was a great help in the revival of the industry which is now flourishing, though to my regret, the delicate embroidery has been dispensed with.

The people in the Tonk had built up all kinds of stories of me. How I, like a modern Razia Sultana was in the habit of roaming the streets in disguise (in *burkah*) wreaking vengeance on the hoarders and the bad characters, and personally conducting raids. Patterning, but regrettably untrue, except that the stories reflected favourably on the administration headed by me. I still meet up with such anecdotes retold to me with much embellishments about myself. So there is a kind of immortality after all.

My last memory of Tonk is of being ceremonially escorted out of the district on transfer, by the police, and of the tears running down the cheeks of the Station House Officer, Tonk as he saluted a goodbye. We had been through a lot together.

13 V.N. BAHADUR

Sticking the Neck Out

Like James Tod's *Annals and Antiquities of Rajasthan,* the two volumes of Philip Woodruff's *The Men Who Ruled India* were also cherished as a Collector's item for district officials, particularly in the initial independence days. These volumes still find a revered place on the book-shelves of the senior district officials' personal libraries along with the copy of the local gazetteer. Official dinners and farewell parties were often punctuated with an anecdote culled from these pages by careerists, who always hoped that at some time of their service tenure, they would go through similar travails and that some, modern Woodruff would write about their efforts in overcoming the built-in resistance in the system which has always been an important part of a district officer's functioning.

The Syndrome of Polyfunctionality

The administrative environment has today totally changed from what it prevailed in the days of the British Raj when the Collector's authority and office was supreme and his word was law. Public accountability was not so direct as it is today. The District Collector has a variety of functions to perform which in post-independence days have become more complex and wider. The expectations from this office remain high, but the line and staff assistance, quantitatively and qualitatively, have not improved *pari passu.* This hiatus makes the task of the Collector, specially in innovative and crisis situations, even more onerous.

The Collector may be called upon to handle a law and order situation, attend to a VIP, prepare or execute a development project, participate in a seminar, be a member of a working group or reconcile different views in the larger interest of the people. In performing these functions, especially those designed to result in the change of a status quo situation, the Collector confronts resistance within the system at different stages and from varying levels. To overcome this system resistance, the Collector has to resort to a variety of strategies. Unlike a soldier who overcomes resistance across enemy lines, the Collector has to defeat resistance often put up by his 'own' men.

The Multiple Resistances

Resistance to change manifests itself in different forms such as vested interests, political parties, inertia on the part of functionaries to carry out timely the task assigned to them or even inadequate knowledge about rules and procedures, inter-service rivalry, inadequate community or target group motivation and sometimes, personal predilections, either of the Collector or other subordinate officials, which form minor irritants with a potential to develop into an explosive situation. Very often, due to such in-built hurdles, the district administration becomes divided into two opposing groups bringing all productive activity to a standstill, much to the delight of the vested interests.

To overcome resistance emanating from lack of knowledge among the subordinate officers, the Collector is expected to make considerable inroads into his personal time to apprise himself of the latest circulars and government orders and for reconciling different pressure groups in such a manner that the interests of the largest section of the population are served.

Very often, subordinate district officials in the Collectorate have vested interests due to their long tenure in a particular area; officials shift from one district to another in the same zone, sometimes even remain in the same alignments tend to make objectivity a peripheral consideration in their decision-making process.

This input in the form of effort to overcome resistance at different stages of his career can become extremely frustrating. Sometimes, depending on the degree and nature of the failure, the wrong attitudes of a young officer get crystallized to the extent of upsetting his value system which would determine his whole career. On the other hand, success often has a multiplier effect, encouraging the officer to undertake even more involved and important measures to overcome this resistance as he progresses in his career.

To overcome this system resistance, the Collector has to delve into his personal armoury of different techniques and strategies so that his tenure does not go unnoticed. He may have to resort to the use of wit to defuse an explosive law and order situation or assert his authority to ensure the compliance of an order, wield the stick or offer the carrot where any socio-economic change is involved or even use the village elders to ensure that a development scheme meets with the support of the local population.

When Tact Averted Tragedy

Once non-payment of wages to the labourers at a famine camp on account of a small procedural wrangle led to an explosive situation, which had to be overcome more by ready wit and repartee, rather than by threats and use of force. The Assistant Engineer, in charge of the relief works camp, had apparently taken exception to a local budding leader taking up the cause of the labourers who had not been paid their wage bill for the first week. This procedural lapse had been lost sight of in earlier weeks and in order to pre-empt a possible audit objection in future, the AEn now insisted on compliance. Informal enquiries at a later date indicated a difference of opinion between the Engineer and the local leader, which brought the situation to an impasse. The Assistant engineer apparently took exception to the local leader entering his 'area of operation' and thus, eroding his authority. Both the groups lost sight of the need for paying wages to the labourers and in the process, the second week passed.

Repeated requests by the labourers did not beget any positive response from the concerned executive agency. The restive labourers left with no option, one day damaged the office furniture and record and then in a group attempted to assault the Assistant Engineer. The latter managed to escape with minor injuries, but could not save one of his vehicles from being partly burnt. Still not satisfied, the mob chased the official, fully armed with pick-axes and bamboos, on the Collectorate. On the way, the demonstrators which included both men and women, picked up a megaphone and the local leader joined the shouting of slogans and started inciting the already infuriated mob. The incident was developing into a custom-tailored situation for the budding politician, who was using it as a stepping stone for his personal career prospects.

No form of coaxing yielded results and all assurances by me and my subordinate officials were ignored. The AEn's blood had by now become the immediate demand, which was applauded by the crowd, who had forgotten the main cause for their anger. Banks having closed for the day, the possibility of an immediate flow of cash was sealed.

The situation was evolving itself into a proper demonstration of rights and if not nipped in the bud, had potential for flaring up. The speech became fiery and rhetorical and at one stage while demanding justice, the leader shouted, "Let the Collector use bullets, if necessary" and for effect, he actually tore open his shirt exposing his baby's bottom chest. That was when I struck, countering his challenge by saying, "You fool, why waste your shirt, the bullet can pierce that also". The large crowd lapped it up much to the chagrin of the local leader. My 'bullet' had scored a bull's eye. While I had saved the situation from worsening, next morning, as a populist measure, I had to personally supervise the payment of wages to the cheering crowd.

Use of force in such a situation would have made us walk into the trap being laid by the political leader. The situation could have been easily handled at the initial stage if the officials of the executing agency had studied the rules and regulations properly, thus avoiding harassment to the relief camp labourers.

In a simpler situation, repartee saved a sumptuous dinner from turning sour. A VIP after finishing his dinner noticed that the assembly which had welcomed him had trickled down to only the Collector, the Superintendent of Police, and a few other senior officials and their wives. Due to the extreme cold weather, the other officials had just slipped away to the adjoining room, leaving only the VIP and his wife making valiant efforts at conversation with the remaining senior officials and their wives. The VIP was constrained to comment to his wife, "It appears our hosts have left us". Registering the embarrassment, I commented, "Sir, the men that matter are still here". Coffee was served in a warmer atmosphere.

Confronting Vested Interests

In some areas of Rajasthan, the firm hold of the erstwhile feudal aristocracy continued to determine the social relationship pattern. The hold of this vested group has been weakening with the spread of communication and education, but by its very nature, it is an extremely slow process of social metamorphosis. Intermingled with the caste factor, it becomes an extremely important socio-economic force which the district officials have to reckon with. This manipulative socio-economic structuring with caste undertones has developed both consciously and unconsciously. The continuing inequalities in income distribution and the financial maturity of these groups, unconsciously bind them into fostering the need for maintaining status quo. With the decentralization of political institutions, it was hoped that economically and socially weak would rapidly move into the productive mainstream. However, with the spread of education and consequent awareness by the people of their rights, there is a perceptible attitudinal change in these vested groups.

One major consequence of this manipulative socio-economic structure in the backward areas is the total control by these entrenched resistance groups of the vantage points of the district economy. These individuals not only control the sources of finance, but also the main productive and distributive channels. There is a complete identity of interests on the same pattern as exists in the western nations between the political hierarchy and the multinational corporations. Very often, there is a complete nexus between the supplier, the distributor and the sub-agents, wielding total control over the quality, supply and the price of a product, designed in a manner to be totally detrimental to the weaker sections of the rural population. This vested group having geographical heterogeneity is homogeneous as far as self-interests are concerned.

To break this nexus requires considerable tact and maturity on the part of a District Collector. Success often alienates powerful vested groups, resulting in trading charges of alignment with specific groups against the Collector, or even frequent transfers, leading to family dislocation. Failure, on the other hand, in overcoming this alignment, so deeply woven in the social fabric, may result in deep frustration and sometimes ignominy for the individual officer. Education and, more sophisticated, but cheap techniques of communication, would be important method for changing these village-level relationships.

An example of such manipulative socio-economic structuring and how the resistance was overcome was experienced by me in a district, where the consumption of light diesel oil (LDO) was the maximum in the entire division. The villagers complained that every year in the peak agricultural season, the supply of LDO became totally choked and consequently its price rocketed to exorbitant levels. This total dependence on a regular supply of LDO keeps a majority of the cultivators on tenterhooks. The more affluent who could afford to pay the price saved their crops, while the small and marginal farmers ended the season with a poor harvest and a heavier debt, trying to save their crop.

The matter was taken up with the concerned public sector undertaking, but again, hosts of alibis were presented. This was an example, in its most undiluted form, of a perfect nexus between the supplier, the distributor and the sub-agents of LDO in the entire division. An attempt to sort out the situation at the state capital yielded no tangible results, beyond assurances to report back at the earliest possible. The possibility of regular electric supply was also ruled out. The local distributor of LDO was, therefore, summoned who passed the buck by stating that the supplies were being determined by the divisional distributor. At every stage, I was confronted with some form of systems resistance. The irrigation period was ending and the crops had started withering. With no agency suggesting any solution, I was left with no option but to summon the divisional distributor of LDO with the help of Superintendent of Police of that district.

The distributor—an elderly, God-fearing and worldly wise man—gave me polite but non-committal assurances with no exact time schedule for the supply of LDO. After much coaxing, however, he indifferently assured me of two or three wagons to overcome the immediate crisis. This offer was, however, subject to a number of conditions. This was the last straw and I, therefore, threatened the old man with the dire consequence of arrest, if he did not inform me of a precise time schedule before leaving the district. The threat had its immediate effect and after a few immediate trunk calls, he came back with a supply schedule indicating the location where the wagons would dock and the quantities to be supplied. In fact, the old man got so scared that on return to his headquarters, he rang me back to assure that the tank wagons had left and would reach as per the agreed schedule. The LDO arrived, much to the relief of the agriculturists. That year, for the first time, the per barrel price of LDO also registered a decline.

A few days later, I was rather surprised to see a friend from my last place of posting, turning up unannounced. During meals he told me that the distributor was his father, who had not slept since my threat and that he had come to assure me of his good conduct. I told him that I was only trying to overcome resistance to change put up by vested interests. We continue to be friends even today.

The Baneful Obscurantism

Traditionalism and obscurantism are other deep-rooted hurdles to any change. Often, this form of resistance verges on an extreme form of irrationality, seeking refuge in facile and illogical arguments. The most uncanny aspect of a pressure group relying on obscurantism is the large numerical strength that it can muster at short notice. Such a group, often heterogeneous, is propagating a weak cause.

Some cases of death by rabies had started flowing in. Accordingly, the district medical authorities were extremely worried and started an anti-rabies campaign. This involved not only immunization but also rounding up the street dogs and putting them to sleep. In any such campaign, public support is extremely essential. A group of obscurantists suddenly emerged demanding that the campaign be called off. While this pressure group had no objection to vaccination continuing, they strongly objected to the killing of the dogs as this offended their religious sentiments, an argument which I could not comprehend. This form of resistance is not capable of being overcome by logic and reason, and has the worst ramifications as it exploits the ignorance of the masses. All efforts to convince them on the need for continuing the rounding up of street dogs fell on deaf ears. Apparently, they would not tolerate any form of violence. Some families even 'adopted' these dogs in an informal manner by allowing them to feed on their domestic garbage normally dumped in the street. One member of the pressure group even went to the extent of saying that my Brahminical roots, which I had long lost sight of, were being desecrated which would disturb the peace of the souls of my ancestors. While listening to this group, I realized how vociferous could an argument become, particularly when it had no substance. The religious protagonists, however, thought that the volume and tone of arguments were a substitute for their content. The straw that broke the Collector's back was when one of them was lustily cheered when he categorically stated, "We would rather see our children die of rabies than have the dogs killed". Irrationality and obscurantism in their most naked form were reigning supreme and none of the techniques from my bag of tricks succeeded. Consequently, the campaign had to be called off.

First Carrot, Then Stick

The resistance due to lack of knowledge amongst subordinates, coupled with the inadequate motivation to learn, manifests itself in forms often very innocuous and unnoticeable. The wives of officers often call on the Collector's wife in the afternoon casually lamenting how overworked their husbands were, resulting in inadequate attention being paid to their personal lives. Sycophancy expressed by way of performing domestic chores and no office work by lower functionaries was another way in which this resistance strengthened itself. Such forms of resistance have to be tackled with a mixture of first offering the carrot and then, if no results are forthcoming, wielding the stick.

On taking charge of a district, I found a familiar face always hovering around violating my privacy at the slightest pretext. On inquiry, it transpired that he was an office assistant who had never been to the office nor appended his signature to any file in the collectorate for the last fifteen years, although he had been drawing his pay against that post. Instead, all domestic chores of the Collector's residence were being attended to by him. Initially, I politely asked him to stop coming to my residence, and to attend to his office work, since my domestic demands were extremely limited. When pressed to attend to files and spend his official time more productively, he proceeded on leave in the hope that the Collector would get transferred. I however, did not oblige and hence he had to extend his leave. This functionary was given ample opportunity to learn and do his bit, but he resisted to the extent of exerting political pressure so that he may be posted to some office where he could attend to the senior officers' domestic chores as that was the only work he had learnt to do. Not having succeeded even in this strategy, he started a self-pity campaign among the collectorate staff which became a topic of animated conversation leading to the emergence of an undercurrent of opposition and conflict in the collectorate staff. All forms of sympathy and peace offers to get him back to any office seat proved abortive, as he was not used to being put into harness. As the atmosphere was being vitiated by his sense of success, it became necessary to make an example of breaking his resistance and I decided to initiate action to dismiss him from service. Initially, this created a furore in the collectorate with the unions taking up his cause, but to no avail. He had in the previous years been enjoying a privileged position as the Collector's household manager and hence had alienated his union colleagues also, who did not press his cause. The individual was finally dismissed, though during the tenure of my successor. Dead wood had thus been shed.

Discretion and Discreetness

The more entrenched form of resistance is manifest in insistence for following archaic procedures and calling for precedents. Whenever any innovative idea is proposed, the requirements of the statute book are hurled at your face and you are charged with ignorance about rules and regulations. The prosecutor is fully aware of the fact that the need of the hour is a mature decision and quick follow-up action and yet some senior officials in their *obiter dicta* have been heard to state that they raised so many queries that their officer will have to go through all the prescribed rules before he discovers the answers. Sometimes these queries are raised with the objective of preventing possible future audit objections. By the time the creative idea becomes conceptualized and emerges in the shape of a scheme, the estimates become obsolete and the target group gets disinterested. Deep cynicism becomes a self-perpetuating phenomenon, and often one begins to wonder whether all this effort in continually searching for an alternative solution to a crisis situation is worth the effort. This is the moment which has to be overcome because effort really begins when it hurts. Those who give up at this juncture muddle through their careers standing at the complaint-counter. Those that overcome, never get weary.

My district stretched longitudinally with the commercially important sub-divisional headquarters in the centre, the district headquarters totally in the northern end and an important tehsil headquarters on the tail. The road, which was the main artery of the district, was metalled between the sub-divisional and tehsil headquarters, leaving the district headquarters connected only by a *katcha* road. Despite repeated proposals and personally following them up, the efforts to improve communications did not fructify. The concerned Minister did not believe that a good transport and communication system was an important pedestal for economic take-off. Once when another senior Minister visited the district at the peak of winter, it was so arranged that nearing the district headquarters, his car would get stuck in the *katcha* road. The Executive Engineer readily prepared the grounds for this slip-up.

While returning, it was a cold and dreary night and just at the agreed spot, the motorcade came to a halt and the elected representative stepped out in a cloud of dust questioning in anger why the main artery was in such a bad state, to which my reply was that the concerned department was not agreeable to the proposal. When the Minister returned after easing himself, the car had been salvaged from the road depression. As he entered the car, he asked me to ensure that I obtain the sanction—the first thing in the morning. Satisfied that the strategy had worked, as I boarded the jeep, a voice from the dark, prefaced with a hand offering a cigarette spoke, "So you have managed". I noticed that the Minister in charge of the department who had not agreed also entered my jeep. During the remaining part of the drive, we discussed where the road rollers would be procured from for commencing the work at the earliest possible.

Evolving Multidimensionality

One quarter from which the Collector least expects resistance is his own home and family. In the initial stage of being posted as a Collector, the dictates of idealism often result in personal relationships being ignored. The urge to mould the world according to one's desire does not include the partner in the newly entered matrimonial alliance of the Collector. The personal demands of the wife and family are small but are effective forms of resistance to one's official work. They may appear as minor irritants but result in upsetting the working temperament of an official who is not willing to accept this demand on his time. The eagerness to visit new places and meet new persons is an inevitable corollary of a youthful relationship. The Collector must necessarily blend his official duties with his personal commitments in such a manner that his working psyche does not get mutilated to the extent that cynicism and frustration overshadow his interpersonal relationships. Taking the family on tour once in a while effectively serves as an olive branch. Another good way of overcoming this esoteric resistance is a quarterly visit to the state capital.

Enthusiastic Idealism

With the changed working environment, those ideals which were underscored by the 'Founders' and the 'guardians' may not be totally relevant today. The winter camps and the *shikars* were treated as a must for picking up the basic details about the area and the people. The mother of parliaments was too far away. Today, it would be difficult for a District Collector to have a long winter camp, particularly when the Assembly is in session. With the emphasis on conservation and maintenance of an ecological balance, the camera has replaced the 12 bore gun.

The most basic and important resistance which the Collector has to overcome emerges from within. Today, with the strains and stresses on the office of the Collector, the individual finds very little time to develop his personal interests and for keeping abreast with the latest developments in management and technology. The capacity for creative thinking tends to atrophy with the passage of time. Change and innovation lose their lure. Economic circumstances add to this resistance. A District Collector cannot often subscribe to the latest journals and magazines, let alone develop a personal library. It is extremely essential in order to keep his bag of tricks sharpened and updated that the District Collector should reflect on ways and means of overcoming this form of resistance in his career. After spending the better part of your lifetime attempting to tame the thundering river of tradition and conservatism, when you start noticing the twilight hours, you may realize that while the river continues to flow, the gut issue is overcoming self-generated inertia, the resistance to self-discipline, sacrifice and dedication. "It is no profit", wrote Publilius Syrus, "to have learnt well, if you neglect to do well". But, to be able to reach the stage, it is essential that the effort is on a continuing basis rather than a fire-fighting operation. Like Aeschylus said, "When the height is won, there is ease". Often, one may fail, but that should not dampen one's idealism and enthusiasm. Behold the turtle, he makes progress only when he sticks his neck out.

14 MEENAKSHI HOOJA

Their First Lady

19 May 1984. Place: Sirohi Road railway station. A bright afternoon. My mother-in-law, two children and six packing cases getting down the train with me and so many unfamiliar yet familiar faces standing at the platform—some holding garlands, some bouquets and the others just staring away—wondering whether the person they are receiving is really their Collector!

I remember this scene vividly as if it was only yesterday. No doubt, it did not happen very long ago to have assumed some of the golden halo of a hoary past, but even so around three years have passed since I detrained at Sirohi Road with my family to join as Collector and District Magistrate, Sirohi. The feelings that were expressed in the scene at Pindwara railway station continued for some time after I joined there. I was the first lady to be posted as Collector of Sirohi. Quite understandably, the desire to welcome the new Collector was there amongst the officers and the people—but the fact that I was a lady made the welcome a little more ceremonial and everybody appeared to be on his best behaviour. This trend of ceremony, best behaviour, courtesy lasted throughout my stay in Sirohi including the last fortnight of farewells in the end.

An Object of Curiosity

As far as acceptance of a lady as a District Collector is concerned, it took its time. Sirohi is a small compact district with a preponderance of Scheduled Caste and Scheduled Tribe population. Industrialization has just started after it having been declared a 'no-industry' district by the state government entitling entrepreneurs to higher subsidies and incentives. The place, as a whole, is quite behind in the race towards modernization, and old attitudes are very much there. And, certainly, my posting then took everybody by surprise, if not by shock. The stares at the railway station gradually turned into friendly smiles, once they got to know me a little better.

However, the word 'lady' before Collector stuck to me like glue. There were times when I told my colleagues that I was a Collector, belonging to the IAS cadre, and functioned like any other officer who held this post. But this could not go fully down their gullet. As a response to this, I started enjoying all the privileges of a lady that were accorded to me, over and above those due to a Collector.

I began to settle down in the house as well as in the office. One of my first important assignments was to receive His Excellency, the Governor, who was coming to Mt. Abu for his annual visit. As usual, there was a lot of rush at the Abu Road railway station upon his arrival, which was on a hot May afternoon. My sweating must have been due to heat as well as nervousness. However, the whole show went off satisfactorily. A few days later, a sudden awareness dawned upon me when I read in a small item in a newspaper that many women had come to the railway station to see the Governor as well as the new *mahila ziladhish* (lady Collector). I realized that I would be an object of 'seeing' for quite some time and should not feel unduly self-conscious or worried about it.

The Prime Minister's Visit

The challenge of having to make arrangements for the PM's visit (late Smt. Indira Gandhi) planned suddenly within less than a month of my joining, was very thrilling. My only experience of a VVIP visit was that of Mrs Gandhi coming to Ajmer in 1976, when I was doing my district training there. However, in Sirohi, it had to be planned out afresh with a lot of responsibility on my shoulders. It was the first serious test of my administrative capacities after having joined the service in 1975. Rakesh, my husband, also an IAS officer, was there on a tour at Mt. Abu when information about the PM's visit came and this announcement gave him the 'wifely' jitters. I told him to relax and leave it all to me and employ his mind in looking after special schemes (He was then holding the post of Special Secretary to the Government, Agriculture Special Schemes). Once the programme got concretized, then, there was a lot to do; plan, programme, issue orders and as is common in our bureaucratic echelons, follow it up. What I had studied in theory had to be turned into reality—how much to delegate, how much to decentralize, how to establish priorities, how to involve everybody and yet get work out of a solid, small team of officers and how to say a 'no' without being rude.

Mrs Gandhi's visit included a public address to an *adivasi sammelan* at Abu Road, where we had to construct a rest room almost overnight. She spent some of her time with the tribals who had come to perform a dance in her honour, which really encouraged the excited participants. Her visit, on the whole, was a big success, this being her first visit to Mt. Abu and Abu Road. No one, of course, knew then that it would also be her last.

With the VVIP visit, came the major advantage to me of getting to know all the officers, political representatives, non-officials, so early after joining. This paved the way for the coordination and team spirit that was there in the district throughout my tenure. No doubt, I understood quite fast as to which officers and persons were sincere and intelligent ones and those who were not—this might not have been to the liking of the latter.

Business and Busy-ness

After my parents-in-laws and children left Sirohi towards the end of June (after a fairly pleasant one month stay at Mt. Abu), the environment suddenly turned lonely. Living alone in a fairly big house (as it was a modern house, it had no semblance of being ghostly) posed a difficult question to which answers had to be found especially for spending the evenings. Gradually, the answers came slowly like scattered raindrops and then as a heavy downpour. House decoration, cooking, games, music, parties, cards, *ghazal* recitals, picnics, gossip sessions and what have you! In no time boredom turned into a busy schedule, in which at times I myself felt trapped.

The first social evening was a contributory dinner, being a *dabba* (a dish of food contributed by each family) variety prefaced by a cultural evening in my living room lined with *gaddas* and *takiyas*, reason—I had no regular furnished drawing room). Officers from administration, police, judiciary, teaching, medical, banks—all joined it. It all went off very well till the compere announced that the Collector would wind up the programme with a song. I had not touched singing with a barge pole for years and it was a *ghazal* of Ghalib, learnt many years ago from my father, that came to my rescue. I was quite determined, after the evening that in future no such programmes would ever be held again—but as we all know in government, once a scheme starts, vested interests often develop for its further continuation—so in this case, the officers and their families loved the idea of such gatherings, which picked up their own momentum.

By July-August, office schedule had become quite well settled. Meetings, tours, court work, interviews with petitioners, were fixed in a systematic manner. The officers, staff, non-officials and people in general got used to my style of functioning and were less inhibited in discussing their problems.

Faux Pas to Remember

One of the *faux pas* I committed during my meeting with a petitioner is something I will never forget. The Income Tax Officer (ITO) posted in Sirohi was a Muslim. Once he had come to call on me at home in my absence, and hence I did not know him by face. One day, a slip came with a Muslim name and a smart gentleman walked in. I asked him to be seated. He sat down. Thinking that he was the ITO, I dwelt at length on the role of income tax and various organizations where I thought the income tax and state government departments should combine to check tax evasion. He listened very patiently and replied that such exercises would be helpful. While getting up, he said that apart from tax evasion, could I also help in improving the electricity supply in village D…, of which he was a resident! My face just fell at hearing this—I looked again at the slip and knew at once what an oaf I had been! I promised to help with the supply of electricity and saw him walk out, much to my relief. Later, when I met the ITO and his wife, I told them about this incident, remembering which always had me in fits of laughter. At least I had the courage to laugh at myself. Later on, the ITO and his family became very good friends and an integral part of my social life at Sirohi.

Eschewing Imitation

District administration and the office of the Collector and District Magistrate has been much written of and is no doubt one of the most discussed issues in official, non-official and private forums. As a child, my ideas were based largely on my father's experiences, who held charge of as many as seven districts for about eleven years. Later on, as a student of Political Science and Public Administration, we read standard texts as well as biographies and commentaries of British bureaucrats and writers. In the Academy at Mussoorie we received all kinds of instructions and during our training and later holding other posts, we were directly exposed to officers functioning as Collectors. When my husband was Collector at Sikar, I could only visit him occasionally at weekends and thus did not really get an idea of the Collector's work. As such, over the years, many ideas about the office of the Collector had developed in my mind with a crystallized set of do's and don'ts. However, I realized very early after joining that one cannot and should not entirely be guided by what one has read; the style to be adopted, priorities to be assigned and goals to be set, have to generate from the environment of the district—social, economic, political. To be successful, the Collector and his thinking should adjust to the local needs and potential, without compromising on general principles of efficiency and integrity. Answers to problems lie, not merely in what one has read, heard or seen, but many times in the problem itself.

As a Collector, I had the onerous task of not only performing well in the eyes of the people and officers of the district, the state government, etc., but also competing withing the family. Apart from my father (who has had one of the longest spells as Collector in the Rajasthan cadre), my father-in-law and husband had held this distinguished office and were always ready to advise (a more sophisticated way of saying 'criticize') on all and sundry issues, including how to dress up, what to eat, what to read and whom to meet. Only my mother-in-law came to my support and said that I should be left free to run my district the way I wanted: women's liberation in practice.

A Mistaken Adventure

Combined with a desire to do what I wanted as also to ensure that I was not less than any of my breed, including the ICS, I decided to go in for some adventure and heights. Mt. Abu is not only a beautiful hill station situated within Sirohi district, but also a place full of temples and sacred places. The temple of Adhav Devi, the presiding deity of the Abu hills, is located in the caves and has about 200 steps of ascent. The *prasad* of coconut and *elaichi dana* that is offered there satisfies not merely the feeling of *bhakti,* but also the bodily needs after the tough climb. Another sacred place is the Gomukh, which has an eternal spring and is supposed to be the place of origin of the Rajputs *(Agnikula)* from the fire. I went there with the SDO and his family, going down and then climbing up 700 steps. It was a fairly exhausting but totally rewarding adventure rejuvenated by the *shikanji* of the Baba at the Hanuman temple. A few more visits here and there, and then came the peak. We had gone to Anadra dak bungalow for a picnic, inspired by the SP and his wife. Anadra is a point from where the local villagers, including tribals, climb a steep six kilometres path to reach Mt. Abu at a height of approximately 5,000 ft. Mt. Abu did not seem far from Anadra at all and I decided that I just had to go there by walking up the old bridle path. On such occasions, it is good to know you are the Collector and District Magistrate—everyone obeys you. So, the SP, Divisional Forest Officer and the District Judge's wife, along with a few forest and police guards, agreed to obey their whimsical Collector—with the exception of the District Judge's wife who did not have to, but was inspired by the same spirit of adventure as the lady Collector's. A bold beginning in the adventure was followed by a simple middle—the only thing that kept me going were the periodical replies of the forest guards that Mt. Abu was very near. Of course, it made us feel frustrated when these replies kept coming from them for hours.

We had started around 4 o'clock in the afternoon and by 6 o'clock it appeared as if the adventure was all a mistake. But, battles begun have to be fought and won, especially by the Collector. So, the climb went on the SP and District Forest Officer had marched far ahead (these are not the days of chivalry) and by 7 p.m. we also saw the Honeymoon Point of Mt. Abu, where the path ends. On reaching there, we felt elated, reminding me particularly of the trail to Gomukh and Tapovan above Gangotri which we had gone to from the Mussoorie Academy during our probationer days. The climb was the topic of discussion amongst officers at Sirohi for a few days and many persons thought it fit to even congratulate us on this.

The festivals of Dashera and Diwali are occasions when one likes to be with one's own family. As it was not possible for me to leave headquarters during these days, my husband and children came over to Sirohi (with breaks) and the whole month of October was spent in festivities and social get-togethers. As the weather was also turning beautiful, it was very easy to combine office work, together with a fairly hectic social life. On Diwali, I had to even go round the market to adjudge the best decorated shops and face a lot of stares, generated perhaps by my heavy *sari* in which I was not seen anywhere else.

Tragedy and Anguish

Things seemed to be going all too well, when suddenly on 31 October, we heard of Mrs Gandhi's assassination. The news came during an inspection of my office being conducted by a Member, Board of Revenue. For the first time, I had to completely forget my role as Collector or a Development Officer and concentrate purely on law and order duties as District Magistrate to maintain peace in the area, and later to see that order was maintained at the railway stations where her ashes came for *darshan* of the people. It was impossible to believe that the woman who had just come a few days ago to Mt. Abu was no more and it was her ashes which were in the urn. This time, we were preparing not to receive her, but the ashes or *phool* of her assassinated body. It was only in due course that administration returned to normal; but for me, the photographs of her first and last visit to Mt. Abu became a highly nostalgic and treasured item, which I keep with a lot of care.

Preparing for the Poll

As expected, elections to Parliament were announced thereafter and the government machinery had to gear itself to conducting them on the basis of a one-day poll. I had attempted in the past few months to evolve a system of holding regular meetings, say monthly, on fixed dates of revenue officers, on tribal area, Standing Committee of Bankers, coordination meetings with police and prosecution, municipalities, and other departments. I also attended tehsil level and panchayat samiti level meeting with as much regularity as was possible. It was as a result of these meetings and extensive touring that I knew the area, the people and the officers and even the vehicles quite well. This knowledge came in very handy during the elections and it was a pleasure to organize the elections as District Election Officer. The amount of cooperation that I got from the officers and those roped in to perform election duties (by and large, teachers) is something I will never forget. Later on, on 26 January, India's Republic Day, we even gave merit certificates to those who had worked hard to make these elections a smooth affair. The elections to the Assembly which were held in March, became relatively easy to organize. During the Assembly elections, we managed to send some vehicles to the neighbouring Pali district, where as my ADM and Deputy Electoral Officers later revealed, it was considered a new thing in the history of administration that the district Sirohi was exporting instead of importing vehicles! The new Prime Minister Rajiv Gandhi also made a short election tour to Sirohi during the Assembly elections. This visit put no one under any stress, as by now elections and VVIP visits were something everybody had got used to.

It would not be wrong to say that Sirohi is known largely because of Mt. Abu, the only hill station in Rajasthan, also still very popular amongst our Gujarati neighbours. Many VIPs from the state and outside visit it during summer as well as winter. During my stay there, apart from Mrs Gandhi, the President and Vice-President of India and Governor of Gujarat also visited the hill resort and the Governor of Rajasthan camped there for about a month during the summers. The Raj Bhawan at Mt. Abu is very beautifully located and those who have privilege of staying there must consider themselves extremely lucky. Of course, for us, the best thing during VVIP visits was the delicious eats, which the Raj Bhawan staff turned out so ingeniously round the clock.

Comaraderie and Team Spirit

Tours, village visits, gram sabhas and night halts are considered integral parts of the functioning of the Collector. I wanted to visit as many villages of the district as possible in order to get a first-hand knowledge of the problems and issues involved. Normally, one or two officers accompanied me on these visits and they had the onerous responsibility of noting down the points that came up and then preparing a visit note based on them.

Many times, these drafts were amended in a very big way by me. If ever these officers felt hurt by these corrections and amendments, they never said so and I just liked to think that they were not too unhappy about it. Similarly, as I made my night halts quite religiously and regularly, a lot of energy of the officers must have gone into making necessary arrangements. But, ultimately, the atmosphere of comaraderie and team spirit that emerged from these tours and visits not only helped in improving performance, but also made work a pleasure. In one case, I remember, my officers and I had to walk about 3 km to reach a village cut off by rains but when we did get there, we met all the people and got their views and could understand the problems in their correct context. Such visits are far more useful in analyzing a problem or situation than a mere study of files with indifferently written reports.

The inevitable question that everyone asks a lady officers is: How is her family life harmonized with a career and officer work. Let me say at the outset, that such a combination is difficult. In Sirohi, I was staying alone while my family was at Jaipur; whenever I thought about this I could not decide whether to place myself in the category of the erstwhile British ICS Collectors who kept their families back home in England or the tehsildar/girdavar/patwari whose families always stayed behind in the village and they made their once in a month *ghar sambhalnewali* (to look after the families) visits! However, my husband did not give me much chance to portray a 'single woman' image and take advantage of it, as his visits as those of the children were quite frequent. He made sure that my identity of Mrs Rakesh Hooja never got lost in files or village visits. In the long run, this image did enable me to enjoy my work as well as the social life at Sirohi and finally when I did get transferred after about a year, I could leave the place, amidst farewells with mixed feelings and lot of satisfaction and happiness.

The Return

Just as I was beginning to adopt myself to the life of Secretariat and home at Jaipur, I was asked to go on duty to a village in Sirohi, which the Prime Minster, Rajiv Gandhi was due to visit. It was so pleasant and wonderful to go back to the district and meet all the officers, friends and people and see the beautiful scenery of hills and colourful bright flowers. A few days later, the government announced the award of a merit certificate to me on Independence Day for revenue work during my tenure as Collector of Sirohi. Behind this recognition was the support of my team members who always put in their best with ungrudging smiles. What more could I expect?

III

Afterword: What is Desirable in the Civil Service

SECTIONAL INTRODUCTION

IAS Espirit de Corps

Rakesh Hooja

In April 1947, Sardar Vallabhbhai Patel, then Home Member, Government of India, addressed the first batch of the IAS at the All-India Administrative Service Training School at Metcalfe House, Delhi. He indicated that the All-India Administrative Service had been brought into being, wherein the officers should be guided by a real spirit of service in their day-to-day administration. Towards the conclusion of his address Sardar Patel said: "Above all I would advise you to maintain to the utmost the impartiality and incorruptibility of administration. A civil servant cannot afford to, and must not, take part in politics. Nor must he involve himself in communal wrangles. To depart from the path of rectitude in either of these respects is to debase public service and to lower its dignity. Similarly, no service worth the name can claim to exist if it does not have in view the achievement of the highest standard of integrity.... I hope that you ... would render your service without fear or favour and without any expectations of extraneous rewards".

Sardar Patel's address was delivered on April 21, 1947. Almost 60 years later Government of India decided to start celebrating April 21 as Civil Service Day. Prime Minister Manmohan Singh has been addressing the Civil Service Day gathering each year at the Vigyan Bhawan in New Delhi. At the Second Civil Service Day in 2007 he said: "The civil service is a professional service and forms the backbone of our government structure. It must remain politically neutral and professionally competent. It must also aim to maintain the highest standards of personal integrity and probity. It must remain ... faithful and loyal to the value system for nation building as enshrined in our Constitution.... I sincerely hope we can root out corruption in the civil service and raise the morale of our officers so that they can give their very best to our country. Senior civil servants have a special responsibility to promote a culture of excellence, probity in public conduct and concern for social equity".

Similarly at the third Civil Service Day in 2008, Prime Minister Manmohan Singh lauded the civil service for its contribution to the process of nation building, for remaining loyal to India's pluralist traditions and to the secular fabric of India's polity, for being supportive of the deepening of democracy and of empowerment of local government and of civil society action, for ensuring free and fair elections time and again, for accelerating the pace of progress and for making the growth process inclusive, for greater attention being paid to pubic service delivery systems in numerous spheres, for being fair honest and efficient, for working in a professional manner, for demonstrating a renewed commitment to knowledge, for placing itself on the side of the disadvantaged in society, for paying attention to improving its humane face, for being innovative responsive and change oriented, and for its versatility. The above indicated some characteristics which Dr Manmohan Singh considers desirable in the civil service. He felt that the All India Services had validated Sardar Patel's vision that they are an imperative for a strong, stable and free India, but that Nehrus vision of ending poverty, ignorance, disease and inequality of opportunity is a challenge that continues to persist.

Singh went on to state that "The challenge now is for effective public management of our resources and to create open, transparent and accountable systems, of delivery. The challenge now is one of increasing professionalism [so] that our civil services are amongst the best in the world when it comes to delivering public services to one sixth of humanity [though] our civil services operate in a much more complex environment than before".

Many from the high and the mighty to the common man have their own ideas and visions of what is desirable from the civil service, and many express them publically in various forums.

Many of them even have negative views about the civil service including even some in service or who have retired from the IAS. Some feel that in the first two or three decades after independence the IAS had lived up to expectations, but then thereafter a decline commenced.

One retired IAS officer recruited in the early 1950s, who recently wrote a book about 50 years of the IAS which has been referred to in the introduction to this book, feels that the IAS has never been able to develop an espirit de corps *from the very beginning; a view that can be debated. However, this is what Sanjoy Bagchi has expressed "The IAS has not succeeded in developing collectively a common ethos of functioning. It does not observe any code of professional ethics. Its officers have often failed to practice decent standards of behaviour. They are generally acquisitive of perks and creature comforts; they are usually arrogant or petty minded in their attitudes towards their colleagues and the public; they frequently reveal their selfish nature in their dealings with government; and are now well known for vulgar displays of sycophancy. The IAS officers show these undesirable characteristics because in many cases they don't realize that their behaviour is reprehensible. Neither the academy nor their superiors in the states have impressed on them the need for a proper code of conduct". Bagchi has perhaps adopted an unduly harsh attitude. He calls for the development of espirit de corps in the IAS.*

This writer feels that a proper civil service ethos is still being inculcated at the Mussoorie Academy (and earlier at Metcalfe House), at the State Administrative Training Institutes like HCM RIPA in Rajasthan which arranges and coordinates the State and district training of the IAS Probationers, by the district Collectors to whom the probationers are attached for field training, and by senior officers at the state level on whom the Probationers make courtesy calls when reporting for State and district training where conversations can often start with statements like "we have a tradition of accessability and responsiveness to the common man", or "make sure you never develop a sense of arrogance", or "I never made a request for a particular assignment in service and I would urge you probationers never to do so yourself", or "make sure you develop a habit of hard work and putting in long hours in the service of the people", and so on. This is in the tradition of the British ICS for which David Gilmour states "I am aware that there was a civil service ethos imbibed at Haileybury and Oxford [where the ICS trained] and later reinforced in the provincial capitals of Bombay, Lahore and elsewhere. Similar ideas percolated in the clubs and in the Secretariats". (Of course, the tradition of clubs for the officers has now gradually died out.)

In this concluding section of this anthology, we have included the views, based upon his experiences while in service, of one of those who has contributed his service recollections in Section I of this book and was Chief Secretary in the State when he initially set forth his views (recently revised), on the spirit of the civil service or a certain minimum set of qualities expected from the civil service.

15 ARUN KUMAR

The Spirit of the Civil Service

I am reminded of the earlier years of my career when some talk had already started about the relevance of a civil service which the country had inherited from a colonial power to the new dimensions of governance. Doubts were being expressed whether the civil service would be able to meet the challenges of a developing country as well as a welfare state. Whether the civil services will be able to adjust to their new roles and discard the old mantle of a basically regulatory body. Though the controversy has not completely died down, I am glad the civil services have not only survived all these years but have also risen up to the demands placed on them and by and large have performed well. We have all adapted to the new requirements and acquired necessary skills for handling new problems and new situations. I think this has been possible largely because there were some basic fundamental attributes that the civil service had acquired, which facilitated acquisition of new qualities required with changing times. Though the expectations from a civil service may have undergone a change, the relative importance of different aspects of work may have changed, a totally new type of jobs may have been required to be performed, certain minimum set of qualities expected in a civil servant have remained unchanged and I would think will remain unchanged irrespective of the job one is performing or the organization or the government one is serving. These are some of these basic tenets of civil service which I would like to discuss with you. Whatever part we may have to play in the country's development and progress these essentials will form the foundations of the civil service and if the foundation is strong, the civil service would be able to stand firm and discharge its duties and functions admirably. And if these basics are shaky, the extent of trust reposed on it so far will go down.

Efficiency

When we talk of a civil service, we talk of an efficient civil service. The word 'efficient' is not used but implied. The first and the foremost requirement is therefore efficiency. All members of the civil service have to be individually efficient and the department or the organization of which they are part should be efficient as a whole. If in an organization the individuals are competent, the chances are that the organization would also be efficient. But if the individuals are inefficient, the organization they serve cannot be expected to be efficient. I am talking about efficiency because I notice this aspect being relegated from its pre-eminent position which it should occupy in a civil service to a position of less importance. What exactly is meant by efficiency is also sometimes not clearly understood.

I do not want to enter into an academic discussion on what is efficiency or what is lack of it but I do want to dwell a little on this purely from a practical point of view. Broadly speaking, what an administrator does can be divided into two parts. One, what he does himself and two, what he gets done by his assistants, followers or team. The first relates to his personal efficiency and the second to his capacity to mobilize his team and get the maximum out of it for the organization. Right from the beginning, we all have to work with a group of people and as we go along our career, we start leading a section, or a wing or a department or an organization. Apart from your personal efficiency, your success now depends largely on the extent to which you are able to develop leadership qualities. You have to develop professional ability, the art of taking decisions, and the capacity to motivate and inspire your team for higher levels of performance. A host of other qualities necessary for administrative leadership have to be acquired and developed. I do not propose to discuss this second aspect relating to man management and leadership but I do want to discuss a little the first aspect of personal efficiency.

Who is an efficient administrator? Different answers may be given to this question and different traits of personality may be emphasized to different degrees by different persons. I find there is a lot of confusion as well about the meaning of efficiency. There are four simple basic requirements of efficiency:

(1) First is the *quality of work*. The performance or the output of a worker must be of good quality. It must be free from mistakes, accurate and well considered. A worker must learn the technique of his job, he must be thorough and his superior must be able to rely on the quality of his output. When we say that the quality of work must be high, it presupposes certain other things. The worker must possess full knowledge about the facts, rules and regulations applicable to them, he must be able to think of various alternatives and the pros and cons of the different alternatives, and

must be able to arrive at a sound decision. Then only his output would be of good quality.

(2) The second essential ingredient of efficiency is the *speed at which the work is done.* A ten-minute job must be finished in ten minutes and not in twenty. In other words, an efficient worker has a large output per unit of time.

At this stage, I may also make it clear that the speed in working is not acquired at the cost of quality but in addition to it. Quality, accuracy or excellence is an indispensable condition of good work and it should not be sacrificed to quickness of performance. Herein lie the basic requisites of an efficient worker: he is both accurate in his work, quality of work is of a high order and at the same time he is also fast. His disposal is quick.

For improving both the quality of work and the speed of doing it, one has to acquire full knowledge about the job he has to perform. Reading books, manuals and old record, interacting with experienced people, and learning from one's own experience are some of the ways of enhancing specialized knowledge. Apportioning available time to different parts of your work is extremely important for improving your pace of working. You must develop the ability to distinguish between what is important and what is not, what is urgent and what can wait, and which decision is going to have a wide repercussion and which will be confined to that particular matter. You must determine your priorities and spend time in dealing with a subject in proportion to its significance. You will find efficient time management to be an indispensable tool for speeding up your disposal.

Knowing relative significance of various activities in your organization and identifying the crucial ones is necessary for having and effective control on your organization. You need to keep a watch only on the critical ones instead of wasting time in overseeing work that is of no consequence.

All through your career you will be dealing with files which will take up most of your time. It is very essential that you learn the knack of laying your finger on papers that really matter in taking a view on the subject being dealt with. There is no great virtue in going through a file from cover to cover. You have to acquire the skill of reading a file quickly and saving time.

These are some of the ways of improving speed of disposal.

I am telling you all this because I have observed that a large number of workers do not realize these two basic essentials of efficiency. A number of people work for long hours with little output. They have not understood the importance of speed of working. An efficient worker is both accurate and fast. Delay, in fact, is a sure sign of inefficiency.

(3) The third factor of efficiency is the *use of minimum effort in doing one's work.* This means that in the day-to-day work an efficient worker feels little or no fatigue. This implies that he is able to put in long hours of work without getting tired.

There are many ways of working without getting tired at the end of the day and one has to learn them.

Thus, a worker who has these three qualities can turn out more and more work of high standard with less and less fatigue.

(4) And finally, the highest level of efficiency is *originality in one's work.* An efficient worker must not merely carry on the routine work or continue to do what he was doing before but must be able to produce new ideas, initiate new schemes, make improvements in systems of working, and introduce time, labour or money-saving devices. He must simplify procedures. He must plan for the future development of his organization. This is the real contribution one can make to his/her work and organization.

Thus, these are the four basic requirements of efficiency: quality, speed, expenditure of minimum effort and creativity. You will do well to remember this. One must strive to be personally efficient in whatever one does. Then only would he be equipped to assume higher leadership positions. At this stage of your career developing personal efficiency is of greatest importance.

Placement

From the very beginning of our career we are all concerned about our postings and rightly so. Where we are posted and what we do affects our career as well as our personal life. It is natural to be concerned about it. But we must realize that once we have joined a service, all posts encadred in it are the possible posts where one can be posted. There is no need to be choosy about it. In fact, a trend now noticeable about civil servants trying to secure particular postings for themselves goes against the basic concept of civil service. All posts are equally important. No work is inferior or superior to the other. In fact, for you, the job currently assigned to you is the most important of all jobs and you must do your best at it. While working on a particular job casting covetous eyes on the job of another is rather demeaning. I am reminded of a *sloka* in the 'Gita' which advises against forsaking duty assigned to an individual: "Better one's own duty though destitute or merit, than the duty of another well discharged. Better death in the discharge of one's duty, the duty of another is full of danger".

Of course, there can be no objection to doing things necessary for improving one's prospects in life. I also realize that at times it may be difficult to go to a particular place of posting due to personal problems like illness in the family or children's education or other reasons. There is no harm in explaining your personal problems to your seniors. But, we must understand that approaching other persons, particularly political leaders, for this purpose is bound to compromise your position. No favour is bestowed without seeking a return. And, the first thing which becomes a casualty is your own self-respect.

On every post you have a certain duty which you must discharge to the best of your ability. The only way to qualify for better jobs and senior assignments is to give full attention to one's present job and do it as well as possible. Please remember no jobs are good or bad. And, how can you expect another colleague of yours to take up a job which you are not prepared to do? You must approach a job with a feeling of not what it can give to you but what you can contribute while on it. It is not the job from which you derive your importance but it is you who lend prestige and glory to the chair you occupy. That is the right approach.

Neutrality

In a democratic set-up, there are broadly two executive wings of the government. The first is the political leadership and the second is the civil service. It is extremely essential for a good government that the relationship between the two is smooth and harmonious. Any conflict results in a sharp decline in the quality of governance and jeopardizes the very working of the government. It is, therefore, necessary that both work together and supplement each other for the common good of the people. Here, one or two aspects of this relationship may be discussed.

All civil servants, whether at the junior level or at the top of the ladder, have to face politicians. While working on field assignments in the districts or other jobs, political workers approach you with recommendations for transfers of petty officials and other small works. All such works which fit in the norms and guidelines or rules and regulations may be done. It is obvious but I am saying this because I have seen some of my colleagues reacting sharply to any approach by politicians. Even if they would have done that work in the normal course, they would not do it only because a political worker has recommended it. This is to my mind not a right approach. But, the problem arises when the recommendation made is about something which cannot be done being against the rules/regulations or against established procedures and guidelines. It is worse when the person approaching you comes from the ruling political party. Members of the ruling party tend to believe that they have a right to get things done the way they want it. This really creates problems for you. But, I think, in a situation like this also, the answer is obvious: one must learn to say 'no' politely but firmly. Half the time people would understand if you explain to them why it is not possible to do a particular work. But sometimes they do not see reason and keep on pestering you. We then have to face it and withstand pressure. In this regard, the seniors have to support their juniors.

But, the problem really arises when an impression is created that an officer would do things if the request comes from a particular quarter and would not do similar things if the request comes from the opposite group. This impression of being partisan or being inclined favourably towards someone or being against someone immediately tarnishes one's reputation and leads to various other problems. This is one thing which all of us have to guard against. In fact, if one learns to say 'no' and applies the same standards to all, irrespective of their political affiliation, people generally come to appreciate such a virtue and respect the individual.

At the senior levels also, one has to maintain his neutrality. The political government has its manifesto which it would like to implement. In a democratic set-up, as civil servants, it would be our duty to assist the political leadership in implementing its policies but here again one has to be very careful in not aligning himself/herself with any political party or a political leader. Sometime ago, there was a lot of talk about a committed civil service. We should very clearly understand that we have to be committed to uphold the Constitution and the rule of law and to implement the directions of the government of the day but it is not the same thing as being identified with a political party or a political leader. Though the distinction is fine, we have to maintain it and the civil service must remain a non-political body.

This was the basic tenet of civil service all along but it has assumed greater relevance in the present rapidly changing political situation. We see that the government at the Centre may be headed by one party at one point of time and another party or a group of parties at another point of time. In the states so many different parties and their combinations are in power and the changes are so frequent that one tends to forget which state is being ruled by whom. In such a situation, you would appreciate the significance of the civil service remaining totally neutral and dedicated to the progress of the country. We must uphold this basic political independence of the civil service.

Freedom of Expression

At the senior and policy making level, civil servants have to interact directly with the political leadership comprising ministers/Chief Minister. They are involved in decisions having far-reaching consequences and policy implications. Even otherwise, important decisions having financial angles may be required to be taken. As civil servants, we must analyse the problem thoroughly and tender the best advice in the circumstances. We must not be afraid of likes or dislikes of our political masters. Whether the advice would be palatable or not, we must be frank in expressing our view, both orally and in writing. What I am saying is very obvious but the need of saying so has arisen because a different trend is now visible. Quite a few of us look to the political masters for ascertaining what they want and try to do their bidding. Before expressing their views or recording a note they would like to talk to the minister and elicit his views and then tailor their own views to suit the political leadership. To my mind this is an incorrect approach. Sometimes, the minister may call the officer for discussion and disclose his mind how he expects a particular matter to be handled. Yet it does not mean that one should follow all that a minister says. One must point out the pitfalls in his suggestions and advice him suitably.

We must clearly understand the role of civil service vis-à-vis the political leadership. The final decision-making authority rests with the minister. But, the bureaucracy has a greater role in advising the minister correctly. As I mentioned earlier, the pros and cons of various alternatives available in a given situation have to be brought out clearly, implications of a particular decision have to be anticipated and a well thought out line of action is to be suggested. Let the political leader then take a decision. He has the authority to overrule you and if you still think that a wrong decision is being taken, it is your duty to point it out and submit it for reconsideration. Only then would you have discharged your responsibility as a good civil servant.

I think, for a civil servant, the right to express his views without any fear or favour is the right to be cherished most. Of course, the decision lies with the political leadership and one should not be afraid of being overruled but one should not surrender one of his basic rights to advise. One should have to strength of his conviction to withstand political pressure irrespective of the consequences. And, I may assure you the consequences will not be anything more than a transfer which, as I said earlier, should be of no significance to you. Any post is good enough for an upright officer. There is no greater reward than the satisfaction of having done the right thing.

Integrity in Public Services

Public services are the backbone of the government. It is as necessary for them to be honest as to be efficient. And, for administrative leadership, unimpeachable honesty is an essential qualification. No executive can command respect of his subordinates or fellow workers unless he is scrupulously honest in his words and deeds. He must set a high example for others to follow. He must be thoroughly upright in money matters. He should shun not only bribery and graft but also subtler forms of corruption such as awarding contracts to friends and relatives, circumventing rules for the sake of personal gain or in order to benefit someone else.

In its wider connotation, integrity would include intellectual honesty, a free and frank expression of one's views, a scientific attitude of mind, a high degree of objectivity, and a high sense of justice. All such things are necessary in an administrator.

Unfortunately, an impression has gained ground and not without reason, that the bureaucracy is inefficient and corrupt. Some of the criticism may be justified but I think that the bulk of the civil service is still honest and it is only a small percentage of people which brings a bad name to the entire service. But this group, however small, is large enough to cause grave concern to all of us. We must give deep thought to this problem. Of course, there are no easy solutions but we cannot give up.

The criticism of the bureaucracy being corrupt has to be looked at in a wider context of the general socio-economic climate in which we are living. The civil service is after all only a cross-section of society. In the matter of integrity, it cannot be expected to rise to a level much above that of the rest of intelligentsia. If the standard of integrity among public servants is to be raised, it will have to be done in case of other professions as well such as lawyers, doctors, businessmen, industrialists, publicmen and politicians. In fact, the need today is to raise the moral values of the society at large. A permanent and long-term solution to the problem of integrity in public service will therefore be inculcation of this virtue in the coming generations at the right impressionable age. Much more emphasis will have to be laid on moral values and character building and it has to start in the homes, in the families, schools and colleges. But precept alone will not do. There have to be men and women of sterling character who can serve as models and whom the coming generation may emulate. It is a difficult task but a beginning has to be made.

Another important fact to be remembered is that being personally honest is not enough. You are responsible for the conduct of your subordinates as well. You have to evolve measures which minimize the opportunity available to your subordinates to exploit people. One can think of organizational arrangements and close supervision over the work of the subordinates which make it difficult, if not impossible, to indulge in malpractices. I would like to discuss some of such measures.

As mentioned earlier, delays in work are a sign of inefficiency. They are also symptoms of corruption. Orders passed on files are not communicated for days together. Delays in sanctioning licences or in issuing them, delays in payments—all such delays are warning signals. A host of other instances of delay in transaction of government business may just arise from unavoidable causes or sheer slackness or may be intentionally created to cause harassment in order to extract a benefit. It should be remembered that delays, whether intentional or due to inefficiency, equally provide opportunity to unscrupulous people to extort illegal gratification. If we want to stamp out corruption from our offices, we must first eradicate delays on which it thrives. We must go into the causes of delay and try to remove them.

The second danger signal of possible existence of corruption is the frequent change of orders. Penalties are first imposed on contractors and suppliers and later on cancelled or reduced; transfer orders are issued but subsequently revised; objections are first raised on bills but afterwards withdrawn and payments made; someone is arrested but later released for want of evidence. Such changes in order readily lend themselves to corruption. To avoid such a situation, one should take great care that the decisions one takes are sound and firm and one should be slow in changing them. Revising decisions readily on receipt of recommendations or pressure exposes the organization to corrupt practices at the hands of the unscrupulous. Always be on guard against such practices.

Another factor, which helps in curbing malpractices, is your accessibility to complainants. If your subordinates know that the harassment they cause will come to your notice and you may pull them up, they will desist from it. You should, therefore, make yourself easily approachable. A time for receiving visitors daily may be fixed and as far as possible no other engagements should be fixed during such visiting hours. Free accessibility does help not only in checking malpractices but also in remedying other complaints of various types. A word of caution must also be said about asking people to meet at the residence. For official business one would like to see you in your office and not at your residence. There is no reason why representatives of staff, contractors or public should be received at the house and not in the office. Emergency apart, it is a sound practice to meet people only in the office for official work.

For a public servant it is not enough to be honest; he must also be known to be honest. In other words, he must have a reputation for integrity. A man's reputation travels far ahead of him and anyone who has established a reputation for honesty, is seldom if ever approached by tempters. Acquisition of a good reputation is therefore also essential for a drive against corruption.

No doubt, reputation is an intangible thing and depends on what others think and talk about a person. A question may be raised how does a man create a reputation for himself if it largely depends on others' perception. Well, friends, there are certain measures which do help in building up a reputation.

As already mentioned, delays and frequent changes in orders are possible areas for corruption to flourish. These two factors spoil the reputation of an administrator. One has to check these two things. As an old saying goes, "a man is known by the company he keeps". Being seen with or keeping company of persons of a doubtful reputation is liable to besmirch your own reputation. There is also danger of such persons exploiting your relationship with them. There is need to exercise utmost caution in accepting recommendations of such persons. For the same reason, it is dangerous to have any favourites among your subordinates. Some of them may trade on your obvious kindness to them injuring your reputation. Though not many people realize, great harm is done to one's reputation by backing wrong or undeserving persons. Extending protection to wrong persons, when they are in trouble or supporting them for promotion, posting or preferment of any other kind, damages your reputation also. One must desist from it.

In the end, I would like to say that we have to prepare ourselves for the challenges ahead. We have to be thoroughly professional in our jobs and have to maintain highest standard of efficiency and integrity. We must continue to learn and acquire new knowledge and skills. Only then we may be up to the mark and also able to face the assaults on the civil service. The turmoil at the political level and new alignments emphasize the need for impartiality and neutrality of civil service. There are certain other new developments which have a bearing on the functioning of civil service and cannot be ignored. The media has emerged as a powerful segment trying to mould the functioning of both the political as well as the bureaucratic set-up. We are all aware of how on the basis of reports in the media several actions are initiated or a new dimension is added. There is yet another group of the NGOs and activists taking up issues of public importance, particularly in the field of social justice. Human rights activists, women's organizations and the like are trying to influence the working of the government. We have to take into account all these groups and their close interaction today with the government. I am confident, the civil service will be able to perform its role admirably with total dedication to the progress of the country.

Contributors

V.N. Bahadur is a keen photographer who served with distinction in the IAS at both Central and State Government levels.

P.N. Bhandari has become a practising lawyer in the High Court after a distinguished IAS career.

T.N. Chaturvedi served in the Government of Rajasthan, Government of India, and the Union Territories of Delhi and Chandigarh. He has been Union Home Secretary, Comptroller and Auditor General of India, a Member of Parliament, and Governor of the State of Karnataka. For many years he edited *Indian Journal of Public Administration* and has also edited a number of books on varying aspects of Public Administration. He is presently Chairman, Indian Institute of Public Administration, New Delhi.

Bhupendra Hooja (late) studied in Lahore before partition and worked in All India Radio, in BBC (London) and Delhi Administration before joining the IAS serving mostly in Rajasthan and also in Himachal Pradesh. He was very active post-retirement as a seminarist, writer, editor, pamphleteer inspiration and mentor for many NGOs and authors, and for 21 years as editor of *Indian Book Chronicle*. His edited and annotated book of Bhagat Singh's jail notebook *A Martyr's Notebook* has been published in many languages and many English editions by various publishers. He has written on a variety of subjects throughout his life.

Meenakshi Hooja serving IAS officer is presently Additional Chief Secretary attached to the Governor of Rajasthan. She has worked in both Government of India and Government of Rajasthan. She is also a published poet in both English and Hindi. Besides three published books of Hindi poetry, she has also authored a couple of books on Panchayati Raj and on tribal development. For six years she was an honorary member of an international editional board on "A Global Dialogue on Federalism in 21st Century" coordinated by Forum of Federations Canada, which has brought out a number of books. She has also been a visiting fellow at Queen Elizabeth House, University of Oxford (U.K.).

Rakesh Hooja continues to serve in the IAS and has worked as Additional Chief Secretary and Chairman, Board of Revenue. For almost seven years he worked as Joint Secretary, Government of India's Department of Jammu & Kashmir Affairs in the Union Home Ministry. Besides serving as an administrator, he has authored or edited 27 books and a number of monographs and almost 390 articles, research papers and reviews on various aspects of development, administration, planning, water and land management, governance, training, federalism and Panchayati Raj. Two of his books have won state government cash awards and merit certificates. He has also been actively involved in the editing of a number of journals and a book reviews' magazine.

Inderjeet Khanna served in Government of India, Government of Rajasthan and as a faculty at Indian Institute of Management, Ahmedabad while in the IAS, where his last assignment was as Chief Secretary, Government of Rajasthan. He subsequently worked on the constitutional post of State Selector Commissioner of Rajasthan.

Arun Kumar retired as Chief Secretary and then served a full term as Chairman of the State Electricity Regulatory Commission of Rajasthan.

R.S. Kumat has been active in education and rural development related NGOs. His IAS career had culminated in his working as Chairman, Board of Revenue. He also has been writing on themes related to rural development and education.

V. Nath (late) had worked in Planning Commission before joining the IAS. He left the IAS early and subsequently worked as a university teacher in USA and on UN assignments in various countries. A geographer, he wrote extensively especially on urban issues and city planning, administration, development, and regional and multi-level planning. Many of his essays and articles are now being republished in series of books containing his writings.

Kusum Prasad served both Government of India and Government of Rajasthan. She now lives in New Delhi.

V.I. Rajagopal remained involved into various government assignments including working as Vice Chancellor, University of Rajasthan, Jaipur after he retired from IAS as Home Secretary, Government of Rajasthan.

K.K. Saxena rose to be Chairman, Board of Revenue for Rajasthan. He now spends considerable time conforting patients in a hospital.

I.C. Srivastava served as Chairman, Board of Revenue before retiring as Chairman, Rajasthan Mines & Minerals Limited. Since then he has authored two books on his experiences while in the IAS. He occasionally writes on administrative topics.

R.D. Thapar came as a refugee at the time of partition and was a class II officer in Central Government before joining IAS. He rose to become Chief Secretary, Rajasthan before retiring as Commerce Secretary, Government of India.